# THE AUSCHWITZ VOLUNTEER:
## BEYOND BRAVERY

# THE AUSCHWITZ VOLUNTEER

Beyond Bravery

*by* *Captain Witold Pilecki*

*Translated by* Jarek Garliński

**AQUILA POLONICA (U.S.) LTD.**
10850 Wilshire Boulevard, Suite 300, Los Angeles, California 90024, U.S.A.

www.AquilaPolonica.com

First published 2012.

ISBN (Cloth): 978-1-60772-009-6
20 19 18 17 16 15 14 13 12      1 2 3 4 5 6 7 8 9 10

ISBN (Trade Paperback): 978-1-60772-010-2
20 19 18 17 16 15 14 13 12      1 2 3 4 5 6 7 8 9 10

Printed in the U.S.A.

Library of Congress Control Number 2012931262

**Acknowledgements:**

Cover design, interior book design and maps in this Aquila Polonica edition are by Stefan Mucha, and are reproduced with permission. Photographs and other illustrative material are reproduced with permission, and are from the collections of the following:

The Archive of the Auschwitz-Birkenau State Museum ("ABM"); Bundesarchiv; Jarek Garliński ("JG"); Stefan Mucha ("SM"); Narodowe Archiwum Cyfrowe ("NAC"); Zofia Pilecka-Optułowicz and Andrzej Pilecki ("Pilecki Family"); The Polish Underground Movement (1939-1945) Study Trust ("PUMST"); United States Holocaust Memorial Museum ("USHMM"); and Yad Vashem ("YV").

The publishers wish to extend special thanks to Zofia Pilecka-Optułowicz and Andrzej Pilecki for sharing their family photos for use in this book, and for the cooperation of the Instytut Pamięci Narodowej ("IPN") and the Muzeum Woli ("MW") in providing access to such photos.

The U.S. National Archives and Records Administration is abbreviated as "NARA."

The views or opinions expressed in this work, and the context in which the images are used, do not necessarily reflect the views or policy of, nor imply approval or endorsement by, the United States Holocaust Memorial Museum.

*The game which I was now playing in Auschwitz was dangerous. This sentence does not really convey the reality; in fact, I had gone far beyond what people in the real world would consider dangerous...*

— Captain Witold Pilecki

# EUROPE 1939

# CONTENTS

*Page*

Introduction by Norman Davies ........................ *xi*

Foreword by Rabbi Michael Schudrich, Chief Rabbi
of Poland .......................................... *xv*

Translator's Introductory Note ........................ *xix*

Publisher's Note ..................................... *xxiii*

Selected Highlights from Pilecki's 1945 Report ............. *xxix*

List of Maps ......................................... *xxxi*

Historical Horizon
    *Captain Witold Pilecki: The Report, the Mission, the Man* .. *xxxiii*

**Captain Pilecki's Covering Letter
    to Major General Tadeusz Pełczyński** .................. 1

**Captain Witold Pilecki's 1945 Auschwitz Report** ............ 5

**CONTENTS**
Continued

## Appendices

1  Glossary of English, German and Polish Terms
   and Acronyms ....................................... 335

2  German-Language Positions and Ranks at Auschwitz
   Mentioned by Pilecki ............................. 343

3  Index of People and Places Referred to by Pilecki
   with Either a Code Number or Letter ................ 345

4  Chronology of Pilecki's 1945 Report ................. 355

Index ..................................................... 365
Discussion Questions ................................... 397

# POLAND – SEPTEMBER 1939

- - - - - - - - - - - - - German-Soviet Demarcation Line

**1st of September 1939** – German forces invade Poland from the north, west and south.

**17th of September 1939** – Soviet forces invade Poland from the east.

**28th of September 1939** – Germany and the Soviet Union agree on the demarcation line partitioning Poland between them.

# OCCUPIED POLAND 1939–1941

Territories of Poland annexed by Germany.

German-administered Generalgouvernement.

Territories of Poland annexed by the Soviet Union. These territories were later occupied by the Germans following the invasion of the Soviet Union by Axis forces in June 1941.

Poland pre-September 1939.

# INTRODUCTION

Misconceptions about the Second World War in Europe appear to be endless; everyone, including the most advanced experts, can always learn something more and increase the precision of their understanding. One basic misconception, for example, concerns the moral framework of the war; many Westerners imagine that the war in Europe saw just one evil regime, the Third Reich of Adolf Hitler, which was opposed by a coalition of democratic allies dedicated to freedom, law and justice. In reality, the largest combatant power of the war, the Soviet Union of Joseph Stalin, despite its differences from Nazism, can only be included in the criminal, mass-murdering category. Stalin began the war in September 1939 as Hitler's partner in crime, and made no effort to restrict his evil practices when the Soviet Union had been attacked by Germany in June 1941. All the countries like Poland which lay between Germany and the Soviet Union felt the lash of both their neighbours, and at war's end they were denied any meaningful liberation. As Captain Pilecki[1] understood very well, the only valid moral stance was to oppose Nazism and Stalinism alike.

---

[1] The name Witold Pilecki is pronounced VEE-told pee-LETS-kee.

Another common misconception concerns the scourge of the concentration camps. Many Westerners continue to imagine that concentration camps were somehow a monopoly of the Nazis; they equally fail to make the important distinction between concentration camps, like Dachau or Majdanek and fully fledged death camps, like Treblinka. Few of them realise that the Soviet 'liberators of Auschwitz' were busy running a massive network of concentration camps of their own. In reality, the Russian acronym, the GULag, stands for "State Board of Concentration Camps". All the indications are that Soviet instruments of repression consumed more human beings than their Nazi counterparts.

Pilecki's third Report on Auschwitz was written in 1945 at a time when his fight against German tyranny had ended and when his fight against Soviet tyranny was about to begin. It is a poignant reminder of the double threat which Europe faced in the mid-20th Century.

I myself became fully aware of the greatness of Witold Pilecki while conducting research on the Warsaw Rising of 1944. Here was a man, who almost single-handedly had held up the German panzers on one of Warsaw's main thoroughfares for a fortnight; using the pseudonym 'Roman', he then disappeared into his dugout and continued the struggle until the Rising capitulated over two months later. Only then did I realise that this was the same heroic character, who four years earlier had deliberately arranged to be arrested by the SS and be transported to Auschwitz. In 1943, having engineered his escape, he wrote the first version of his Report on Auschwitz, which I had read and which had been the first of several attempts to inform the outside world of what was really happening. Pilecki was a Polish officer and Catholic who viewed his fight against his country's oppression as synonymous with his patriotic and religious duty. If ever there was an Allied hero who deserved to be remembered and celebrated, this was a person with few peers.

Yet Pilecki's astonishing career did not end with the declaration of peace. He was put to death by an act of judicial murder, destroyed by a Communist regime which was working for Stalin's interests and which treated all non-Communist resistance fighters as traitors and Nazi-lovers. Pilecki's name mirrors the tragic fate of millions whom the West forgot. Only when one grasps the true horror of his fate can one comprehend what the Second World War in Europe was really about.

*Norman Davies, FBA*
*Oxford, Great Britain*
*February 2012*

Witold Pilecki–1922.

# FOREWORD

During World War II, a time of unprecedented darkness on earth, heroic men and women rose up and, calling upon the highest resources of the human spirit, took action against evil. Many such people were thrust unwillingly into situations that challenged them physically, emotionally and morally, but they rose to meet the challenge. Others, a much smaller number, actively courted danger in order to battle the evil.

One who stands out in that unique, smaller company of heroes is Polish Army Captain Witold Pilecki, who volunteered for an almost certainly suicidal undercover mission at Auschwitz.

Pilecki is a shining example of heroism that transcends religion, race and time. Yet his story, one of the most dramatic missions by an Ally in World War II, is virtually unknown in the West.

Why isn't Pilecki better known? There is a simple answer: his story was intentionally suppressed by the postwar communist regime in Poland—because Pilecki's heroism did not stop with his nearly three-year-long Auschwitz mission.

After his escape from Auschwitz, Pilecki worked in intelligence with the Polish Home Army, fought in the Warsaw Uprising of 1944, and was taken prisoner by the Germans. He ended the war in a German prisoner of war camp. Then in late 1945, he volunteered for another undercover mission: to return to Poland, where conditions were chaotic at war's end as the communists were asserting control, and secretly gather intelligence for the Polish government-in-exile.

This, tragically, became his final mission. Pilecki was arrested as a Western spy by the Polish communist regime, tortured, and executed in 1948 at age 47. His heroic exploits were expunged from Polish history.

Now, for the first time, English-language readers will have a chance to discover, through his own words, this remarkable man who risked everything to organize against the unspeakable evil of Auschwitz and tell the world about the horrible realities of this now-infamous death camp. If heeded, Pilecki's early warnings might have changed the course of history.

Pilecki's eyewitness account covers the early period in Auschwitz's existence: from September 1940, shortly after the Germans opened the Auschwitz concentration camp, through April 1943 when Pilecki escaped. His report provides firsthand information about less well-known aspects of Auschwitz—e.g., its initial function as a concentration camp for Polish political prisoners; the extermination of Soviet soldiers taken as prisoners of war; the first intimations and subsequent execution of the Nazi German "final solution" for Jews, which began in earnest in 1942.

Pilecki's experience and observations provide a perspective that fills in the overall picture of Auschwitz. This book is essential reading for anyone interested in the Holocaust. It is also, perhaps unintentionally, the portrait of a man of conscience faced with unimaginable horrors, as Pilecki opens what is supposed to be a strictly factual account with these words:

> They have told me: "The more you stick to the bare facts without any kind of commentary, the more valuable it all will be."
>
> Well, here I go... but we were not made out of wood, let alone stone, though it sometimes seemed as if even a stone would have broken out in a sweat.

When God created the human being, God had in mind that we should all be like Captain Witold Pilecki, of blessed memory. May the life of Witold Pilecki inspire us all to do one more good deed, of any kind, each and every day of our lives.

*Rabbi Michael Schudrich, Chief Rabbi of Poland*

*Warsaw, Poland*

*December 2011*

Witold Pilecki–1930's.

# TRANSLATOR'S INTRODUCTORY NOTE

This translation is based on the original typescript of Captain Witold Pilecki's 1945 Report held at the Polish Underground Movement Study Trust in London.

In fact, this report was the third and most comprehensive one that Pilecki wrote on his time in Auschwitz. In June 1943, shortly after his escape from the camp, while staying with the Serafińskis in Nowy Wiśnicz, Pilecki wrote an eleven-and-a-half-page initial report. A few months later, in the autumn of 1943, in Warsaw, he wrote an amplified version, called *Raport W*, and he wrote the full Report, here translated, in the summer of 1945 in Italy where he was serving with the Polish Second Corps, under overall British command. This report, as Pilecki's covering letter to General Pełczyński makes clear, was written primarily for military purposes.

Throughout both *Raport W* and the 1945 Report, but only in some places in the June 1943 report, Pilecki replaced the names of most of the people to whom he refers in the text, whether camp inmates or others, and of many of the places, by numbers and sometimes letters. This was done to protect their and their families' identities, which continued to be relevant even after the war had ended in 1945. Pilecki's own keys to the June 1943 and the 1945 Report have never been recovered. Painstaking research by a number of scholars, including my late father Józef Garliński and Adam Cyra of the Auschwitz-Birkenau Museum, managed to break the 1945 code and establish the names of most of the people mentioned.

In the spring of 1991, some years after much of the original detective work had been done, an almost complete key to the names (over 200 out of 235) in the autumn 1943 *Raport W* was discovered in archives in Warsaw. It was returned to Pilecki's son Andrzej, together with some of his father's other papers which had been taken at the time of his arrest in 1947. However, the numbers in this key do not correspond to the numbers in the 1945 Report: for instance, in the 1945 Report, Colonel Władysław Surmacki is no. 1, in *Raport W* he is no. 8; Colonel Juliusz Gilewicz is no. 121 in the 1945 Report and no. 72 in *Raport W*.

There are also a few factual discrepancies between the three reports, and I have noted the main ones in footnotes to the text. I have used Adam Cyra's invaluable book, *Ochotnik do Auschwitz: Witold Pilecki (1901–1948)* (Oświęcim: Chrześcijańskie Stowarzyszenie Rodzin Oświęcimskich, 2000), as the most up-to-date source for the identified names, which I have included in the body of the text in square brackets.

In this translation I have chosen to retain Pilecki's somewhat staccato style, with many words and phrases in parentheses and quotation marks. I have tried to be as faithful to the original as possible, retaining Pilecki's colloquialisms and inconsistencies, bearing in mind that the Report was written quite hastily. However, I have taken the liberty, in one or two instances, of introducing a new paragraph or section where Pilecki did not, but where a radical change in subject matter appears to warrant it.

Occasionally Pilecki's memory plays him false and I have taken the liberty of pointing this out in footnotes. I have also corrected the spelling of the odd German word or two. Where he has used a German word or camp argot, I have nearly always used them too, translating where it has seemed to me to be appropriate.

A word about place names, Polish being well known for its daunting tongue twisters, such as Brzeszcze, Brzezinka, Oświęcim, Wiśnicz. Where there are accepted English-language versions I have used them, examples being Birkenau, Minsk, the Vistula, Warsaw. However, I use the more evocative Kraków in place of the rather flat English rendering Cracow, for which I have never much cared. Following the same principle that one does not, for instance, translate the "Bois de Boulogne" into English as the "Boulogne Wood," I have not translated street names, although I have used the English word "Street" in lieu of the Polish "Ulica."

While it has become common of late to refer to the Warsaw Rising of 1944, I must confess to preferring the older form, Warsaw Uprising.

It was my late father, Józef Garliński, himself an inmate (number 121421) in Auschwitz for a few months in 1943, which he spent in the Penal Company, who first brought Witold Pilecki to the attention of a wider audience in his ground-breaking book *Oświęcim Walczący* published in 1974. It appeared a year later in English as *Fighting Auschwitz*. It was in fact the first work by a serious historian on the resistance movement in Auschwitz and involved much detective work in breaking Pilecki's name code. Hence my great debt to him.

I should like to conclude by thanking Dr. Krzysztof Stoliński of The Polish Underground Movement Study Trust in London for his kindness in making the text of the Report available and for his patience in answering some follow-up email questions. Dr. Adam Cyra of the Auschwitz-Birkenau

Museum has also patiently responded to my queries. Finally, many thanks to my editors at Aquila Polonica, Terry Tegnazian and Stefan Mucha, for their helpful suggestions and attention to detail.

*Jarek Garliński*
*Texas*
*February 2012*

## PUBLISHER'S NOTE

### This Edition

*The Auschwitz Volunteer: Beyond Bravery* presented us as publishers with an editing challenge. Captain Witold Pilecki's original 1945 Report was not written for publication—it was written for his Polish Army superiors, and done rather hurriedly as Pilecki was preparing to embark on another (ultimately fatal) secret mission into postwar Poland where a virtual state of civil war raged between the Soviet-backed Polish communist regime and the various anti-communist resistance organizations scattered throughout the country.

Pilecki did not have time to edit, revise or polish his writing. As a result, this report of his Auschwitz mission has a rare immediacy and a particularly personal voice—it reads almost as if Pilecki were sitting in the room with us, telling us his story.

Translator Jarek Garliński wanted to preserve this special energy and authenticity of Pilecki's Report, and we agreed with him.

As a result, we have for the most part left uncorrected the numerous inconsistencies in style, formatting, punctuation and references that would normally have been corrected during the editing process.

While Pilecki wrote his Report in Polish, he also uses a number of German words throughout, because German was the language of the Nazi German concentration camps. Contrary to proper German-language standards, Pilecki either does not capitalize the German nouns or does so inconsistently. Instead, he incorporates the German words into his writing as if they were Polish words and in Polish, as in English, common nouns are not capitalized. Further, Pilecki adds Polish word endings to form plurals or other parts of speech as needed. At that time, both Pilecki and his Polish Army superiors would have known German well enough to understand the Report without need for a translation, and they would not have found this practice regarding language unusual.

We have for the most part followed Pilecki's idiosyncratic capitalization of the German words in this translation of his Report. We also generally form plurals of the German words as if they were English, by adding an "s" at the end—similar to Pilecki's practice in incorporating the German words into his Polish narrative. Except for proper nouns, dialogue and quoted material, we italicize the German words the first time they appear. Recognizing that many English-language readers will not be fluent in German, in most cases we follow such words throughout the text with an English translation, unless the meaning is clear from the context. In addition, we have included a Glossary.

Pilecki occasionally uses the Polish shorthand date notation, which we have translated to a form that would be more familiar in English. For example, Pilecki's 16.ii.43 is translated as 16 Feb. '43.

In writing about his friends and comrades, Pilecki frequently refers to them by nickname or a diminutive (e.g., Tadek for Tadeusz; Janek, Jasiek, Jaś or Jasio for Jan).

Also, as Mr. Garliński describes in more detail in his Translator's Introductory Note, in most cases Pilecki replaced names with code numbers or letters to protect people. Therefore, in addition to the general index, we have included an index of the code numbers and/or letters and the names associated with them to the extent they have been identified, which also gives the related nicknames or diminutives, if any, used by Pilecki for each such person.

The true names of people and the translations of German words are inserted throughout the text in square brackets, to distinguish from the regular parentheses used by Pilecki.

The Report is roughly chronological, but was written as one long piece without chapter divisions or section headings. We maintain this unbroken form of Pilecki's narrative, but to help orient readers, we indicate the year in the running head, and include both a brief selection of highlights from Pilecki's 1945 Report in the front material of the book and a more detailed chronology of the Report in the Appendices.

Translating Pilecki's Report was a demanding project. The original Report is more than one hundred pages of single-spaced lines, with miniscule margins, typed on a manual typewriter with numerous handwritten interlineations. In this translation of Pilecki's Report, we benefit not only from Mr. Garliński's linguistic skills, but also from the added dimension of his extensive scholarship and knowledge of literature, history and the military, as well as his personal connection to the material.

Pilecki's 1945 Report had no formal title; we have chosen to call this translation *The Auschwitz Volunteer: Beyond Bravery*. Since Pilecki was, by all accounts, a modest person, it is doubtful that he would have chosen such a title himself. We have done so to honor this most extraordinary and courageous man.

Captain Witold Pilecki's 1945 Report occupies a unique place in the history and literature about Auschwitz. It is with great pride that we publish this essential primary source in English for the first time.

## The Polish Language

In *The Auschwitz Volunteer: Beyond Bravery*, Polish names and words are written in the Polish language which, with its strings of consonants, diacritical marks and that strange "l with a slash" ("ł"), can appear impenetrable to most native English speakers. Below is a very abbreviated pronunciation guide which may help to demystify the language.

Polish is fairly phonetic in its spelling (i.e., unlike English, the way a Polish word is spelled is usually how it is pronounced); therefore each sound is represented by one letter or a standard combination of letters. Polish and English both use the Latin alphabet, so the Polish alphabet is similar to, although not exactly the same as, the English alphabet— here are a few of the principal differences:

1) There is no letter "v" in the Polish alphabet, so Polish uses the letter "w" for the "v" sound. When "w" is the last letter of a word, it is pronounced more like an "f."

2) The "w" sound, in turn, is represented by the Polish letter "l with a slash" ("ł").

3) There is no letter "q" in the Polish alphabet, so Polish uses the letter "k" for the "q" sound.

4) The Polish "j" sounds like the "y" in "yes."

5) The Polish "c" sounds like the "ts" in "cats."

6) The strings of consonants, sometimes with an accompanying vowel, generally break down into standard clusters, each of which represents a certain sound. Some of the major clusters are:

"ch"—like the "h" in "hand"

"ci"—like the "ch" in "cheap"

"cz"—like "tch" in "itch"

"drz"—like the "j" in "just"

"dz"—like the "ds" in "beds"

"dzi"—a softer version of "dz," similar to the "j" in "jeep"

"rz"—like the "s" in "pleasure"

"sz"—like the "sh" in "show"

7) The diacritical marks under or over certain vowels and consonants change their pronunciation; for example, "ę" is pronounced like "en" as in "ten" or as "em" before certain consonants; "ó" like "oo" as in "moon"; the "ć" as a soft "tch."

The accent on Polish words of more than one syllable is usually on the penultimate, or next to last, syllable.

So, for example, "Warszawa" (the Polish word for "Warsaw") is pronounced: var-SHA-va. People who live in Warsaw are called "Varsovians" in English—derived from the Latin word for Warsaw, "Varsovia," and perhaps from the pronunciation of the Polish "Warszawa."

This is how some of the names in *The Auschwitz Volunteer: Beyond Bravery* would be pronounced:

Witold Pilecki—VEE-told pee-LETS-kee

Oświęcim—osh-vee-EM-cheem

Tomasz Serafiński—TO-mash se-ra-FEEN-skee

Sławek Szpakowski—SWA-vek shpa-KOV-skee

Władysław Surmacki—vwa-DIH-swaf sur-MATS-kee

*Aquila Polonica Publishing*

Witold Pilecki with his wife Maria in Legionowo–1944.

## SELECTED HIGHLIGHTS
## FROM PILECKI'S 1945 REPORT

(A more detailed chronology of Pilecki's 1945 Report is included as Appendix 4.)

*Page*

**1940...**                                                              11–80

-   Deliberately walks into a German SS street round-up in Warsaw—transported to Auschwitz, inmate no. 4859
-   Begins setting up a military organization: the first "five"
-   Serious killing starts up again. Weakening, but could not admit to others
-   Christmas: the first parcels from home—no food allowed

**1941...**                                                              80–155

-   Sick: in the hospital, overrun by lice
-   New meaning for "organize"
-   Camp orchestra formed
-   New camp word: "Muselmann"
-   Collective responsibility for escapes
-   First Bolshevik prisoners of war
-   Second Christmas in Auschwitz

**1942...**                                                              155–254

-   Change in attitude toward Jews
-   Typhus-infected lice cultivated and released on SS men
-   Builds a radio transmitter; broadcasts until autumn 1942
-   First women prisoners brought in

**SELECTED HIGHLIGHTS**
Continued

*Page*

**1942 (continued) . . .**

– Transports: mostly Jews from throughout Europe, sent directly to the gas chambers at Rajsko-Birkenau

– "Canada"

– Typhus: recovering thanks to comrades' care

– "Able to take over the camp on more or less a daily basis"—awaiting orders from Home Army High Command

– Germans begin sexual experiments on inmates

– Third Christmas in Auschwitz

**1943 . . .**                                                           247–326

– Gypsies brought to Rajsko-Birkenau

– Avoids transport to other camps

– Escape

– On the outside, meeting the real Tomasz Serafiński

– Return to Warsaw: working in Home Army High Command

**1944 . . .**                                                           326–328

– A few post-Auschwitz experiences

# LIST OF MAPS

Page

Europe 1939 ......................................... *vi*

Poland–September 1939 ............................... *ix*

Occupied Poland 1939–1941 ........................... *x*

Auschwitz and Environs .............................. 9

KL Auschwitz I ...................................... 10

Pilecki's Escape Route from Auschwitz ................ 300

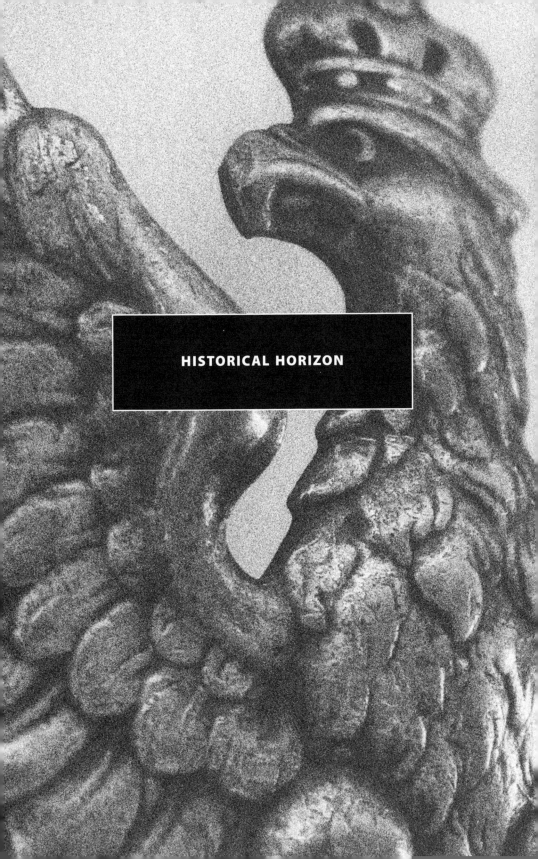

**HISTORICAL HORIZON**

## HISTORICAL HORIZON

*Captain Witold Pilecki: The Report, the Mission, the Man*

### The Report

Witold Pilecki's 1945 Report is a powerful document. It is powerful not because of cadences of prose or striking imagery. Indeed, it was never meant to be a work of literature. Pilecki wrote it in Italy in the second half of 1945 as a report to his military superiors, which Pilecki's covering letter to General Pełczyński makes clear. In his report Pilecki often uses short sentences and paragraphs, and he freely admits that, had he had the time, he might have spent more time polishing it. Yet it is powerful because of its immediacy and because it illuminates the savagely perverted world of Auschwitz in a way that only someone with recent firsthand experience of it could have done.

Pilecki was not a sociologist trying to fit Auschwitz into neat little boxes or theories, nor did he over-intellectualize his experiences there. He was an honest, by all accounts unassuming man, without any political or ideological axe to grind except love of his own country and his Catholic faith, who followed the code of "Bóg, Honor, Ojczyzna" ("God, Honor, Country") and who wrote down what he had personally seen and felt, occasionally venturing into the realm of philosophy and self-reflection.

By any stretch of the imagination, he was also an extraordinary man. Endowed with great physical resilience and courage, he showed remarkable presence of mind and common sense in quite appalling circumstances, and a complete absence of self-pity. While most inmates of Auschwitz not slated for immediate death were barely able to survive, he had enough reserves of strength and determination left to help others and to build up an underground resistance organization within the camp. Not only that, he managed to keep a clear head at all times and recognize what he needed to do in order to stay alive which, for instance, often meant fighting his own physiological impulses and saving some food for the following day: a task requiring almost superhuman willpower. He also enjoyed a fair portion of luck and even had time for some wry irony, noting that the inner and outer pairs of digits of his own camp number 4859 both added up to thirteen!

He claims to have attained quite quickly an almost spiritual state of serenity. He felt "happiness" at the solidarity which the camp's terrible conditions had created amongst the Poles: "Then, I felt a single thought coursing through these Poles standing shoulder to shoulder, I felt that finally we were all united by the same anger, a desire for revenge, I felt myself in an environment perfectly suited to begin my work here and discovered within me a semblance of happiness..." There is even a hint of the mystical, Solzhenitsyn-like belief that only those who have experienced a labor camp can really understand the deeper meaning of life. He writes: "We were cut with a sharp instrument. Its blade bit painfully into our bodies, yet, in our souls, it found fields to till...," and later: "A man was seen and valued for what he really was..."

The Report is powerful, too, because it highlights an aspect of Auschwitz less well known outside Poland and the world

Cavalry Officer
Second Lieutenant
Witold Pilecki

Witold Pilecki–Auschwitz inmate no. 4859

of concentration camp survivors and historians. While most people have heard of Auschwitz in German-occupied Poland in the context of the Holocaust and know of the abomination of the gas chambers and the unspeakable crime of gassing living human beings, fewer know that in the first stage of the camp's existence most of its victims were Christian Poles, many of whom were savagely killed or worked to death. Indeed, Auschwitz was initially set up in 1940 as a camp for Polish political prisoners, and only later was it turned into a death camp for the Jews of Europe. Moreover, how many people in the West, outside the academic community, know that Soviet prisoners of war were sent to the camp to be killed?[1] The Report describes, sometimes in chilling detail, the relentless, ceaseless and at times almost casual brutality where no moral limits were recognized. Indeed, it shows to what depths human beings can sink when there are simply no moral rules.

At the same time, the Report also represents a beacon of hope, in that it demonstrates that even in the midst of so much cruelty and degradation there were those who held to the basic virtues of honesty, compassion and courage. Pilecki describes men who were able to rise above their circumstances and who, while recognizing the need to save their own lives, were not prepared to do so at the expense of others. He writes too: "... but there we also developed respect for this strange human nature, stronger for possessing a soul, and containing something apparently immortal within itself." While Pilecki was indeed a believer, his Report is not a testament per se to Christian values, but rather a reminder of the universal human virtues to which all faiths and religions subscribe.

---

[1] On the Eastern Front, unlike in the West, little respect was shown for the Geneva Conventions which, in any case, the USSR had never signed.

Yet he expresses anger at a world that could have sunk so far: "We have strayed, my friends, we have strayed dreadfully. What's worse is that there are no words to describe it... I would like to say that we have become animals... but no, we are a whole level of hell worse than animals!" He wonders which world is real: the perverted one of the camp, or the uncaring and shallow world outside.

Christian though he is, Pilecki also makes it clear that fire must be fought with fire. Exceptionally cruel *Kapos* (inmates serving as camp "trusties" or supervisors), SS men and informers were killed without compunction by the camp inmates, as often as not in the hospital. Although Pilecki does not·mention it, his underground organization, the ZOW (Związek Organizacji Wojskowych—The Union of Military Organizations)[2] in fact set up a kind of court.[3] It was a brutal fight for survival in which the timid, the selfish or the fainthearted stood no chance.

Perhaps the most extraordinary episode described is the shooting of two hundred or so young Polish men who knowingly marched to their deaths without a guard, understanding full well that the sole result of any attempt on their part to revolt would be brutal reprisals against their families. Nevertheless, Pilecki states that had these men indeed decided to revolt, his organization would have taken a stand and made a fight of it.

Pilecki's achievement was considerable. Not only did he establish an organization capable of helping people to survive the camp, but his efforts led to a rapprochement between the Polish political parties represented in the camp: no mean

---

[2] Sometimes written Związek Organizacji Wojskowej (the Union of Military Organization) which seems less logical.

[3] Many cases were actually reviewed by a couple of inmates who were jurists in order to retain some semblance of legality.

feat, given the interwar tensions and animosities. He notes wryly: "So one had to show Poles daily a mountain of Polish corpses in order for them to reconcile..." Given his very junior military rank and the fact that he was a complete political unknown, this was a remarkable accomplishment and a testament to his character.

His organization also sent a number of reports to the Polish government-in-exile in London by way of the Polish Home Army (the Armia Krajowa, or AK) on conditions in the camp, including the first details of the gassing of Jews in large numbers. It is a measure of the Nazi Germans' violation of all human and moral codes that even men like Pilecki, who were actually there and saw terrible things happening around them, could not initially comprehend the enormity and scale of the crime which would later become known as the Holocaust. Little wonder, perhaps, that the outside world was slow to react to the news.

Yet Pilecki's Report ends on a note of frustration, if not anger. Pilecki, who, it must be remembered, had gone voluntarily to Auschwitz, was upset that the Home Army commanders, and for that matter the other Allies, were unwilling to organize any kind of military attack on Auschwitz to take advantage of the organization he had built up there: "Should there be an airborne assault or an arms drop... Neither we nor our Allies contemplated such a thing—or even conceived of it—so our enemies did." Indeed, he felt that they were more or less indifferent to the suffering in the camp and he writes about the outside world's "continual, ignorant silence."

There is also more than one somewhat disparaging comment about those who had spent the war in less arduous billets: "So, fine people were going to their deaths here [Auschwitz] and losing their lives so as not to implicate anyone outside, while far weaker people than us were casually calling us skeletons." He writes with some scorn of his reaction after his escape to people on the outside: "At times I felt that I was wandering through a great house and would suddenly open the door to a room in which there were only children: '... Ah, the children are playing...' " Or: "The boundary between honesty and common dishonesty had been meticulously blurred."

## The Mission

Pilecki's organization had three principal goals: to boost morale by obtaining and distributing to its members news from outside and extra supplies; to send out reports about the camp; and to prepare for an armed uprising. In the short term, it focused on helping inmates to cope with the frightful conditions. Through well-placed contacts, men were assigned to easier indoor work details (*Kommandos* in the camp jargon, the camp's official language being German), sick men were brought into the hospital, extra food and clothing were scrounged or, to use the camp vernacular, "organized." He claims that by early 1942 his organization had penetrated, he uses the phrase "taken over," every Kommando but one.

Indeed, the story of how enterprising political prisoners[4] were able eventually to wrest control of the top positions throughout the concentration camp system from the mostly German criminal prisoners who initially held them is extraordinary, but is not part of Pilecki's tale. As the war progressed, the German authorities found political prisoners better able to handle the administrative complexities of a huge camp like Auschwitz than the criminals who had originally held

---

[4] These were often communists, who were by and large the best-organized group in the camps.

those posts. Even during Pilecki's time in the camp, he points out that conditions did improve marginally for a variety of reasons, not least of which was a lessening of the German criminals' hold on power.

However, the organization's longer-term goal was to recruit and organize a body of men who could, when the circumstances were right, rise up and take over the camp. This would have been necessary if, for instance, the SS had shown signs of wanting to liquidate all the inmates. While such a group was indeed ready, and Pilecki states that it was in fact prepared to take over the camp ("for some months now we had been able to take over the camp on more or less a daily basis"), it never received the outside assistance without which it would have had little chance of success.

Pilecki envisaged a land operation, perhaps supported by the Polish Parachute Brigade from England and using weapons parachuted into the camp—both of which were quite unrealistic expectations at the time, given Auschwitz's location. However, he was only too aware that any premature action on his part could have considerable repercussions outside the camp in terms of local reprisals and, as a military man, he was not prepared to take such a major decision without orders.

The Polish Home Army did in fact consider attacking the camp, but was never strong enough to do so, since it calculated that it could hold off the German SS garrison, which was several thousand strong,[5] only long enough to enable between two hundred and three hundred inmates to get away in safety. The remaining inmates, perhaps as many as one hundred thousand, would have had to fend for themselves, leading to

---

[5] As late as August 1944, the SS garrison still consisted of 3,250 men. The Germans could have also pulled in additional forces. The Home Army could have gathered no more than a few hundred armed men, if that.

a bloody massacre. There was also a strong likelihood that the Germans would then wreak vengeance on the local Polish population. Nonetheless, the thought that the Germans might want to murder all the remaining inmates as the Red Army approached continued to worry the Home Army. In the summer of 1944, one of the Polish SOE-trained operatives (*cichociemni* in Polish), Second Lieutenant Stefan Jasieński, carried out a reconnaissance of the area around the camp, but was picked up in September and imprisoned in the camp. While his subsequent fate is unclear, there were reports that he in fact survived Auschwitz. No attack on the camp was ever launched and the SS never carried out a final mass slaughter of the remaining inmates.

## The Man

Witold Pilecki was born on the 13th of May (the 30th of April, Old Style[6]) 1901 into a patriotic Polish family in Olonets, a small town in Karelia near the Finnish border in what was then the Russian Empire, Poland having been partitioned by Russia, Prussia and Austria at the end of the 18th century. Educated in Wilno (today Vilnius) and Oryol, at an early age Pilecki became used to conspiratorial Polish organizations proscribed by the Russians, including the Polish scouting movement. He later took part in military operations against the Bolsheviks in the Polish–Bolshevik War of 1919–1920.

In 1921, forced to abandon his studies in Fine Art at the Stefan Batory University in Wilno (in newly independent Poland) for lack of funds, he joined the Association for the Nation's Security (Związek Bezpieczeństwa Kraju),

---

[6] The pre-revolutionary Julian Russian calendar (known as Old Style) was 13 days behind the Western Gregorian calendar by the 20th century. Bolshevik Russia adopted the Gregorian calendar in 1918, when the 14th of February followed the 31st of January.

Below:
Witold Pilecki–Wilno
(Vilnius), 1923.

Above:
Sukurcze Manor, the Pilecki
family estate.

Below:
Witold Pilecki with the youth of
the Lida district at a gathering in
Warsaw–1930s.

All photos on this page: Pilecki Family

Left:
Witold Pilecki–1920s.

Left:
Witold Pilecki leading a cavalry parade in Lida.

Below:
Witold Pilecki with his wife Maria and son Andrzej at Ostrów Mazowiecka, 1932 or 1933.

Left:
Witold Pilecki with his wife and children, Zofia and Andrzej, 1934.

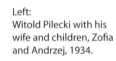

Right:
Second Lieutenant Witold Pilecki (*seated left*) with Major Jan Włodarkiewicz, Commanding Officer of TAP (Tajna Armia Polska—the Polish Secret Army).

a semi-volunteer organization, in which he served for a couple of years. A man of many talents who wrote poetry, painted and played the guitar, Pilecki was posted in 1926 to the 26th Uhlan Regiment and promoted reserve second lieutenant in the cavalry. He was to hold this rank until promoted first lieutenant in November 1941 while in Auschwitz (a departure from the Home Army's usual practice of not promoting men in camps), his final promotion to cavalry captain coming in February 1944.

In the 1920s he took over the running of his small family estate, which lay in what is today Belarus, and married a local schoolteacher, Maria Ostrowska in 1931.[7] They had two children. He was much attracted to matters military and formed a volunteer cavalry unit which was eventually integrated into the regular order of battle, and it has been surmised that he worked for military intelligence or counter-intelligence in the thirties.

Like many Poles of his generation, he was profoundly patriotic and Catholic, and appears to have been emotionally in tune with many of the views of Marshal Piłsudski—Poland's de facto leader until his death in 1935. While never particularly political, Pilecki does appear to echo some of Piłsudski's frustrations with politicians and the rather messy democratic process as it played out in interwar Poland.

Mobilized in August 1939 shortly before the Germans attacked Poland, Pilecki fought in his cavalry unit, attached to the 19th Infantry Division, which was defeated by the Germans on the 6th of September. He then fought on with various units as late as the 17th of October, long after the Soviet invasion of Poland, the fall of Warsaw and the

---

[7] She died aged 96 in 2002.

formation of a new Polish government-in-exile in Paris. The unit was then disbanded.

Together with a number of army officers and several civilians, in November 1939 Pilecki helped to set up an underground military resistance organization: the TAP (Tajna Armia Polska—the Polish Secret Army). Founded on patriotic and Christian principles, the TAP had no political party affiliation and grew to supposedly between eight thousand and twelve thousand members before it was amalgamated at the end of 1941 with the ZWZ (Związek Walki Zbrojnej—The Union for Armed Combat), which in 1942 became better known as the AK (Armia Krajowa—Home Army).[8]

Having volunteered to get himself arrested and sent to Auschwitz as a prisoner in order to carry out his secret mission for the Polish Underground, Pilecki deliberately walked into a German street round-up in Warsaw on the 19th of September 1940. He arrived in Auschwitz during the night of the 21st–22nd of September, in the second Warsaw transport (the first having gone in August), under the assumed name of Tomasz Serafiński—a real person whom Pilecki did not know, but whose identity papers had been found in a Warsaw "safe house" where Serafiński had stayed and which Pilecki had been using. Despite the terrible conditions in the camp and the constant need to stay alert and alive, Pilecki quickly sought out other imprisoned TAP members to form the nucleus of his new organization.

Using the TAP as a model, his Auschwitz organization, ZOW (Związek Organizacji Wojskowych—The Union of Military Organizations), was set up on the principle of "cells," or what Pilecki called "fives" (sometimes a "five" had more

---

[8] Interestingly enough, the Home Army often hid its identity under the acronym PZP (Polski Związek Powstańczy—the Polish Insurrectionary Organization).

Right:
Standing from the left: Jan Redzej, Witold Pilecki, Edward Ciesielski —escapees from Auschwitz. Here, standing in front of the Serafiński family house in Nowy Wiśnicz, summer 1943.

All photos on this page: Pilecki Family

Left:
Witold Pilecki–1943.

Below:
From the left: Second Lieutenant Marian Szyszko-Bohusz, Maria Szelągowska and Cavalry Captain Witold Pilecki–Rome, 1945.

Above:
Witold Pilecki in front of "Koryznówka," the Serafiński family house, 1943.

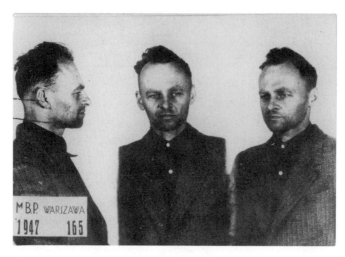

All photos on this page: Pilecki Family

Above:
On the 8th of May 1947, Pilecki was arrested by the Ministry of Public Security (Ministerstwo Bezpieczeństwa Publicznego or MBP) and charged with being a "Western spy".

Left:
A pistol and ammunition alleged to have belonged to Pilecki.

Above:
On the 15th of May 1948, following a show trial, Pilecki was sentenced to death and was executed ten days later at the Mokotów Prison in Warsaw.

*l*

than five members). The "fives" operated independently of one another so that in the event of the Germans getting hold of some of the members and torturing them, it was impossible for one person to betray the whole organization. The "cells" then recruited further "fives," who in turn went about recruiting others. He set up the first "top five" as he called it, as early as October 1940.

There is some dispute as to when he set up his second "top five." In June 1943, just after his escape, Pilecki stated that it was in November 1940, while later that year and in 1945 he put it in March 1941. He then set up the third "top five" in May 1941, the fourth one in October of the same year and the fifth in November. There are some discrepancies as to the membership of these "top fives" in Pilecki's own writings, as in other sources. However, ultimate proof of the efficacy of his structure is the fact that Pilecki himself was never picked up or indeed identified by the camp authorities as the ZOW's primary organizer.

The organization almost immediately started sending out information on conditions in Auschwitz to the Polish Underground authorities. Pilecki's first report was sent out in October 1940 by way of a released inmate, eventually reaching the Polish government-in-exile in London in March 1941. Indeed, it was Pilecki's organization which provided the outside Polish authorities with information on the inhumane treatment of Soviet POWs in Auschwitz and the start of the mass murder of Jews (the Holocaust) in Birkenau/Brzezinka, information which the Polish government-in-exile then passed on to the other Allies. Pilecki in his messages urged the Polish Underground to attack Auschwitz, but never received any reply to this request.

In addition to the military and self-help dimension of his work, Pilecki, who emphasized his own apolitical approach, managed to contribute to the forming towards the end of 1941 of a Political Committee embracing all the different political groupings represented in the camp: a notable achievement, given lingering prewar antipathies and the prevailing conditions in the camp. Eventually accused by other inmates of wanting to create an organization in order to feed his own ego (a quite unjustified assertion), Pilecki turned over command of the ZOW to the commander of the ZWZ/AK group in the camp, Lieutenant Colonel Kazimierz Rawicz, who was in the camp under the assumed name of Jan Hilkner.

Concerned eventually that too many good Poles had been shipped out to other camps and that the Polish Underground authorities appeared to be turning a deaf ear to his pleas for help in liberating the camp, Pilecki escaped in April 1943 from the camp bakery together with two other inmates, in order to plead his case in person. The local and regional AK commanders, skeptical of his story, were unwilling to take up his call to attack the camp and free the inmates.

Pilecki later worked in AK High Command in Warsaw, became a member of the anti-communist deep-cover underground organization NIE (Niepodległość—Independence), which was to operate when the Red Army arrived, and he fought with distinction in the 1944 Warsaw Uprising.[9] Taken prisoner by the Germans, he then spent time in Lamsdorf and Murnau POW camps, after which he joined the Polish Second Corps in Italy. It was there that he wrote the 1945 Report and from there that he began his fateful final mission to Poland.

---

[9] To be distinguished from the uprising in the Warsaw Ghetto in 1943.

Pilecki set about his task in the camp with astonishing single-mindedness. While he talks freely of his friends, he never once mentions his wife and children, and from the Report it is unclear where they were during his time inside and whether he even saw them after his escape. He makes only passing references to his family in terms of receiving parcels, worrying that his relatives might buy him out of Auschwitz while he was still absorbed in setting up his resistance network, and writing to them from time to time.

This absorption in what Pilecki saw as an existential struggle for the survival of the Polish nation is the nub of a terrible moral dilemma, doubtlessly faced by many people who have families and who have chosen to join resistance movements. Should they become involved in activities which might endanger their loved ones? There is of course no correct answer, and I believe that we, from the comfort of our retrospective armchairs, have little standing to judge such people one way or another. They did what they felt to be right at the time, and we can but admire them for even asking the question in the first place. How much easier it would have been simply to lower the brim of one's trilby and take the quiet route to anonymous obscurity.

That was not Pilecki's way. Indeed, once he had volunteered to go to Auschwitz to set up a resistance movement there, it was unlikely that he would ever have been willing to lead a life of quiet compromise. It was this trait which led ultimately to the tragic culmination of his life which, while beyond the scope of the Report, is essential for an understanding of the whole man.

After the war, Pilecki, like most Poles, was opposed to the Soviet-imposed atheist, communist régime in Poland. Therefore, in 1945 he undertook a mission to liaise with anti-communist resistance organizations within Poland

and report on conditions to General Władysław Anders, commander of Polish Second Corps under British command, who was emerging as the Poles' leader in the West. Pilecki's wife and children were in Poland and he was able to visit them. Ignoring orders from Anders to leave the country when it was clear that the communist authorities were on to him, he was eventually arrested on the 8th of May 1947 and tortured by the Polish secret police, later telling a family member during a prison visit that Auschwitz had been child's play (*igraszka*) compared to his treatment at the hands of his Soviet-trained countrymen.

Accused of spying and preparing armed attacks on members of the Polish secret police, charges he vehemently denied, he was tried in a Military Court, convicted and finally executed in the Mokotów Prison on Rakowiecka Street in Warsaw in the evening of the 25th of May 1948 . . . by his own countrymen.

It is hard to imagine a more terrible ending to a life for which St. Paul's moving words to St. Timothy are, perhaps, a most fitting epitaph:

> I have fought the good fight,
> I have stayed the course,
> I have kept the faith.

Pilecki's final resting place is unknown. He was fully exonerated posthumously in the 1990s and is now treated as an heroic figure in modern Poland.

*Jarek Garliński*

CAPTAIN WITOLD PILECKI'S
COVERING LETTER TO
MAJOR GENERAL TADEUSZ PEŁCZYŃSKI

*Preceding page:*

Montage of Pilecki's photo and his handwritten
covering letter to General Pełczyński.

*Letter*: PUMST
*Photo*: Pilecki Family

Dear Sir,

I deliver my paper to you, Sir, because I am unable to take it with me,[1] and because Senior Officers and Commanders of our underground forces in Poland might find interesting these details of an area of Home Army work which is completely unknown. I have been offered a commercial deal to publish this for big bucks in America, but for the time being I have not decided to take this step because I have not had the time to polish the style and also because I would feel remorse at selling it for money. There have been others who have wanted to get hold of it from me, but in my opinion the right thing to do is to put this in your hands, General. Perhaps someone in London might also find it interesting. Please do not treat this as (exclusively) sensationalism, for these are the experiences at the very highest level of a number of honest Poles. Not everything has been related here, for it was not possible to do so in a short time. Nothing has been "overdone"; even the smallest fib would profane the memory of those fine people who lost their lives there.

Tomasz of Auschwitz
Cavalry Captain Witold
who reported to you a few days ago.

19 Oct. 1945

---

[1] One assumes that he means back to Poland, on his final, fateful mission. Translator's note.

3

**CAPTAIN WITOLD PILECKI'S**

**1945 AUSCHWITZ REPORT**

# SUMMER  1945

So, I am to write down the driest of facts, which is what my friends want me to do.

They have told me: "The more you stick to the bare facts without any kind of commentary, the more valuable it all will be."

Well, here I go...but we were not made out of wood, let alone stone, though it sometimes seemed as if even a stone would have broken out in a sweat.

Therefore, now and again I shall insert a thought amongst these facts to indicate what one was feeling.

I do not know whether this must by definition devalue the description.

One was not made out of stone, though I often envied it; one still had a heart beating, sometimes in one's mouth, and certainly, running around one's brain was the odd thought which I sometimes with difficulty grasped...

I think that inserting a sentence or two from time to time about this is needed in order to present a true picture.

# AUSCHWITZ AND ENVIRONS

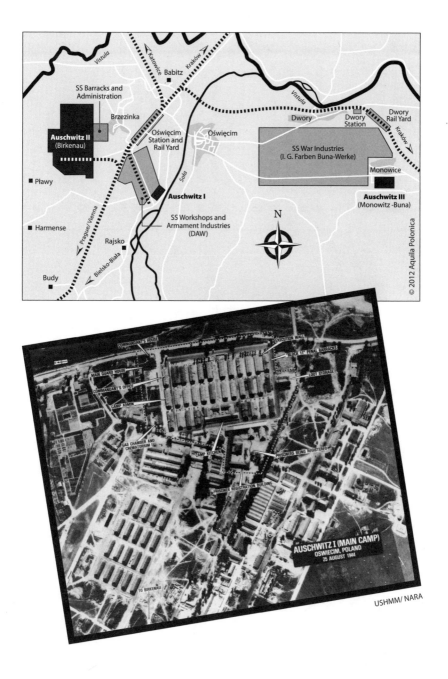

Above: A schematic of Auschwitz and environs dating from 1944, juxtaposed against an aerial photo of the camp taken by Allied reconnaissance units in August 1944.

# KL AUSCHWITZ I

- – Soviet POW camp (old block nos. 1–9), October 1941–March 1942
- ⊠ – Watchtowers
- **24** – Camp block numbers
- ⁹⁄ – Old block numbers
- **A** – Camp Commandant's house
- **B** – Main guardroom
- **C** – Camp Commandant's offices
- **D** – Camp administrative offices
- **E** – SS hospital
- **F** – Camp Political Department's (Gestapo's) offices
- **G** – Administrative Building
- **H** – Prisoners' hospitals
- **I** – Kitchen
- **J** – Main gate ("Arbeit macht frei")
- **K1** – Gas chamber and Crematorium No. I
- **L** – Gravel pit—place of execution
- **M** – Storeroom of possessions seized from murdered people
- **N** – Spot where the camp orchestra played
- **O** – SS laundry hut
- **P** – Blockführers' (SS block supervisors') hut
- **S** – The wall of death
- **T** – Gallows
- ⁄⁄ – Railroad

Support barracks and workshops

Oświęcim town center ▶

RIVER SOŁA

▶ Oświęcim train station

▶ Birkenau

N

▶ Rajsko, Brzeszcze, Bielsko-Biała

**SEPTEMBER 1940...**

The 19th of September 1940—the second street round-up in Warsaw.

There are a few people still alive who saw me go alone at 6:00 a.m. to the corner of Aleja Wojska and Felińskiego Street and join the "fives" of captured men drawn up by the SS.

On Plac Wilsona we were then loaded onto trucks and taken to the Light Horse Guards Barracks.

After having our particulars taken down in the temporary office there, being relieved of sharp objects and threatened with being shot if so much as a razor was later found on us, we were led out into the riding school arena where we remained throughout the 19th and the 20th.

During those two days some of us made the acquaintance of a rubber truncheon on the head. However, this was more or less within acceptable bounds for those accustomed to guardians of the peace using such methods to keep order.

Meanwhile, some families were buying their loved ones' freedom, paying the SS huge sums of money.

At night, we all slept side by side on the ground.

The arena was lit by a huge spotlight set up right next to the entrance.

SS men with automatic weapons were stationed on all four sides.

There were about one thousand eight hundred or so of us.

11

What really annoyed me the most was the passivity of this group of Poles. All those picked up were already showing signs of crowd psychology, the result being that our whole crowd behaved like a herd of passive sheep.

A simple thought kept nagging me: stir up everyone and get this mass of people moving.

I suggested to my comrade, Sławek Szpakowski (who I know was living in Warsaw up to the Uprising),[1] a joint operation during the night: take over the crowd, attack the sentry posts while I, on my way to the lavatory, would "bump" into the spotlight and smash it.

However, I had a different reason for being there.

This would have been a much less important objective.

While he—thought the idea was total madness.

On the morning of the 21st we were put onto trucks and, escorted by motorcycles with automatic weapons, were taken off to the western railroad station and loaded onto freight cars.

The railroad cars must have been used before for carrying lime, for the floors were covered in it.

The cars were shut. We travelled for a whole day. We were given nothing to eat or drink. In any case, no one wanted to eat. The previous day we had been issued some bread, which we did not yet know how to eat or to treasure. We were just very thirsty. The lime, when disturbed, turned into a powder. It filled the air, irritating our nostrils and throats. We got nothing to drink.

We could see through the cracks between the boards covering the windows that we were being taken in the direction of Częstochowa.

---

[1] Pilecki is referring to the Warsaw Uprising of 1944, not the Warsaw Ghetto Uprising of 1943. Translator's note.

Around 10:00 p.m. (22:00 hours) the train stopped some-where and went no further. We could hear shouting and yelling, the cars being opened up and the baying of dogs.

I consider this place in my story to be the moment when I bade farewell to everything I had hitherto known on this earth and entered something seemingly no longer of it.

This is not an attempt on my part to use unusual words or terms. Quite the contrary, I believe that I do not need to attempt to use any irrelevant or pretty little word.

This is how it was.

We were struck over the head not only by SS rifle butts, but also by something far greater.

Our concepts of law and order and of what was normal, all those ideas to which we had become accustomed on this earth, were given a brutal kicking.

Everything came to an end.

The idea was to hit us as hard as possible. To break us psychologically as speedily as possible.

A hubbub and the sound of yelling voices gradually drew near. Eventually, the doors of our freight car were wrenched open. Lights shone in, blinding us.

"Heraus!rrraus!rrraus!...," the SS belabored us with epithets and rifle butts to our shoulders, backs and heads. The idea was to get out as quickly as possible.

I leapt out, managing somehow to avoid being hit, and joined the "fives" in the center of the column.

A larger group of SS was hitting, kicking and screaming: "Zu fünfen! [Form up in fives!]"

Dogs urged on by the crazed soldiery rushed at those on the outside of the column.

Blinded by the lights, shoved, beaten, kicked, and rushed by the dogs, we had suddenly found ourselves in conditions which I doubt any of us had ever experienced. The weaker ones were so overwhelmed that they simply fell into a stupor.

We were urged on towards a larger cluster of lights.

On the way, one of us was told to run to a post at the side of the road; he was followed by a burst of automatic weapons fire and mown down. Ten men were then dragged out of the ranks at random and shot with pistols as "collective responsibility" for the "escape," which the SS themselves had staged.

All eleven of them were then dragged along by leg straps. The dogs were teased with the bloody corpses and set on them.

All this to the accompaniment of laughter and joking.

We approached a gate in a wire fence over which could be seen the sign "Arbeit macht frei" ["Work Liberates You"].

It was only later that we learned to understand it properly.

Beyond the fence stood rows of brick huts amidst which could be seen a large parade ground.

Entering between the rows of SS men right in front of the gate we experienced a short interlude of peace. The dogs were led away, we were ordered to form up by fives. Here we were carefully counted, the dragged corpses being added at the end.

The high, at that time only, barbed-wire fence and the gate filled with SS somehow brought to mind a Chinese saying which I had read somewhere: "Entering, think of the return, and on leaving you will be whole . . . " An ironic smile arose somewhere within me and died . . . there would be little use for that here . . .

Inside the wire, on the great parade ground we beheld quite another sight. In the somewhat eerie light crawling over us from the spotlights on all sides we could see beings resembling people, but whose behavior was more like that of wild animals (I absolutely see animals here, our language still has no word for such creatures). They were wearing strange striped

# 1940...

All those entering the main camp at Auschwitz were greeted by the sign "Arbeit macht frei" ("Work Liberates You").

A section of the electrified perimeter double fence surrounding Auschwitz.

Concentration camp inmates (here, at roll call in Buchenwald) were identified by their blue and white striped prison clothing. Also visible in this photo are the colored triangular patches called "winkels" with inmate numbers written on a white patch, which were stitched onto the left breast of the jacket and the right leg of the trouser.

The first Auschwitz inmates to have a number tattooed on their body were Soviet POWs in the autumn of 1941, and from then onwards all new prisoners not selected for immediate death were also tattooed. A program to tattoo earlier inmates did not start until the spring of 1943.

clothes, like those one had seen in films of Sing Sing, with what in the flickering light appeared to be medals on colored ribbons, with clubs in their hands attacking our comrades with wild laughter, hitting them over the head, kicking them on the ground in the kidneys and other tender spots, jumping on their chests and stomachs with their boots, dealing death with an outlandish giggle.

"So they've put us in a lunatic asylum!" the thought ran through my brain, "How fiendish!" I was still thinking in earthly categories. These were people who had been caught in a street round-up, and so even in the Germans' mind not accused of any crime against the Third Reich.

The words of Janek W. [Jan Włodarkiewicz], spoken after the first round-up in August in Warsaw, lit up in my brain. "There, see, you've missed a grand opportunity, people picked up in round-ups are not accused of any political crimes; it's the safest way to get into a camp."

How naive we were there in faraway Warsaw about the Poles who had been shipped off to the camps.

Here on the ground you didn't need to be a "political" to lose your life.

They killed whoever was at hand.

The first thing was a question thrown out in German by a striped man with a club: "Was bist du von zivil? [Hey you, what's your civilian job?]"

Replying priest, judge, lawyer, at that time meant being beaten to death.

When asked, the fellow standing in the row in front of me replied in German "Richter [a judge]," as his clothes were grasped under his throat.

It was a disastrous mistake. Within moments he was on the ground being beaten and kicked.

So, they were going out of their way to kill the professional classes.

After this observation, I changed my mind somewhat.

Perhaps there was a method to this insanity and this was some terrible way of murdering Poles beginning with the intelligentsia.

We were desperately thirsty.

Pots with some liquid arrived. These same striped murderers carried mugs with liquid through our ranks, asking "Was bist du von zivil?"

We got the desired and wet liquid by naming some manual job or craft.

Hitting and kicking, these strange "semi-humans" sometimes yelled: "Hier ist KL Auschwitz, mein lieber Mann. [This is Auschwitz Concentration Camp, my dear sir!]"

We asked each other what could this mean. Some knew that this meant Oświęcim, to us this meant only the name of a small Polish town, for the camp's terrible reputation had not yet managed to reach Warsaw, nor was it known to the world at large.

Only some time later would this single word freeze the blood in free men's veins and drive sleep from the eyes of prisoners in the Pawiak, Montelupich, Wiśnicz and Lublin prisons.

One of us explained that we were in the barracks of the 5th Regiment of Horse Artillery near the small town of Oświęcim.

We discovered that we were a *zugang* of Polish bandits, who had been attacking the peaceful German population and who were to receive their just deserts here.

Everything that arrived in the camp, every new transport, was called a zugang.

Meanwhile, the roll was called, the names we had given in Warsaw being called out, to which we had to reply quickly and loudly "Hier [Present]." This was accompanied by much harassment and beatings.

After roll call we were sent off in groups of a hundred for a grandly sounding "bath."

That is how they greeted a transport of people who had been caught on the streets of Warsaw and who were supposedly to be sent for labor to Germany; that is how they greeted every transport in the first few months after the camp at Auschwitz was opened on the 14th of June 1940.

Out of the darkness, somewhere overhead, from above the kitchen, the butcher Seidler [Fritz Seidler],[2] spoke as follows:

"Let none of you imagine that he will ever leave this place alive... It has been worked out that you will survive for six weeks; anyone who lives longer... must be stealing, and anyone who is stealing, will be sent to the SK [Strafkompanie (Penal Company)], where you won't live very long." This was translated into Polish by the camp interpreter Baworowski [Władysław Baworowski].

The idea was to break us psychologically as quickly as possible.

On the parade ground we put all the bread we had into wheelbarrows and onto a cart which had been brought over. No one much minded doing this; no one was thinking of food.

Later, the mere thought of this moment made one salivate and curse. Several wheelbarrows and a cart filled with bread! What a pity we couldn't eat ourselves sick...

Together with my hundred I at last found myself in front

---

[2] At that time, Fritz Seidler was Acting Deputy Camp Commandant. He later became Deputy Camp Commandant. Translator's note.

of the *baderaum* [communal washing facilities] (Block 18 using the old numbering system).[3]

Here we put everything into great sacks which had appropriate numbers attached.

Here our head and body hair were shaved and a few drops of almost cold water were sprinkled over us.

Here I had my two front teeth knocked out because I was holding my prison number written on a card in my hand and not between my teeth, as the *bademeister* [washroom supervisor] required that day.

I was hit on the chin with a heavy club.

I spat out the two teeth. I bled a little... Par for the course.

From that moment on we were just numbers. Our formal name was: "Schutzhäftling no. such and such..."[4]

My number was 4859. The two thirteens (composed by the inner and outer digits) convinced my comrades that I would die; the numbers cheered me up.

We were issued with blue and white striped prison clothing, the same sort that had struck us during the night.

By now it was morning (22 Sept. 1940). A number of things now lost their terrible nighttime appearance.

The "semi-humans" wore yellow armbands on their left arm with the black letters K A P O, and instead of what had seemed to me in the flickering nighttime lights to be colorful ribbons with medals, on their left breast they wore a colored triangle (here known as a *winkel*[5]) beneath which there was a

---

[3] As the central camp expanded and eight new blocks were added in the summer of 1941, some of the blocks had their numbers changed: e.g., Block 18 became Block 26. Translator's note.

[4] Technically, a *Schutzhäftling* was an inmate or prisoner held under indefinite detention pursuant to the Nazi German law of *Schutzhaft* (protective custody), while a *Häftling* was held for a definite term of incarceration. Except in formal situations, the term Häftling was generally used for all the inmates in Auschwitz. Translator's note.

[5] *Winkel* in German and *winkiel* in Polish. Translator's note.

# 1940...

"My number was 4859. The two thirteens (composed by the inner and outer digits) convinced my comrades that I would die; the numbers cheered me up."

**Wincenty Gawron (Pilecki's comrade—code no. 44) with the red triangular "winkel" of a political prisoner and his inmate number sewn onto his prison uniform.**

JG

21

**Fritz Seidler in SS uniform.**

**The SS Totenkopf
(Death's Head) cap
badge, 1934-1945.**

small black number written on a white patch just as on the ribbon.

There were five colors of winkel.

Political prisoners wore a red one; criminals—green; those refusing to work in the Third Reich wore black; Jehovah's Witnesses[6]—purple; and homosexuals—pink.

All us Poles, who had been picked up on a Warsaw street supposedly to be sent to labor in Germany, were given red winkels, as political prisoners.

I must confess that out of all these colors, this one suited me the best.

Dressed in our striped prison uniforms, with no caps and socks (I was issued socks on the 8th of December and a cap on the 15th) and with clogs which kept falling off, we were led onto the parade ground used for roll calls and divided into two halves.

One group went to Block 10 and we went to the first floor of Block 17.

A group of *häftlings* [inmates] was accommodated both on the ground floor and first floor of individual barracks, each with its own arrangements and administrative support, forming a separate "block." To distinguish them, each upstairs barrack room had the letter "a" added to its number.

So we were sent off to Block 17a into the care of "Aloiz," later known as "Bloody Aloiz."

A German—a communist—with a red winkel, a degenerate who had already spent about six years in camps, he beat, tormented and tortured, with several corpses to his personal account every day.

A lover of order and military discipline, he would line up the ranks on the parade ground beating us with his club.

---

[6] Also known as conscientious objectors. Translator's note.

Formed up in 10 ranks our "block," thus dressed in the military sense of the word by Aloiz running through the ranks with a great club, could have served in the future as a model of dressed lines.

This morning he ran through our lines for the first time.

He was forming our zugang into a new block.

He sought out amongst these unknown faces people able to maintain order on the block.

Fate decreed that he picked me, Karol Świętorzecki (a reserve officer from the 13th Uhlans), Witold Różycki (not the Różycki of infamous repute,[7] but a decent fellow from Ładysława Street in Warsaw) and a couple of others.

He quickly led us in and upstairs, ordered us to line up along the wall, do an about-turn and bend over.

He gave each of us as hard as possible "five of the best" with his club in that spot which is apparently there for that reason.

One had to grit one's teeth hard to prevent the slightest groan escaping.

I think I passed the test well.

"Just so you know what it tastes like and just so you use your clubs like that, ensuring cleanliness and discipline on the block."

So I became a *stubendienst* [room supervisor], but not for long.

Although we maintained exemplary order and cleanliness on the block, Aloiz did not care for the methods we used to achieve this.

He warned us several times himself and also through "Kazik" (an intimate of his), and when this got him nowhere,

---

[7] Pilecki is here referring to Adam Różycki, a *Kapo* with a murderous reputation. Translator's note.

he exploded and kicked several of us out into the main camp for three days saying: "Just so you see what it tastes like to work in the camp and get to appreciate better the comfort and peace you have here on the block."

I had noticed that fewer people returned from work every day, and I knew that they had been "finished off" at one task or another, but now I was to discover the hard way what a day "in the camp" looked like for a normal häftling.

Everyone had to work.

Only the stubendiensts [room supervisors] could remain on the block.

We all slept side by side on straw mattresses laid out on the floor. Initially we had no bunks at all.

Everyone's day began with a gong at 4:20 a.m. in summer and at 5:20 a.m. in winter.

At this sound, summoning us with its seemingly inexorable command, everyone came to their feet.

We quickly folded our blanket, boxing it carefully. The mattresses had to be carried to one end of the room where they were grabbed by the "mattress orderlies" to make a mattress pile. On leaving the room we handed in our blanket to the "blanket orderly." We finished dressing in the corridor.

Everything was done at the double and in a rush, for Bloody Aloiz, shouting "Open the windows," would charge into the room with his club and we needed to hurry to get in line for the toilet.

Initially we had no toilets in the blocks. We all ran to a number of latrines where there were very long queues, sometimes of one hundred to two hundred men. There were few actual toilets. Inside stood a *kapo* with a club who counted to five and hit over the head anyone slow getting up. More than one häftling fell into the latrine.

After the latrine we all ran to the pumps, of which there were a number on the parade ground. Initially, there was no *waschraum* [washroom] on the blocks.

Several thousand people had to wash under these few pumps.

This was obviously impossible.

You forced your way to the pump and caught a little water in your canteen.

However, in the evening we had to have clean feet. The block chiefs, going around the room in the evening while a "room supervisor" would report on the condition and number of häftlings lying on their mattresses, would simultaneously check the cleanliness of our feet, which had to be held up from under the blanket so that the sole was visible. If a foot was not sufficiently clean, or if the block chief thought it was not, the culprit was beaten on the table. He would receive between 10 and 20 strokes.

This was one way to wear us down, all under the beautiful cloak of hygiene.

Another way to wear us down was the destruction of our constitution in the latrines by having to do everything at the double and to order, or the nerve-jangling chaos at the pumps, or the endless rush and *laufschritt* [doing things at the double] employed everywhere during the camp's initial phase.

From the pump everyone ran to the block for so-called coffee or tea. A warm liquid was brought into the room in large pots—a pale imitation of these beverages.

A wretched häftling hardly ever saw any sugar.

When I saw that some of my comrades who had been there for a few months had swelled faces and feet, the medical men whom I asked told me that this was due to a surfeit of liquids. Kidneys or the heart were failing. The body's enormous effort when doing physical labor while ingesting only liquids: coffees, tea, *awo* [a sort of broth] and soup; I resolved to avoid liquids which brought me no benefit and stick to just awo and soups.

One had to control one's desires.

Some did not want to forgo warm liquids, on account of the cold.

Smoking was even worse. Because, during the initial stages of his time in the camp, a häftling had no money, for at first letters could not be sent. He waited a long time for that. Then before any kind of reply could arrive, about three months would elapse.

Anyone who could not overcome this and who sold bread for cigarettes was "digging his own grave."

I knew a great many like this; every one of them died.

There were no graves. All the bodies were burned in the newly constructed crematorium.

So I did not race back to the block for hot dishwater; others pushed their way through, earning blows and kicks.

If a häftling with swollen feet then managed to get a better work assignment and food, he regained his strength and the swelling would subside, but suppurating boils would form on his feet, oozing a stinking fluid and sometimes phlegmon, which I saw here for the first time.

Eschewing liquids, I successfully managed to avoid this.

Before everyone had managed to get some hot dishwater, the "room supervisor" was using his club to empty the barrack room, which had to be tidied up before roll call.

Meanwhile the mattresses and blankets had been arranged according to the style in fashion in that block, and the blocks competed amongst themselves in arranging their "bedclothes."

Now the floor still had to washed.

The gong for morning roll call was sounded at 5:45 a.m.

At 6 o'clock we were all standing in dressed lines (each block formed up in lines of 10 to make counting easier).

Everyone had to attend roll call.

If someone was missing, not because he had escaped, but because some new arrival had naively hidden himself, or someone else had simply overslept and the numbers did not match the camp's roll, a search was begun, the man was dragged onto the parade ground and almost always publicly killed.

Occasionally a häftling was absent: he had hanged himself somewhere in an attic, or right during roll call he "went for the wires," then shots rang out from a sentry in a watchtower and the inmate fell riddled with bullets.

Inmates usually "went for the wires" in the morning, before another day's torment; before nightfall, when there was a break of a few hours in the agony, this happened more rarely.

There was an official order which forbade inmates preventing their comrades from taking their own life. If caught "preventing," a häftling was punished with a stint in the "bunker."

All the camp's internal authorities were recruited exclusively from among the inmates. Initially they were Germans, but then other nationalities began to clamber up to responsible posts.

The block chief (wearing a red armband with the word "Blockältester" in white on his right arm) wore down an inmate on the block with strict discipline and his club. He was responsible for the block, but had nothing to do with a häftling's work.

However, a kapo wore down an inmate with work and his

# 1940...

**An inmate shot by guards as he "went for the wires."**

Lagerältester (Head Inmate) Bruno Brodniewitsch—Inmate No. 1.

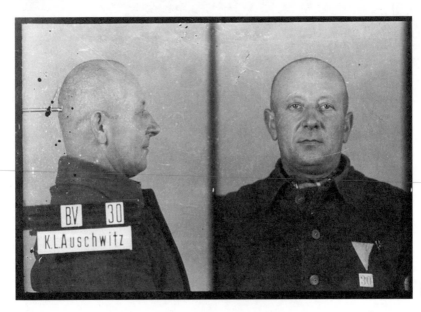

Lagerältester (Head Inmate) Leo Wietschorek—Inmate No. 30.

club in a *kommando* (work detail) and was responsible for that kommando's work.

The highest authority in the camp was the so-called Lagerältester [Head Inmate].

Initially, there were two of them: Bruno and Leo, both inmates.

They were two bastards before whom everyone trembled in fear.

They murdered in front of everyone, sometimes using clubs or fists.

The first one's real name was Bronisław Brodniewicz [also written Brodniewitsch], the other's—Leon Wieczorek [also written Wietschorek]; both ex-Poles working for the Germans...

Dressed differently than everyone else in high boots, navy-blue trousers, jackets and berets. (A black armband with white lettering on their left arm.)

They were an evil pair, often seen together.

However, all these internal camp authorities, recruited from "people inside the wire," were as nothing before any SS man, to whose question they would reply only after removing their cap and standing at attention.

Just imagine how much less significant was an ordinary gray häftling...

These "super-human" authorities in military uniform, the SS, lived outside the wires in barracks and the town.

I return to the daily camp routine.

Roll call. We stood, clubbed into lines straight as a wall (in fact I yearned for the well-dressed Polish lines of 1939).

We were transfixed by the terrible scene before us.

In front of us were the ranks from Block 13 (old numbering system)—the SK [Strafkompanie (Penal Company)], being dressed by the block chief Krankenmann [Krankemann in some sources] using a radical method—a simple knife.

At that time all the Jews, priests and some condemned Poles went straight to the Penal Company.

It was Krankenmann's responsibility to finish off as quickly as possible the almost daily intakes of häftlings. Clearly this man's character was well suited to his duties.

If someone inadvertently moved a few centimeters too far forward, Krankenmann would plunge the knife carried in his right sleeve into the victim's stomach.

He who, through an excess of caution, moved too far back, received a thrust in the kidneys from this murderer running around the ranks.

The sight of the falling man kicking the sand and screaming drove Krankenmann into a rage. He would jump onto the man's chest, kick him in the kidneys, in his private parts, finishing him off as quickly as possible, which forced us to stay silent.

This sight ran through us like an electric current.

Then, I felt a single thought coursing through these Poles standing shoulder to shoulder, I felt that finally we were all united by the same anger, a desire for revenge, I felt myself in an environment perfectly suited to begin my work here and discovered within me a semblance of happiness...

A moment later I was afraid that I had taken leave of my

senses. To feel happiness here, for whatever reason, was absurd...abnormal!

I looked carefully inside myself and now felt happiness with full certainty, above all because I wanted to start work and so I had not cracked.

This was a key psychological breakthrough.

In medicine we would say that the crisis had successfully passed.

However, for the time being, all my efforts were needed to stay alive.

The gong after roll call meant: "Arbeitskommando formieren! [Work kommandos fall in!]"

On this order everyone rushed to whichever kommando seemed best.

There was still chaos with assignments (not like later when everyone quietly went to the detail where his number was registered), inmates ran in all directions, crisscrossing, which was the cue for the kapos, block chiefs and SS to stick out a foot, to push and club the running and tripping men, always kicking the most tender spots.

I was to spend the three days Aloiz had punished me by sending me into the camp carrying gravel in wheelbarrows.

Simply not knowing where to stand and not having a chosen kommando, I joined the "fives" of the hundred taken off to do this work.

For the most part Warsaw lads were working here.

The older "numbers," in other words, those who had been there longer, those who had survived so far, had already taken the better "jobs."

Those of us from Warsaw were ground down en masse by all manner of tasks, sometimes by carrying gravel from one pit to another and then back again.

I was among those who were carrying gravel needed to complete the construction of the crematorium.

We were building the crematorium for ourselves.

The scaffolding around the chimney rose ever higher.

We had to move quickly with a wheelbarrow filled by the *vorarbeiteren* [foremen], toadies who showed us no mercy, and then push the wheelbarrows at the double over planking.

Every 15 to 20 paces stood a kapo with a club, which he used to beat the passing inmates shouting "Laufschritt! [Move at the double!]"

We pushed the wheelbarrows up slowly. With an empty wheelbarrow, laufschritt applied all the way.

Here muscles, cunning and eyes competed in the battle to stay alive.

You needed strength to push the wheelbarrow, you had to know how to keep it on the planks, you had to see and pick a suitable moment "to take a breather" to help one's tired lungs.

It was here that I saw how a great many members of our intelligentsia were unable to cope with difficult and merciless conditions.

Yes—we were going through a harsh selection process.

Sport, and my early physical training, were coming in very handy here.

The intellectual, looking helplessly around seeking better treatment or help from someone, as if almost demanding it because he was a lawyer or an engineer, now came face to face with a hard club.

Here is some lawyer with a tummy, or a landowner clumsily pushing his wheelbarrow which falls off the planking into the sand and he cannot pull it back up.

There a teacher in glasses, or an older gentleman, present a pitiful sight of helplessness.

All those who were unsuited to the work, or who had no strength to run with a wheelbarrow, were beaten, and when they fell over with their wheelbarrow they were beaten to death with clubs and boots.

It was at moments like this, when someone ahead was killed, that like a real animal one would stop for a couple of minutes and draw some breath into one's overworked lungs and slow down one's racing heart.

Fortunately, in the Third Reich's orderly world overtaking those ahead had not been foreseen.

The lunch gong was greeted with joy by everyone in the camp and was, I think, in those days sounded at 11:20 a.m.

Between 11:30 and 12:00 the midday roll call was held, usually quite quickly and from 12:00 to 13:00 was the time assigned to lunch.

After lunch, a gong again summoned everyone to his arbeitskommando and the misery continued until the gong for evening roll call.

I worked like this for three days "on the barrows."

On the third day, after lunch I thought that the gong would never come.

I was by now very tired and I understood that when they ran out of weaker people to kill, my turn would come.

Bloody Aloiz, who was satisfied with our efforts on the block to maintain order and cleanliness, generously agreed to take us back after three days' hard labor in the camp saying: "Now you know what work in the camp means. Paßt auf [take care] with your work on the block, or I'll kick you back out into the camp for good."

In my case he quickly made good on his threat.

I did not use on my comrades the methods demanded by him and recommended by Kazik, and was kicked off the block with a bang, under circumstances which I shall relate below.

I now want to write about the early stages of the work I was starting there.

The main task was:

To set up here a military organization in order to:

— keep up my comrades' spirits by providing and distributing news from outside;

— by organizing, whenever possible, additional food and distributing clothes amongst the members;

— send information out of the camp; and, as the crowning glory,

— prepare our own detachments to take over the camp when the time came in the form of an order to parachute in arms or troops.

I began my work the same way I had in '39 in Warsaw and even, with a few small exceptions, with the same people whom I had brought into the TAP[8] in Warsaw.

I now set up the first "five" to which I swore in Colonel 1 [Władysław Surmacki], Captain Dr. 2 [Władysław Dering],[9]

---

[8] Tajna Armia Polska (The Polish Secret Army) was an underground resistance organization formed on the 9th of November 1939. It eventually became integrated into the ZWZ (Związek Walki Zbrojnej [The Union for Armed Combat]—the precursor of the Armia Krajowa (AK, or Home Army). Translator's note.

[9] Dr. Władysław Dering was a controversial figure who in 1964 sued the writer Leon Uris in Britain for libel, Uris having claimed in his novel *Exodus* that Dering had performed 17,000 medical experiments without anesthetics on inmates in Auschwitz. Although Dering won the case after an eighteen-day trial, the court awarded him minimal damages and ordered him to pay costs. Translator's note.

Cavalry Captain 3 [Jerzy de Virion], Second Lieutenant 4 [Alfred Stössel], as well as 5 [Roman Zagner] (I am writing a separate key to the numbers).[10]

Colonel 1 [Władysław Surmacki] commanded the "five"; it was Dr. 2's [Władysław Dering's] responsibility to take over the prison hospital where he was already working as a *pfleger* [nurse]. Poles were not officially permitted to work as doctors and could only be nurses.

In November, I sent my first report to High Command in Warsaw through Second Lieutenant 6 [Tadeusz Burski][11] (he was living at 58, Raszyńska Street in Warsaw before the Uprising), who had worked in Intelligence and who had been bought out of Auschwitz.

Colonel 1 [Władysław Surmacki] moved his operations to the *baubüro* [construction site office].

Later I set up a further four "fives." Each of these "fives" knew nothing of the existence of the other "fives," believing itself to be the apex of an organization which it developed downwards as extensively as the sum of its individual members' abilities and energy allowed.

I did this as a precaution so that if a "five" was rolled up, it would not bring down the next one.

Eventually, the expanding "fives" began to make contact and sound out one another.

Then on more than one occasion members would come to me to report that "you know, there's some other organization working out there." I would reassure them that they needn't worry about this.

---

[10] The key to this 1945 Report has not been found; see Translator's Introductory Note. In his autumn 1943 report (*Raport W*), Pilecki has Eugeniusz Obojski instead of Alfred Stössel in his first "five." Translator's note.

[11] A mistake on the part of Pilecki. In fact the report was carried by Aleksander Wielopolski, and indeed Burski appears later in this 1945 Report. Translator's note.

But this all lay in the future. For the time being there was only a single "five."

Meanwhile, back at the block, one day after morning roll call I went to report to Aloiz that there were three sick men on the block, who could not go out to work (they were almost completely done in).

Bloody Aloiz flew into a rage. "A sick man on my block?!!...I don't have sick men!...Everyone works...you too! Enough!" He rushed into the room behind me with his club. "Where are they?"

Two of them were lying by the wall panting heavily, the third one was kneeling in the corner praying.

"Was macht er? [What's he doing?]" he shouted at me.

"Er betet [He's praying]."

"He's praying?!! Who taught him to do that?"

"Das weiss ich nicht [I don't know]," I replied.

He rushed over to the praying man and started to insult him and shout at him that he was an idiot...that there was no God...that he, not God, gave him bread...and so on, but he did not strike him.

He then ran over to the two men lying by the wall and began to kick them in the kidneys and so on, screaming "Auf!!! [Get up] auf!!!..." until they, seeing death before them, dragged themselves to their feet with what little strength they still had left.

Then he began screaming at me: "See! I told you they weren't sick!...They can walk, they can work. Weg!!! [Get out!!!] Off to work! And you too!"

Thus he threw me out to work in the camp.

He himself took the one praying to the hospital.

He was a strange man, that communist.

On the parade ground I found myself in an odd position.

Everyone was already standing in his kommando waiting to march out. To run over and join the "fives" as a tardy häftling was asking for a beating and a kicking from the kapos and SS.

I noticed that on the parade ground around me stood a detachment of those who did not belong to work details. At that time those inmates not required for work (the camp was still being built and there were few kommandos) "did PE" [physical exercise] on the parade ground.

For the moment there was no sign of kapos or SS busy around them forming up arbeitskommando columns.

I ran over and stood on the parade ground in a circle to "do PE."

I used to enjoy PE, but after Auschwitz I don't quite have the same appetite for it.

From six in the morning, sometimes for hours on end, we stood around freezing dreadfully.

Without caps or socks and wearing thin prison clothes, in that autumn of '40 we trembled from the cold in that foothills climate, the mornings almost always misty.

Our feet and hands, sticking out from trouser legs and sleeves cut short, turned blue.

We were left alone.

We had to stand and freeze.

The cold hastened our exhaustion.

Passing kapos and block chiefs (often Aloiz) stopped, laughed and said with a knowing hand gesture imitating rising steam: "...und das Leben fliiiiieeegt [...life's just seeping away]...Ha, ha!"

When the mist dissipated, the sun shone through and it became somewhat warmer and it appeared that lunch could not be far off, a pack of kapos began to get us "doing PE"; it might just as well have been called heavy physical punishment.

For this type of PE there was still far too much time before lunch.

"Hüpfen! [Hop!], rollen! [roll!], tanzen! [dance!], kniebeugen! [do squats!]"

Just one of those "hüpfens" could do you in.

It was impossible to frog-hop around the large parade ground, not because we were in clogs, for we were holding them, not because we were barefoot and the gravel ripped the skin of our feet till we bled, but because our muscles were unable to accomplish such a feat.

Here again my past involvement in sport saved me.

Here again the weak intellectuals with tummies, for whom frog-hopping even a short distance was beyond them, were finished off.

Here again clubs crashed down on the heads of those who kept falling over every few steps. There was more beating and merciless finishing off.

And again, like an animal, one would take advantage of a pause to get one's breath while the pack with clubs pounced on some new victim.

After lunch—part two.

By evening a great many corpses and semi-corpses, who quickly succumbed in the hospital, were dragged off.

Two rollers were working alongside us on the parade ground. They were supposedly levelling the parade ground.

They were working to finish off the people pulling them.

To one of them, the smaller, were harnessed priests with a few other inmates—Poles, altogether about 20–25 men.

About 50 Jews were harnessed to the second one—the larger.

On the rollers' towing bars stood Krankenmann and some other kapo, who with their own weight increased the load, pressing the towing bar into the backs and shoulders of the inmates pulling the rollers.

From time to time the kapo or block chief Krankenmann with philosophical calm smashed down his club on someone's head or struck out at some other human beast of burden with such force that he sometimes felled him immediately, or he pushed the stunned man under the roller, beating the other inmates not to stop.

Over the course of a day from this little factory of corpses a great many were pulled out by their legs and laid out in a row to be counted during roll call.

Towards evening, Krankenmann, walking around the parade ground with his hands behind his back, looked with a smile of pleasure at these former inmates now lying peacefully.

I did this "PE," called the "circle of death," for two days.

On the morning of the third day, I was standing in the circle wondering what percentage of those still "doing PE" were weaker and less fit than I was, and calculating how much longer I could go on, when suddenly my situation changed abruptly.

The kommandos were marching out to work. Some of them to work inside the wires and some marched out to work beyond the fence.

The Lagerführer [Camp Head], together with a group of SS men, was standing near the gate at a lectern. He was reviewing the departing kommandos and checking their numbers against the roster.

Next to him stood an *arbeitsdienst* [work assignment leader], Otto [Otto Küsel] (a German who never struck a Pole). His duty was to assign specific inmates to work. He was responsible for filling specific kommandos with workers.

Standing in the arc of the circle nearest to the gate I noticed that Otto was running straight towards us.

I instinctively moved even closer.

The arbeitsdienst, with a worried look, charged straight into me: "Vielleicht bist du ein Ofensetzer? [You're not by any chance a stove fitter?]"

"Ja wohl. Ich bin ein Ofensetzer [Yes, sir. I'm a stove fitter]," I replied without a thought.

"Aber ein guter Meister? [But are you a good one?]"

"Gewiß, ein guter Meister. [Of course, I'm a good one.]"

"Also schnell!. . . [Quickly then!. . . ]"

He told me to take four others out of the circle and to follow him at the double to the gate to Block 9 (old numbering system); they gave us buckets, trowels, bricklayers' hammers, lime, and our "five" lined up before the lectern of the Lagerführer, who at the time was Fritsch [Karl Fritzsch].

Only now did I look at the faces of my chance companions.

I knew none of them.

"Fünf Ofensetzer [Five stove fitters]," reported Otto, out of breath.

They assigned two SS men as guards and we marched out of the gate towards the town.

It turned out that Otto had been meant to line up a few fitters to change out the stoves in some SS man's apartment, that he had forgotten and had saved the day at the last minute by bringing in the five of us, while the earlier kommandos were being counted at the gate.

# 1940...

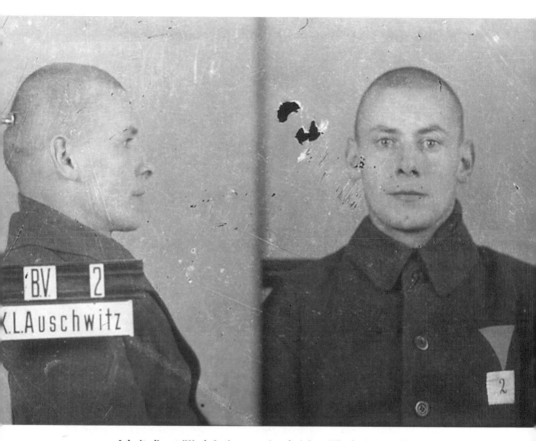

**Arbeitsdienst (Work Assignment Leader) Otto Küsel—Inmate No. 2.**

Inmates working on one of the many new buildings being constructed at Auschwitz.

Female inmates, brought to Auschwitz beginning in 1942, digging the foundations for one of the new buildings next to the main camp.

ABM/ SS Dietrich Kamann

The guards were now taking us to an SS man's flat.

In one of the houses in town, the flat's owner, an SS man, addressed us in German, but in a normal tone of voice, which by now sounded odd.

He asked who was the foreman and he then explained to me that he was gutting the kitchen. His wife was coming, he wanted to move the ceramic tiles here and the stove to another room. He thought that there were too many of us, but above all he wanted the job to be done well, so we could all work there, and if a couple of us had nothing to do, we could tidy up the attic. He would stop by every day to check on our work. Then he left.

I checked whether any of the others knew anything about stoves and when it turned out that no one did, I set the four of them to bringing water, digging clay, dismantling and so on.

The two soldiers stood guard outside.

I was on my own. What did I do with the stove? The less said the better.

A man fighting for his life can do more than he ever imagined he could.

I took the stove to pieces carefully so as not to break the tiles, and I carefully noted where the flues went and how they were assembled.

Then I installed the stove and the range in the indicated spots.

I spent four days on it.

However, when on the fifth day I was to go and lay a trial fire in the stove, I lost myself so successfully in the camp, that although I heard them calling for the foreman stove fitter, they did not find me.

No one thought to look among the gardeners in the Camp Commandant's garden...

No one had taken our numbers, for at that time even kommando kapos did not always take down numbers of "fives."

I never did find out whether the stoves worked well, or smoked…

Let me return to the moment when I first found myself in the SS man's apartment in town.

I am supposed to stick to dry facts…

I had already seen some terrible sights in Auschwitz; nothing had managed to break me.

And now here, where no club or kick threatened me, I suddenly felt my heart rise into my throat and I felt worse than I had before…

I know… no need to remind me, that I am to describe only facts, so I am describing it just as it really was. However, this comes from within me and perhaps that is why it's not so dry.

I was alone with my "stove problem," but this was not a stove issue… What—was there still a world outside where people lived normal lives?

Here there were houses, gardens, flowers. Happy voices. Games.

Yet right next door—hell, murder and the destruction of everything human, everything good…

There, this same SS man was a murderer, a torturer; here, he pretended to be human.

So where did the truth lie? There… or here?

At home he was arranging his nest. His wife was coming, so he occasionally had to have some feelings.

Church bells, people praying, loving and giving birth, and right next door. . . all this killing.

It was then that an urge to fight back arose within me.

It was a moment of powerful struggle.

Then four days going to work on the stoves and, for a change, seeing this hell, this patch of earth, was like being continually shoved into heat and then back into cold.

Yes! This tempered me!

Meanwhile the "first five" took a few steps forward and a few new members were sworn in.

One of them was Captain 7. His name was Michał [Michał Romanowicz].

Captain Michał's method was to help form up the ranks going out to work in the morning. In the presence of the kapos he would curse at and berate his comrades, quickly dressing the ranks and sparing many an inmate a kapo's blows, while making a great deal of commotion and noise, and giving everyone a knowing wink when the kapo's back was turned.

The kapos decided that he was suitable to command a "twenty" and assigned him four "fives," making him a vorarbeiter [foreman].

It was Michał who saved me on that critical day when I had to avoid the kapos, by packing me off to the "twenty" of a friend of his, an *unterkapo* [deputy kapo], which was one of the kommandos going to work outside the wires.

I ended up in a detail working in the fields next to the Camp Commandant's villa.

Meanwhile they were looking for the ofensetzer back in the camp until Otto grabbed another inmate and the "five" set off for the stoves, as usual.

All day long it rained and the wind blew.

Working in the field out of which we were hastily making a garden for the Commandant we were all soaked, so it seemed, to the very core and it seemed too as if the wind blew right through our bodies. Not a dry stitch was on us. The wind turned us around, since one couldn't stand facing it for long. It froze the blood in our veins and only rapid motion with a spade eked out a little heat from our own reserves of energy. And we had to husband our energy, since it was not certain we would be able to replenish it.

We were told to take off our prison clothes. In our shirts, without socks, our clogs bogging down in the mud, without caps, our heads and faces streamed with water and whenever the rain stopped we steamed like horses after a run.

The year 1940, and especially the autumn with its frequent rain, especially at roll call, had it in for the inmates of Auschwitz. Roll call in the rain became a regular occurrence. Even on a good day which could be put in the fine weather column. Everyone got soaked at roll call: those who had worked outside all day in the fields, as well as those who had been working indoors.

"Old numbers," in other words those who had arrived two or at most three months before us,[12] got the jobs indoors.

These three months made a huge difference in "jobs" (for all the indoor ones had been filled) and also in experience.

In general, an inmate who came a month later, was not different because he had spent 30 fewer days there, but because he had not experienced the same torture methods which had been used barely a month before; the methods kept changing and yet the whole constellation of supervisors, whippers-in

---

[12] The first transport of Polish inmates arrived in June 1940. Translator's note.

and other shady sorts who wanted in this disgusting way to ingratiate themselves with the authorities still had plenty.

It was the same during the succeeding years. However, no one then was thinking in terms of years. Kazik (in Block 17) once told us: "The worst is getting through the first year." Some smiled politely. "A year? We'll be home by Christmas. The Germans won't last! England, etc., etc.!" (Sławek Szpakowski)... filled others with foreboding. "A year? Who could survive a year here?" When one played blind man's bluff with death on a daily basis... not today... perhaps tomorrow!—and a day sometimes seemed as long as a year.

Stranger still, a day dragged by like an endless nightmare. At times, when one ran out of steam for work, which nonetheless had to be done, an hour seemed like an age, while the weeks passed quickly. It was all strange and yet that is how it was—sometimes one felt that either time or one's senses were at fault...

That our senses were no longer those of ordinary people... those of people way out there in the real world... was a given.

We died the same people who had once walked the earth, but we were becoming someone else.

Not infrequently we heard one of us cry out, summing up his life in words: "What a fool I was!"

So, after some difficult moments we had grown together and the experience of hitherto unimagined stress had tightened the bonds of friendship more strongly than in the real world...

...When you had your "pals" who helped one another, sometimes at the risk of losing their own life... and then suddenly, my friend... before your very eyes, one of your pals is killed, is murdered in the most frightful way... what then?!...

There appeared to be but one course of action...rush the killer and all die together... Indeed that was tried once or twice, but only led to just another death...

No, that was not a solution! That way we'd all be dead in no time...

So we watched a comrade's slow death and one died, as it were, with him... watching, one felt oneself to be dying with him... and yet... one went on living... one recovered, one revived... one survived.

And if one dies like that, let us say if only ninety times, then, no way for it, one becomes someone else.

But thousands of us were dying there... tens of thousands... later, hundreds of thousands.

So the outside world and the people in it seemed to us comical, busy with what in our eyes were irrelevant matters.

Thus did we tie ourselves up in emotional knots.

Not everyone reacted like that.

Camp was a proving ground of character.

Some—slithered into a moral swamp.

Others—chiseled themselves a character of finest crystal.

We were cut with a sharp instrument. Its blade bit painfully into our bodies, yet, in our souls, it found fields to till...

Everyone eventually went through this process of transformation.

Like soil turned by the plough, some already ploughed into fertile ridges on the right, while on the left lay earth which would be turned only during the next pass.

From time to time the plough would bounce over an inner stone leaving some of the soil unturned and infertile—a useless strip—a barren patch...

We lost all our titles...

Ranks, diplomas were left far behind in the world outside...

As if already in the spirit world, we looked at these shapes still clothed in earthly inessentials, we could see all our pals in their former lives: this one with this and that one with that title, and one could but smile indulgently the way one does at children...

We were all by now on first-name terms.

We addressed formally only zugangs, for they as yet understood nothing.

To do so amongst ourselves was usually meant as an insult.

Colonel R [Tadeusz Reklewski], whom I inadvertently addressed as "sir," turned on me saying: "Will you just drop that..."

How different things are in the outside world.

There, some Tom, Dick or Harry would boast to his friends that he was on first-name terms with someone two ranks higher.

Here—all that had vanished without trace.

We had all become just our bare essence.

A man was seen and valued for what he really was...

I worked for two days in the Commandant's garden.

We levelled and laid out flowerbeds, paths. We shifted soil from the deeply sunken paths. We filled in depressions with thick layers of crushed brick. We also demolished a couple of small houses nearby. In fact, all the houses near the camp, and especially those in the belt between the *kleine postenkette* [inner security perimeter] and the *große postenkette* [outer security perimeter], an area with a radius of several kilometers, had to be demolished.

The German supervisors attacked these structures built by Poles with special zeal and even fury.

Expensive villas and modest, yet trim, cottages which some Polish working man had spent a lifetime building disappeared, demolished by hand by the inmates—Poles urged on by clubs, beaten and abused with a whole flurry of "damns."

Work in the garden and on demolishing the houses provided an endless opportunity for beating and kicking.

After tearing off the roofs, and taking down the walls, the hardest job was to remove the foundations, which were to disappear without trace. The holes were filled in and the owner, should he ever return, would be hard-pressed to find where his family nest had once stood.

Why, we even dug up some of the trees. Nothing remained of the whole farmyard.

While we were demolishing one of these farms I noticed a picture of Our Lady hanging on a bush and which, so it seemed to me, rested there alone and yet at peace, still intact amidst all this chaos and destruction.

None of us wanted to destroy it.

In the kapos' minds just such a spot, exposed to the rain, snow and frost, would condemn it fastest to a life of misery.

Much later, one could still see the picture in the snow-covered bush, encrusted with rime, its gold glittering and only the face and eyes showing through the central piece of glass which had not steamed up, affording our lads, who that winter were chased to work amidst hoarse shouting and kicking, a sight which led their thoughts to wing homewards, for some to wives, for others to mothers.

Soaked at work, soaked at roll call, at night we put our wet prison clothes under our heads for a pillow.

In the morning, you put on your wet clothes and went off

barefoot in clogs that were falling off, without a cap, once again into the rain or the biting wind.

It was already November.

From time to time it snowed...

Some of the fellows were flagging. They went to the hospital and never returned.

Odd this: I was no Hercules, but I never had so much as a sniffle.

After I had worked a few days in the garden Michał fitted me into his "twenty," which he was allowed to handpick.

He tended to choose men who had already been sworn in [to Pilecki's organization], or those who, one could assume, would join our organization: worthwhile people, who deserved to be saved.

Our "twenty" belonged to a "hundred," which joined a dozen or so other "hundreds" going to Industriehof II.[13]

There, a number of kapos were going nuts: Black August, Sigrod [Johann Siegruth], Bonitz [Bernard Bonitz], White August and others.

There were a few teenage "whippersnappers," *volksdeutsch*,[14] helping the Germans and who took special delight in hitting inmates on the face, beating them with clubs and so on.

One of them went too far and a few days later he was found hanged in one of the barracks: "He must have hanged himself, no one stopped him," which was in line with the clear camp instructions.

Michał, as vorarbeiter [foreman], and his "twenty" was given one of the small houses in a field to dismantle.

---

[13] An area alongside a railroad siding where building materials were unloaded and stored. Translator's note.

[14] They were likely to have been Polish citizens of German descent. Translator's note.

There he took us and there we "slaved away" for a few weeks.

We sat amongst the ruins of the house's foundations and took it easy after work, occasionally using a pickaxe so that some sounds of work could be heard.

From time to time a couple of us would carry out on a stretcher some of the rubble into which the walls and foundations of the demolished house were turning.

This rubble was then used to build a road a few hundred meters away.

No one in authority bothered to come over to this house lying a long way from the work of the other "hundreds."

The kapos had their hands so full finishing off a dozen or so "hundreds" filled with "damned Polish dogs" that they forgot about us, or just did not want to struggle across the muddy fields.

Michał stood on guard watching carefully. If any SS man or kapo appeared in the immediate vicinity, then a couple of us with stretchers would move out, and the pickaxes would briskly strike the foundations' cement and the cellar roofs.

During work I stood next to Sławek Szpakowski. Our conversation revolved for the most part around culinary matters. We were both optimists. We came to the conclusion that we had almost identical taste in food. So Sławek devised the menu with which he would one day entertain me at his house in Warsaw, after we got out of the camp.

From time to time, when the cold got to us and the rain would trickle inside our collars, we would take work a little more seriously and break off great slabs of concrete.

In our "stripes," with pickaxes and hammers, we presented a sight worthy only of a line from the song "hammer in hand, at the rock face we stand..."[15] and Sławek promised, after getting out of this inferno, to paint my portrait wearing my "stripes" and with a pickaxe.

It must have been our optimism which kept us going, for everything else—reality—was very grim.

Hunger was now gnawing at our entrails.

Oh, if only we could have had that bread which we had put into those wheelbarrows on the day of our arrival at the camp.

We had not yet learnt the true value of bread.

Near our worksite, beyond the wire lying at the edge of the outer security perimeter, a cow and two goats were grazing and happily munching on cabbage leaves growing on the other side of the wire.

There were no cabbage leaves on our side. They had all been eaten. Not by cows, but by creatures still somewhat resembling humans, by häftlings, by us.

We ate raw mangelwurzels.[16]

We envied the cows for they could eat mangelwurzels. A very high percentage of us had stomach problems. *Durchfall* ("the runs" or dysentery) was rife among the häftlings and was spreading to an ever larger number of inmates.

For some reason I did not have stomach problems.

Basic as it may seem—a healthy stomach was so important in the camp.

Anyone who fell sick—had to show great willpower by not eating anything at all for a short time.

A special diet was out of the question. It could be followed in the hospital, but it was initially very difficult to get

---

[15] From the song "Nie dbam jaka spadnie kara" ("I don't care how they punish me"), the lyrics of which were written by the celebrated Polish poet Adam Mickiewicz and date from the 1830s when Poles were exiled to Siberia by the Russian Tsarist authorities after the failed insurrection of 1830–31. Translator's note.

[16] An edible root. Translator's note.

admitted there and few returned—usually leaving by way of the crematorium chimney.

Willpower, so critical, sometimes in these cases was not enough.

Even when an inmate controlled himself and gave away his lunch and dried the bread, leaving it for the following day, or burnt it in the coals and then ate it to stop diarrhea, he had become so weakened by bowel movements that at work in a kommando, under the eye of a sadist with a club, this lack of strength meant that he was labelled "ein fauler Hund [a lazy dog]" and was beaten to death.

Returning to camp for the noon and evening roll calls, twice a day, we all had to carry bricks.

At first, for two days, we each carried 7 bricks, then for a few days it was 6 and eventually a norm of 5 was established.

There were six two-story and fourteen single-story huts within the camp wire at the time we arrived. Eight new two-story blocks were being built on the parade ground and all the single-story ones were having a floor added.

We carried all the building materials (bricks, iron, lime) by hand for several kilometers.

Before the building work had been finished, many thousands of häftlings lost their lives on this project.

Work in Michał's "twenty" spared us all much effort.

Honest Michał, guarding our safety outside the house, caught cold, contracted pneumonia and died in the hospital. He died in December.

When he left us for the *krankenbau* [hospital], it was still the end of November; we were quickly "taken in hand" like all the other "twenties" and "hundreds."

The serious killing started up again.

We were unloading freight cars, shunted onto a siding.

Iron, glass, bricks, piping, iron drainage pipes.

All the materials needed to expand the camp were brought in. The railroad cars had to be unloaded quickly. So once again to the accompaniment of clubs we all hurried, carried, stumbled, fell under the weight, sometimes doubled up under a two-ton beam or rail.

Even those who did not fall were using up their reserves of energy, stored up evidently some time before.

For them it was a daily surprise that they were still alive and walking, when we seemed to have crossed far beyond the threshold of what the strongest man could endure.

Yes, we now developed on the one hand, a kind of great disdain for those who, owing to their physical bodies, had to be considered humans for better or worse and members of the human race, but there we also developed respect for this strange human nature, stronger for possessing a soul, and containing something apparently immortal within itself.

To be sure, this was disproved by the dozens of corpses, which we dragged back, four of us to a corpse, to roll call in camp.

The cold feet and hands, by which we held the corpses, were just bone covered in blue skin.

Often indifferent eyes now looked out from the blue, gray and purple faces bearing traces of beatings.

Some of the corpses, still warm, their heads smashed by a spade, swayed to the rhythm of the marching column which had to keep up the pace.

Food, sufficient for someone just idling in a vegetative state, was far from adequate for work, for replenishing the energy used up by our muscles. Even more so when this same energy was also needed to warm our bodies, frozen by work in the open air.

At the Industriehof II, after the loss of Michał, Sławek and I used our wits to weave artfully between the clubs to get ourselves always into the best group.

Once we were set to unloading railroad cars, then in White August's *strassenbaukommando* [road-construction kommando].

When working in this kommando, we had to build a road near the storerooms and our nostrils were hit by a strong smell of smoked meat.

Our sense of smell, sharpened by hunger, was then surprisingly sensitive.

Our imaginations saw vividly rows of hams, bacon and tenderloin hanging.

So what? It was not for us!

These supplies had to be for the "master race."

In any case, so we joked, our sense of smell was evidence that we were no longer even human. The storerooms must have been about 40 meters away. Our noses were those of animals, not people.

One thing always saved us; we never lost our sense of humor.

Yet all these conditions put together began to wear us down for good.

Carrying bricks back to camp, especially in the evening, I walked with an apparently confident step.

In reality—I sometimes lost consciousness and walked several paces quite mechanically... as if in a trance... I was "out of it"... I could see green spots... It would not have taken much for me to stumble...

When my brain started to function again and register my internal state, I would wake up...my thoughts would send a command to my brain: "You are not to give up for anything!"

Then I continued... urged on by willpower alone...

This state of incoherence passed slowly...I entered the camp gate. Now I understood the sign over the gate "Arbeit macht frei."

Oh, indeed... work sets you free... sets you free—of the camp... of consciousness... as I had experienced a moment or two before... sets the soul free of the body... sending that body to—the crematorium.

Yet something had to be devised... something had to be done to arrest this process of weakening.

When the three of us got together, myself and the two Władeks (Colonel 1 [Surmacki] and Dr. 2 [Dering]), Władek 2 would always ask: "Well, Tomasz, how are you feeling?" I would always reply with a cheerful expression that I felt fine.

Initially they were surprised, then they grew accustomed to this and finally they believed that I felt fine.

I could not have answered otherwise. Wanting to do my "work," despite the fact that my comrades had already got down to it with a will and that one of them had managed to strengthen his position in the hospital where he was beginning to have some pull, and another had set up a "five" in the baubüro [construction site office], I still continually had to maintain that our "work" was perfectly feasible and to fight the psychosis to which No. 3 [Jerzy de Virion] was beginning to succumb, that conditions prevented it.

How would it have looked if just once I had complained that I felt bad... or that I was weak... and that I was so overwhelmed with work that I was looking for anything to save myself?

It was obvious that then I would be unable to inspire anyone else or require anything of them.

So I was fine—for the time being only as far as others were concerned—but later, as I describe below, gradually I really did begin to feel fine there, despite the constant danger and nervous tension, and not just superficially for general consumption.

In a manner of speaking I developed a split personality.

Then, while the body underwent torments, at times mentally one felt splendid and not just in some abstract sense.

Satisfaction began to take root somewhere—in one's physical brain both on account of spiritual experiences and of the interesting, purely intellectual, game I was playing.

However, one had to save one's own body, which in order to accomplish anything here, somehow had to be protected from being killed.

Somehow one had to get indoors to prevent being worn down by the weather in the open air.

Sławek's dream was to get into the carving section of the carpenters' shop.

Then he would try to get me in too.

By now there were two carpenters' shops in the camp. There was a large one at Industriehof I and another small one in the main camp in Block 9 (old numbering system).

One of my work colleagues from Warsaw, Captain 8 [Ferdynand Trojnicki], known as Fred, had already managed to get into this shop.

In response to my questions, he informed me that I might be able to get in if I could somehow convince the shop's vorarbeiter [foreman].

The vorarbeiter was a Volksdeutsche, Wilhelm Westrych, who came from Pyry near Warsaw. He was inside for black-market currency dealing and was waiting to be released shortly.

Though a Volksdeutsche, Westrych tried to have it both ways: working for the Germans he sometimes saved Poles, if he felt that there might be something in it for him in the future.

He willingly saved formerly important people, so that if the Germans were defeated, he could call on them to whitewash his time working for the Germans.

Therefore, I had to become someone important.

It was then I decided to "go for the jackpot."

My comrade, Captain 8 [Ferdynand Trojnicki], agreed to prime the vorarbeiter and get him to come out in front of Block 8 (old numbering system) where he lived.

That is where we had our conversation. I told him in a few words that it was not surprising that he did not remember me, for who could have heard of Tomasz... here I gave him my "prison name."

"It's like this, I'm here under an alias."

The Fates now had my life in their hands... I thought of my Sienkiewicz.[17]

All it would take was for the vorabeiter to report or mention to just one of the bunch of SS or kapos, with whom he mixed, that someone was there under an alias, for it to be all up with me.

I won't describe how I then went on to "charm" Westrych...

I did it. He started to "sir" me, which coming from a vorarbeiter to a gray häftling no longer sounded like an insult; quite the opposite. He came to the conclusion that he must have seen me somewhere... perhaps in some pictures from a reception at the Royal Castle in Warsaw or somewhere else but, what was most important, he said that he always rescued decent Poles, for he felt himself to be one too and so on and so

---

[17] Henryk Sienkiewicz (1846–1916) is one of Poland's most beloved novelists. He won the Nobel Prize for Literature in 1905. Among his best-known works is the novel *Quo Vadis*. Translator's note.

on, and that I was to come the next day to the carpenters' shop (the small one) and he would square it with the shop's kapo. I would almost certainly be taken on and he hoped that I would be grateful to him in future.

Our conversation took place in the evening of the 7th of December.

The following day, the 8th of December, I found myself after roll call indoors in the carpenters' shop.

Hitherto, working in the fields, I had not worn a cap or socks. Here, indoors in the warmth, irony of ironies, on the 8th I received socks from Westrych, and on the 15th of December—a cap.

In the shop he introduced me to the shop kapo as a good carpenter (bad ones were not taken on) who, nonetheless, was on probation.

The kapo looked me over and then nodded his agreement.

The workday passed in completely different conditions. It was warm, dry, and the work was clean.

Punishment here was not a beating, but being expelled from these conditions—being thrown out of the carpenters' shop and shoved back into the hell and torment of the camp proper.

However, to be able to work here, you had to be able to do something.

I've never lacked skills in my life, however there was no way round it, I knew nothing about carpentry.

I stood at the workbench of a good carpenter, later to be a member of our organization, Corporal 9 [Czesław Wąsowski], his Christian name was Czesiek.

Copying him and following his instructions I put my hand to movements which came naturally to a real carpenter.

The kapo was in the shop and knew carpentry. Therefore, every movement had to appear professional.

For the time being I was not doing anything major. I was planing boards or sawing with Czesiek, who remarked that for a first attempt it was not bad.

The next day the kapo gave me an individual task. Now I had to come up with something on my own. Fortunately, it was nothing difficult and with Czesiek's help it turned out quite well.

That day we managed also to "wangle" Sławek into the carpenters' shop since the kapo happened to be looking for a carver, and another fellow and I gave Sławek's number as a good woodcarver.

A few days later Czesiek received a new task from the kapo.

Assigned to his workbench, I helped him and followed his instructions. He was quite pleased with me.

No matter, when the kapo himself was dissatisfied with Czesiek's approach to the task, both of us were thrown out of the carpenters' shop with a bang: Czesiek the craftsman and I, his apprentice.

"... Imagine... such a good carpenter messing up on his joints," the other carpenters discussed our sad case. Czesiek had not messed up, he had simply understood that the kapo had not wanted any joints in a custom-made item.

One way or another, this was a hard blow.

We were kicked out into the camp proper for negligence at work and sent to a penal detail "on the barrows" at the Lagerältester's [Head Inmate's] disposal.

The day "on the barrows" in the camp proper began with a hard morning.

Bruno and the *Lagerkapo* (the discipline kapo) cut us no slack.

There was a sharp frost, but laufschritt [doing things at the double] did not permit us to feel the cold.

However, our strength was another matter. Czesiek, having worked some time in the carpenters' shop, had managed to regain his strength. I was saved by the few days' rest in the warmth when I had managed to regain some of my strength.

But we were not complete novices.

Czesiek during the morning and I in the afternoon managed to sneak off for a bit of shelter, each in a different block.

We began to know our way around the camp, which a zugang could not do without risking a beating.

The day somehow passed, but what now?

Czesiek did not return to the small carpenters' shop. I later met him elsewhere.

But Westrych had obviously decided to take a major interest in me...

He informed me through Fred (Captain 8 [Ferdynand Trojnicki]), that I was to come to the carpenters' shop the next morning after roll call.

The following day he explained to the kapo that I had only been following Czesiek's instructions, that I was a decent carpenter and the kapo agreed that I could continue working there.

To ensure that I did not run afoul of the kapo again, Westrych came up with a carpentry job outside the shop. There, the kapo was watching the carpenters' hands and movements, so he led me to Block 5 (old numbering system) and handed me over to the block chief, Baltosiński [Baltaziński in some sources], telling him that I could make him a wooden shoe-scraper, a coal scuttle, repair the window frame and other such minor tasks which did not require a first-class carpenter.

Furthermore, as I learned later from Jurek 10 [name unknown], he told Baltosiński to watch out for me and feed me up a bit, for this might come in handy, given that I was not just anybody. Apparently those pictures from the Castle were still oddly bouncing around in his head and reminding him of me.

I worked on Block 5 in room no. 2 whose master was a barber from Warsaw, Stasiek Polkowski.

There I carried out the previously mentioned tasks.

I repaired, or made new cupboards for the room supervisors from pieces of old cupboards brought from the shop.

They gave me some extra food there in the rooms. Baltosiński sent me "seconds" of soup—I began to regain my strength.

Thus I worked through December and the beginning of January of '41 until the incident with Leo, which I shall recount below.

The year 1940 was drawing to a close.

However, before I turn to 1941 in Auschwitz, I would like to add a few "camp pictures," which are part of 1940.

The German murderers' bestiality, which underscored the depraved instincts of the outcasts and sometime criminals— concentration camp inmates for some years—who were now our superiors in Auschwitz, took the most varied forms.

In the Penal Company these brutes enjoyed themselves crushing testicles, mainly Jews' testicles, with a wooden hammer on a small board.

At Industriehof II an SS man nicknamed "Perełka" ["Pearly"] would train his Alsatian to attack people by using humans for practice, which bothered no one.

The dog would attack häftlings running by at work, knock the weakened victims to the ground, bite into their bodies, tear them with its teeth, rip their testicles and throttle them.

The first inmate to escape from Auschwitz through what

was then still the single wire fence, as yet not electrified, was named, as if to taunt the prison authorities, Wiejowski.[18]

The authorities went berserk.

After it had been established at roll call that an inmate was missing, the camp was kept at attention on the parade ground for 18 hours as a punishment.

It goes without saying that no one could manage to stand at attention.

At the end of this "punishment parade" people were in a pitiful state.

SS men and kapos ran through the ranks which were without food and unable to go to the toilet, beating with clubs those who could no longer stay on their feet.

Some inmates simply collapsed from exhaustion.

To the appeals of the doctor, a German, the Camp Commandant replied:

"Let them die. I'll stand them down when half are dying."

The doctor then began to go through the lines encouraging people to lie down.

When the majority were already lying on the ground and the kapos had got tired of clubbing people, an end was finally called to the "punishment parade."

Over the next few months work was done on perimeter security. A second wire fence was built around the first one at a few meters' distance.

On two sides a high concrete fence was erected outside the wire, preventing anyone outside seeing into the camp.

Much later, the wire fence was heavily electrified.

The camp was surrounded between the concrete and wire fences with wooden watchtowers, which covered the parade

---

[18] Loosely translated as "runaway" or "scarper." The inmate, Tadeusz Wiejowski got away, but was rearrested in the autumn of 1941 and shot. Translator's note.

ground and the camp by virtue of their location and auto-matic weapons and on which soldiers stood careful watch.

Therefore, escape attempts were made not from the camp itself, but from work details which went outside.

Retaliation for escapes gradually relaxed to the extent that we would stand at roll call only so long that, if it was an evening roll call, we could eat some cold food before the night-time gong.

However, there were no rules about this and at times we missed supper or lunch.

The punishment for an escape was not relaxed.

An escapee always paid with his life: he was killed imme-diately after capture, or put in the bunker, or publicly hanged.

A häftling caught trying to escape was dressed up for a joke in a dunce's cap and other fripperies.

A sign was hung around his neck on a piece of string saying "I am a dunce... I tried to escape..." and so on. He would also have a drum fitted around his waist and thus, comically dressed and banging on the drum, he would take his last walk on this earth past his comrades standing in ranks at roll call to the delight of the jeering camp "dogs."

The blocks, lined up for roll call, watched this macabre comedy in complete silence.

Until the culprit was found, the blocks stood "on punish-ment parade."

Several hundred inmates under the supervision of a pack of kapos and packs of dogs went off to find the escapee (escapees), who was hidden usually somewhere between the inner and outer perimeter fences, if he had not yet managed to cross the outer one.

Sentries on watchtowers at the outer perimeter were stood down only when the evening roll call tallied with the number of inmates in the camp that day.

One evening roll call, on an exceptionally cold and rainy day when rain interspersed with snow was falling, a piercing siren rang out with the bad news of a "punishment parade."

It was established that two inmates were missing.

A "punishment parade" was called until the escapees, who had to be hiding somewhere in Industriehof II, were found.

Kapos, and a couple of hundred inmates, were then sent out on a search, which took a long time.

That day the snow, the rain, exhaustion after work, the inmates' inadequate clothing, were painfully finishing us off on "punishment parade."

Finally, the gong signaled that the escapees had been found.

Only the inert bodies of these unfortunates made it back to camp.

One of the thugs, furious at the extension of the workday, had driven a narrow board into the back right through the kidneys and stomach of one of them, who was carried back to the camp, unconscious with a bruised and twisted face, by four thugs.

Yes, escapes did not pay and were an act of great selfishness, since a "punishment parade" by thousands of one's comrades in the cold resulted in hundreds of corpses.

They died, simply from the cold, having used up all their remaining strength.

They were taken to the hospital where they died during the night.

Sometimes, even though no one had escaped, but the weather was dreadful, we were kept at roll call a long time, for several hours, until they got the numbers right.

The authorities went indoors somewhere, supposedly to do some simple arithmetic; we were finished off by the cold, or the rain, or the snow, and the requirement to stand motionlessly in one place.

You had to fight with your whole body, tense your muscles and release them in order to create some warmth and save your own life.

At roll calls an SS man, a *blockführer* [block supervisor], received a report from the block chief. After receiving a report from several blocks, the SS man would go to the desk of the *Rapportführer* [SS officer responsible for discipline and roll calls], who was Obersturmführer[19] Palitzsch [Gerhard Palitzsch].

Palitzsch, whom I shall describe later, was feared like the devil even by the SS. He would send SS men to the bunker at the slightest provocation, and on the basis of a report from him an SS man could be sent to the front.

Hence everyone feared Palitzsch and when he appeared there was silence.

Silesians—people whom I had once taken to be Poles, but who for the most part had recently turned their back on their Polish heritage—now began scrambling up to be block chiefs.

Having formerly had a very good opinion of them, I now could not believe my own eyes. They killed off Poles, no longer seeing them as some of their own, while taking themselves to be some kind of German tribe.

I once asked a vorarbeiter [foreman] from Silesia:

"Why are you beating him, he's a Pole?"

"But I'm no Pole; I'm from Silesia. My parents wanted to make a Pole out of me, but a Silesian—that's a German. Poles live in Warsaw and not in Silesia."

---

[19] Pilecki is mistaken as to Palitzsch's rank. He was not an *Obersturmführer* (the equivalent in the German SS of First Lieutenant), but he was in fact a *Hauptscharführer* (the equivalent in the German SS of Master Sergeant). Translator's note.

And he went on beating the other fellow with his club.

There were two block chiefs, Silesians—Skrzypek [Alfred Skrzypek] and Bednarek [Emil Bednarek]—who were perhaps worse than the worst German.

They clubbed to death such a large number of inmates that even Bloody Aloiz, who in any event had slackened off a bit, could not keep up with these thugs.

Every day standing at evening roll call we could see at the left end of the block wheelbarrows standing next to these killers with inmates' corpses on them.

They boasted of their work to the SS, to whom they reported the numbers present.

However, one cannot generalize, for just as everywhere else, here too there were exceptions to the rule.

An exception was a Silesian who was a good Pole, and when you came across one, you could confidently put your life in his hands—he was your friend for life.

There was such a Silesian, block chief Alfred Włodarczyk and there was Smyczek [Wilhelm Smyczek]; there were also Silesians in our "fives," about which more later.

Bloody Aloiz, whom I have mentioned, was now no longer a block chief.

Block 17a (old numbering system) was used to store sacks with inmates' clothes.

Transports of inmates kept arriving, increasing the numbers on the rolls; but the size of the camp itself did not grow.

The surplus left through the crematorium chimney.

However, our effects—sacks with our earthly possessions which we had once used—were carefully stored.

They now occupied all the spare space in Block 18. Therefore, the space allocated to the *effektenkammer* [storeroom for inmates' personal belongings] was expanded by a floor on

Block 17 (Block 17a), and all the inmates were transferred to different blocks.

From the 26th of October I had been living on Block 3a (on the first floor of Block 3).

The block chief in Block 3a was Koprowiak [Stanisław Koprowiak]; someone had said good things to me about him and his past in another prison.

Here, I saw him beat from time to time; perhaps his nerves were going.

However, he tended to beat only when a German was watching.

Perhaps he wanted to protect his life, or his position. He was one of the best block chiefs as far as Poles were concerned.

On Block 3a I lived in room 1, whose supervisor was Drozd [Franciszek Drozd]. A good fellow, he treated people in the room well, without beatings. In this matter, the block chief left him a free hand.

It was from a first-floor window of this block that one day I saw a sight which has stuck in my mind.

It was a workday on which I remained in camp. I was going to the dispensary where I had been summoned by a note.

On my return I remained on the block.

It was raining and it was a dreary day.

The Penal Company was working on the parade ground carrying gravel which was being dug out of a hole. There was also a kommando standing around, freezing and "doing PE."

Three SS men stood by the hole, and unable to leave out of fear of Palitzsch or the Commandant who was poking around the camp that day, they had devised a game. They were agreeing something and everyone was putting a banknote on a brick.

Then they would bury an inmate head down in the sand covering the upper part of his body in the hole and, looking at their watches, they would see how many minutes his legs would continue to move.

A new form of football pools, I thought to myself.

Clearly he who was closest to guessing how long someone buried in the sand would continue to move his legs before dying, scooped the pot.

Thus did 1940 come to an end.

Before I managed to get into the carpenters' shop with all its advantages, including extra food on Block 5, the hunger twisting my entrails became so powerful that I began to devour with my eyes the bread of those who, already in "good jobs," could save some of theirs for the morning, and I began what I think was the hardest battle in my life with myself.

The whole issue was how to eat now and still leave something for the morning...

But what is the point of writing about hunger for people with full stomachs... or for those who, getting parcels from home or from the Red Cross and not living under the threat of hard labor, complained afterwards how hungry they were.[20]

Ah!...the crisis of hunger arrives in all its different degrees.

There were times when one felt oneself capable of cutting off a piece from a corpse lying outside the hospital.

It was then, just before Christmas, that they began to issue us barley gruel in the morning instead of "tea," which was a great blessing, but I do not know who was responsible. (It continued until the spring.)

---

[20] More than likely this is a veiled allusion to the Polish officers who had spent the war as POWs. Translator's note.

A couple of beautifully lit Christmas trees were put up in the camp for Christmas.

In the evening the kapos laid two häftlings on two benches under the trees and gave them 25 strokes on that part of the body which out in the free world has been called soft.

This was supposed to be a German joke.

Punishments in Auschwitz were graded as follows:

The lightest punishment was a bench beating. It took place in public in the presence of all blocks at roll call.

The "execution block" was prepared—a bench with slots for the hands and legs on both sides.

Two SS thugs stood there (often Seidler himself and sometimes Lagerältester Bruno) and one was beaten on the naked body so as not to spoil one's clothes.

One was beaten with a whip or sometimes a heavy cane.

After a dozen strokes the body was badly cut. Blood spurted and the remaining blows were on raw meat.

I witnessed this on several occasions.

Men sometimes got 50 strokes, even 75.

One day, when the punishment was 100 strokes, the häftling, some poor wretch, expired at around the 90th stroke.

If the victim was still alive, he was then meant to stand up, do a few squats to restore the blood flow and, standing at attention, say thank you for the just punishment.

The next punishment was the bunker.

There were two types of bunker. The normal bunker consisted of cells in the cellars of Block 13 (old numbering system),where inmates were kept usually before interrogation and at the pleasure of the political department,[21] as were also kapos and SS men as a punishment.

---

[21] The political department was run by the Gestapo. Translator's note.

The cells of the normal bunker occupied three parts of the cellar on Block 13; in the last quarter of the cellar was a cell like the others, but without light, and called the "black hole."

At one end of the block the cellar corridor turned ninety degrees right and ended immediately.

In this stub of the corridor there were three quite different small bunkers. They were the three so-called *stehbunker* (standing bunkers).

Beyond a rectangular opening in the wall, through which one could only enter bent double, there was a sort of cupboard 80 cm by 80 cm and 2 meters high,[22] so that one could stand upright easily.

With the help of clubs, four inmates who had been sentenced to the stehbunker were shoved into one of these "cupboards" which was closed with bars and they were left there all night (from 7 in the evening until 6 in the morning).

It appears impossible, and yet there are witnesses and there are those still alive today who were punished in the stehbunker with their comrades, eight at a time.

They were let out in the morning and sent off to work and for the night they were again squeezed in like sardines, locked behind iron bars till morning.

The usual sentence was five nights, but there were also much longer ones.

Those who had no connections among the work detail "higher ups," were usually finished off at work after one or two nights for lack of energy.

Those who could take a break with the kapo's permission during the day at work could somehow get through this punishment.

---

[22] Approximately 31 inches square and 6½ feet high. Translator's note.

The third punishment was the simple "pole" borrowed from the Austrians.

Added to that, the duty SS man would, for the fun of it, from time to time swing the man hanging by his arms tied behind his back. Then the joints creaked and the ropes bit into the body.

The last thing needed was the arrival of "Perełka" and his Alsatian.

Sometimes interrogations were carried out like that, and the hanging man was fed salad dressing, in other words vinegar, to prevent him fainting too soon.

And the fourth, the highest punishment was death by shooting—a quick death and thus more humanitarian and indeed genuinely requested by those tortured for a long time.

"Shooting" is not quite accurate; more accurate would be "shooting down," or even killing.

This also took place on Block 13 (old numbering system).

There was a yard there, hemmed in by Blocks 12 and 13. On the east side it was enclosed by a wall linking the two blocks, called the "wall of tears." On the west side there was also a wall with a gate, usually closed, blocking the view. It was opened for a live victim or in order to toss out bloody corpses.

Passing that way one could often detect the smell of an abattoir.

A red stream ran through the gutter.

The gutter was whitewashed and yet on an almost daily basis a new stream of red flowed between its white sides.

Oh, if only that were not blood... not human blood... not Polish blood... and the best Polish blood too... then... who knows... one could even have admired the contrast of colors...

That was outside.

Inside, however, terrible and dreadful things took place.

There, in the enclosed yard, the executioner Palitzsch, a handsome lad who never beat anyone in the camp (that was not his style), was the principal director of terrifying scenes.

The condemned, in a row, having undressed and now naked, stood one after the other by the "wall of tears" while he would put a small-caliber pistol to the back of their head and end their life.

He would sometimes employ the kind of bolt used to kill cattle.

The spring-loaded bolt would pierce the skull and the brain and kill.

Sometimes a group of civilians who had been tortured and interrogated in the cellars and who had now been handed over to Palitzsch for some fun would be led out.

Palitzsch would order the girls to undress and run in a circle around the enclosed yard.

Standing in the middle of the yard he would take his time picking a victim, then he would aim, shoot and kill them all one by one.

None of them knew who would die next, or who would live for a few more moments, or who might be taken back for further interrogation.

He—improved his aim.

These scenes were witnessed from Block 12 by several block supervisors standing guard to prevent a häftling from approaching the window.

The windows were covered in wire netting, but not thoroughly enough; so everything was visible.

Another time, a family standing in the yard by the "wall of tears" was seen from Block 12.

First of all, Palitzsch shot the father, killing him before the eyes of his wife and two children.

**The "Wall of Tears"**

**In front of the brick wall between Blocks 12 and 13 (old numbering system), the Germans built another removable wall: the "Wall of Tears," also called the "Wall of Death" or the "Black Wall." Made of wood covered with cork painted black, its function was to absorb the bullets of the firing squad—protecting the brickwork and preventing bullets from ricocheting back at the executioners.**

ABM

SS Hauptscharführer Gerhard Palitzsch.

Then he killed the little girl who was gripping her pale mother's hand.

Then he grabbed the small child which the unfortunate woman was cuddling to her breast. He grasped it by the legs and smashed its little head against the wall.

Finally he killed the mother, semi-conscious from grief.

This scene was recounted to me so precisely and so identically by a number of friends who had witnessed it that I have no doubt that that is what happened.

For Christmas of 1940 inmates were for the first time allowed to receive parcels from their families.

But not food parcels, oh no!

We were not allowed to receive food parcels for fear we might have it too easy.

The first parcel arrived at Auschwitz. It was a clothes parcel, containing a number of previously specified items: a sweater, a scarf, gloves, ear muffs, socks.

Nothing more could be sent. Someone's parcel contained underwear—it went to the sack in the effektenkammer [storeroom for inmates' personal belongings] with the inmate's number and stayed there.

That is how it was then.

We later managed to get into everything, with the help of fellows in the know.

There was just one parcel, one a year, at Christmas, with no food, but still valuable because of the warm clothes, and precious because it came from home.

Over Christmas, Westrych and the carpenters' shop kapo managed to wangle for the carpenters some additional cooking pots of an excellent stew from the SS kitchen, and the arriving carpenters were in for a treat in the shop.

These pots came around a number of times and also later, brought in secretly by the SS who received money collected from us by Westrych.

The year 1941 began for me with more carpentry work in Block 5, where I continued to come up with new jobs.

The block chief left me completely alone.

Here I met a friend, Gierych [Bolesław Gierych], the son of friends of mine whose flat in Oryol I had used for clandestine purposes in 1916–1917.

The Lagerältester, Leo [Leon Wietschorek] (inmate number 30), came around to Block 5 almost daily.

If an SS man or the Lagerältester came into the room one had to call out "Achtung" and report.

I would do this faultlessly, adding to my report: "... ein Tischler bei der Arbeit! [... carpenter at his post, sir!]"

This suited Wietschorek. He was not in the least interested in what I had been spending so much time doing there as he strutted around like a peacock.

Block 5 was the "youngsters' block," with boys between the ages of 15 and 18 whom the Third Reich still hoped to bring around.

They took some sort of courses there.

Leo would come around daily, for he liked young people and he liked boys... too much. He was a pervert.

Here he chose victims for his perversions. He fed them, plumped them up, forcing them to comply through favors and the threat of the Penal Company, and when he had had enough of his boy, he would hang him in the toilet, usually at night, so as to avoid having an awkward witness to behavior which was forbidden in the camp.

About the 15th of January I was standing by the window when Leo came into the room.

I failed to notice him and did not call out "Achtung," for my attention was distracted by a zugang outside. I also saw Colonel 11 [Tadeusz Reklewski] through the window.

Leo was visibly displeased with me. He came over and said: "You've been hanging around this block too long. I don't want to see you here tomorrow."

I told Westrych this, but he nonetheless ordered me to go there the next day.

So, on the following day, I again went off to Block 5.

Leo arrived shortly after I did, saw me and fell into a rage.

"Deine Nummer? [Your number?]" he bellowed and unusually he did not strike me. "Rrrrraus! mit dem alles! [Get out! and take your stuff with you!]" he said pointing to my tools.

I got out sharpish and he took my number, shouting after me that I would be kicked out of the carpenters' shop that same day.

Back at the shop I recounted the incident to Westrych.

A moment later Leo burst in.

By a stroke of luck, the kapo was not in the shop. Westrych was acting for him and he let Leo shout to his heart's content and then explained that his carpenter had reported the incident the previous day, but that he had ordered him to go back to Block 5 that morning to collect all the tools. Leo calmed down.

I remained a carpenter, working, just to be on the safe side, in the shop's second room, also on Block 9.

A few days later, Westrych ordered me to take my tools and follow him somewhere in the camp.

He took me to Block 15 (old numbering system).

This was the hospital, which went by the German name krankenbau.

The hospital block chief, a slightly crazy German, wanted things to be tidy, however, on his block.

Westrych had suggested to him only the day before to put slats around the straw mattresses.

There were no beds.

The sick lay side by side on the floor in terrible conditions.

The mattresses, thrown on the floor so that the sick had their heads to the wall, were not always straight and hardly improved matters. So it had been decided to put slats at the end of the mattresses which were arranged along the walls in two rows the length of the ward.

These slats running evenly the length of the ward would create in the center of the floor an evenly framed pathway.

The block chief gave me a good look and asked if I could do a good job. Bad work would mean a beating on the bench; good work would mean daily "seconds."

So I got down to work, and ward after ward I provided every mattress with a frame with slats which I attached to the floor with square blocks.

I was given (Westrych sent him) an engineer from Warsaw to help me.

Both of us got our daily "seconds."

We had plenty of food on the block.

It was issued for everyone, but some of the sick wanted nothing to eat.

The engineer from Warsaw caught the flu here. Admitted to the hospital in the same block in the conditions current in the krankenbau, with its terrible lice, he soon died.

I finished off the slats by myself.

Then my turn came. I either picked up some kind of flu or caught cold at roll call.

The winter was quite severe. To be sure, we had been issued coats even before Christmas, but they were "ersatz" without linings and gave little protection from the frost.

I fought my sickness for several days.

I had a temperature and on some days in the evening it was as high as 39 degrees [Celsius],[23] so that I would have been admitted to the hospital without any inside connections. But I did not want to go to the hospital.

There were two reasons for this: the terrible lice in the hospital, and an end to my job in the carpenters' shop.

I fought as best I could, but the sickness had gripped me and did not want to let go.

The worst was standing at roll call running a temperature and with the wind driving through me.

I have no idea how this struggle would have ended.

Something quite different took a hand.

On the block, in Room 1, conditions were still bearable. After "room supervisor" Drozd, we got a new one—Antek Potocki.

Some of us had various cleaning responsibilities.

Mine were the windows, doors and lights.

Everything might have worked out on the block were it not for the fact that we were all "somewhat" lice-ridden.

Every evening we did some serious hunting in our shirts.

I used to kill about a hundred of them daily on the assumption that more would not appear during the night, but by morning another hundred would be there.

---

[23] Equivalent to 102.2 degrees Fahrenheit. Normal temperature would be 37 degrees Celsius (98.6 degrees Fahrenheit). Translator's note.

Then it was hard to hunt down any more, for the lights went out at a certain time. During the day at work there was no time for this.

At night they would crawl from the blankets onto our shirts. Even if one could have got them all off the blanket during the night, it would have achieved nothing: during the day the blankets were all stacked together and so every day one got another blanket. By the warm fire, these little creatures were only too happy to wander from one blanket to another.

Finally, delousing was ordered.

Unfortunately, this came at a very bad time for me.

I was running a high temperature.

That evening we were told to undress. We handed over our clothes, threaded on a wire, to be steamed.

Then we went naked to take a shower in Block 18 (old numbering system) and then naked to Block 17 (old numbering system). There we spent the whole night naked, several hundred of us to a room, and it was terribly stuffy.

In the morning, we were issued clothes and set off across the parade ground to Block 3 in the wind and the frost.

I had given my coat to Antek Potocki who was also sick.

That night did me in.

I went to the hospital almost unconscious. After again being sprayed with water in the waschraum [washroom], I was put on Block 15 (old numbering system) in Room 7 (where I had been affixing the slats to the floor), which had terrible lice.

The next few nights, doing constant battle with the lice, were, I think, my hardest in the camp.

I did not want to submit and let the lice devour me.

But how was I to defend myself here?

If you looked at the blanket under the light, its whole surface was constantly heaving.

There were all sorts of them: small and large, swollen, elongated, white and gray, red with blood, some had horizontal stripes, others had vertical ones... they crawled slowly up people's backs and then quickly slid off.

I was revolted, and resolved firmly not to allow myself to be eaten by this disgusting horde.

I tied my long johns firmly around my ankles and my waist and buttoned up my shirt at the neck and the wrists.

There was no question of killing them one by one; I crushed whole handfuls with a swift motion, gathering them from my neck and feet.

Exhausted by the temperature and the constant movement, my body craved sleep.

My head fell, but then I dragged myself back.

I could not under any circumstances allow myself to go to sleep.

To fall asleep meant to stop fighting and to allow oneself to be eaten.

Within an hour my hands were stained red from crushing this filth's bloody bodies.

It was a hopeless task to destroy them all.

We lay packed tightly together, our bodies covered in blankets, our backs or sides touching.

Not everyone fought. Some were unconscious, others just wheezed, others were no longer able to fight.

An unconscious older inmate (a highlander) lay next to me. His face, which I shall never manage to forget, was a few dozen centimeters from my head; it was covered in a motionless crust of lice of all sizes which had burrowed into the skin.

To my left lay an inmate (Narkun), who had died. His blanket had been pulled over his head and a stretcher was awaited.

Meanwhile the lice on his blanket started to perk up and head in my direction.

In order to kill the lice in one's own blanket, one would perhaps had to have pounded the blanket time and again with a blunt stone on an even floor.

But trying to protect oneself on either side was almost as fruitless as trying to arrest a stream in full flow: impossible to stop the flow or destroy it completely.

Here I have to admit that for the first time I began to doubt that I had the strength to fight, indeed to want to fight.

My psychological state was dangerous. To doubt one's will to fight was to crack.

Once I became aware of this, I felt better.

I continued to crush lice on my neck and feet.

The corpse was replaced by a new patient, a boy of perhaps eighteen, named Salwa, whose Christian name was Edek.

When I dozed off he would protect me from the stream of invaders coming from the right, sometimes scooping them up with a knife and sometimes a spoon.

He fought his own battle on his own blanket and so I had a neighbor protecting my left flank, providing me with a little more peace.

He would also buy me bread from patients who were too sick to eat.

I ate—everything.

I do have a strange character, as I have discovered more than once.

Others, when running a fever, do not eat; I eat like a horse.

I invite anyone who, on reading this shrugs, to get to know me better, then he might discover that all my life I have done things back to front.

In this ward there were a few fine people, who eased what was left of these sick people's lives.

There were Janek Hrebenda and Tadeusz Burski, both fine, good people working with the sick. There was not much that they could do, but whatever was within their power, then the sick got it.

However, it was obvious that they could not change conditions.

There was a time in the summer when it had been forbidden to open the windows to prevent the sick catching cold and everyone suffocated in the heat and the stench.

Now, when there was a hard frost, all the windows were opened wide twice a day and the place was aired for a long time, the icy air from the windows creeping along the floor, shaking the huddled forms lying under a thin, wretched blanket with a blast of cold.

I struggled with the lice more than with the sickness for three days and two nights.

The third day, almost at the end of my strength, I decided to reveal my weakness to Władek.

Using a new friend, Tadek Burski, I wrote a card to Dr. 2 [Władysław Dering].

All cards in the camp were suspect. They could be interpreted as two inmates who were acting against the interests of the Third Reich trying to get in touch.

I wrote: "If you don't get me out of here at once, then I will use up all my reserves of strength fighting lice. In my present condition I am rapidly approaching the crematorium chimney." I gave my location.

A few hours later, Dr. 2 [Władysław Dering] appeared, assisted by Dr. 12 [Edward Nowak].

Both were officially only pflegers (nurses).

A Pole could not officially be a doctor there.

However, Dr. 2 [Władysław Dering] had so successfully managed to cope that he already had some say in the running of the hospital.

Dr. 2 [Władysław Dering] was going around the ward (it was not his department).

He pretended not to know me.

He turned to Dr. 12 [Edward Nowak] saying: "What's wrong with this fellow? Can you look him over?"

It turned out that I had pneumonia in my left lung.

Dr. 2 [Władysław Dering] announced that the patient needed to be taken for tests and for one of the new injections.

I marched over to Block 20 (old numbering system).

Upstairs, I was given a bed in one of the wards.

I was a new man. There were no lice here. That meant that I found about 40–50 of them in the new underwear I was given and in my blanket, but that didn't count. I killed them and that was that.

They would not climb the bed legs from my neighbor. That, they had not yet learnt to do.

No matter even that they had put me in a bed backed up to a window which was always open and through which the wind blew, the flow of cold air turning the warmer air by the window into a slight mist.

I tried to keep my infected side as far away as possible from the cold.

The following day I was moved to the middle of the ward, I was given four blankets and an injection.

After ten days I had recovered to such an extent that I had to give up my bed to someone sicker than me.

I was again moved to Block 15 where I had been during the first days of my illness, but the lice had gone.

Dr. Władysław Dering (Pilecki's comrade—code no. Captain Dr. 2)—Inmate No. 1723.

ABM

**Maximilian Grabner, head of the camp Gestapo.**

In the meantime the delousing, going block by block, had already reached Block 15.

How extraordinary. The same dreadful, louse-ridden ward, now fumigated and whitewashed, looked quite different.

This was the 1st of February, 1941.

I rested there for a whole month after my illness, helping Tadek [Tadeusz Burski] and Janek Hrebenda.

The fine pfleger, Krzysztof Hofman, would often look in on the ward. Sometimes he would even sleep there.

Heniek Florczyk, a mathematician from Warsaw, was also a patient there.

Tadek Burski (of 56, Raszyńska Street)[24] was released from the camp owing to his sisters' efforts.

I used him to send information to Warsaw.

Despite the change for the better in prison conditions, every day a couple of patients died on the ward.

There was nothing to treat people with and even the pills that Krzyś [Krzysztof Hofman] managed to wangle were just that—pills.

Sometimes people just did not want to live.

They did not want to fight and whoever gave up, very quickly died.

Here, as a convalescent patient, I managed to get into the camp with the help of some friendly nurses (they brought me clothes from Fredek 4 [Alfred Stössel]).

I would sometimes leave the ward unseen by the authorities.

I had more time to set up "fives."

The camp was like a huge mill, turning living people into ashes.

---

[24] Earlier in this 1945 Report, Pilecki gives Burski's address as no. 58. Translator's note.

We, the inmates, were finished off in two ways.

In parallel and independently more than one group worked to finish us off at work or by means of the camp's conditions. Men who were there for serious reasons died alongside others who had been accused of nothing. In any event, outside issues had no influence on what went on here. However, another group independently examined individual cases in the political department. At times an inmate who had managed to "hang on," survive at work, was coping and had even managed to secure some additional food, one day was killed.

His number was read out at morning roll call. He had to go to the principal *schreibstube* [office], whence he was usually led by an SS man to the political department and was frequently shot by Palitzsch on Block 13.

This was the result of ferreting around in the files by that other murderer—Grabner [Maximilian Grabner].

Palitzsch was paid "by the head" for shooting people.

There were often agreements between these two gentlemen.

One picked out the cases, the other did the shot in the head.

The money was shared and the business prospered.

Death, choosing our comrades at random, often struck our network, set up after much work and lengthy observation.

Thus the network kept breaking in different places, and constant repair work was needed.

The men already in the chain felt morally stronger, having a few friendly souls at their backs ready to help one another, and began with growing confidence to scramble slowly into better kommandos.

We were not to mention anything that any of us would have called "organizing" prior to Auschwitz and I banned the word.

Instead, we cheerfully grasped the new meaning of the word and "spread" it widely throughout the camp, until the concept found broader acceptance.

To a certain extent it was our lightning rod.

Here "organizing" meant "illicit scrounging."

Someone would filch some pats of margarine, or a loaf of bread from the stores at night, and it was called "organizing margarine or bread."

Someone else "organized" some boots for himself, another "organized" some tobacco.

The word "organize" now spread openly and was widely used. If the wrong person heard the word used unexpectedly or casually about our underground organization, it was understood in no other way but as referring to stealing or scrounging something.

In our work, the average "link" was not meant to know too much.

The lad knew the "skeleton," a few personal "contacts," and he knew who ran it.

As an organization we began to take over specific kommandos and increase our reach.

I decided to expand and take advantage of the possibilities offered by those German kapos who beat unwillingly (there were some), and I made contact with them through specific members.

In the initial phase of Auschwitz concentration camp's existence, where the killing started the very day the first transport of Poles was brought on the 14th of June 1940, the organization involved in finishing off the inmates consisted of 30 Germans, or aspiring Germans, brought in from Oranienburg in May of '40.

Although they were inmates too, they were chosen to be our tormentors.

They bore the first Auschwitz numbers: 1–30.

The first and last of these, in other words inmate no. 1 Bruno [Bronisław Brodniewitsch] and inmate no. 30 Leo [Leon Wietschorek] received Lagerältester armbands, a few others were given block chief *binden* [armbands] and the rest became kapos.

Amongst this crew of bandits working with coarse brutality or perfidy at murdering inmates, there were a few who beat unwillingly, more out of necessity so as not to fall out with the rest of this gang and the SS.

The inmates very quickly picked up on this.

As an organization we decided to take advantage of this.

Shortly also Otto (inmate no. 2 [Otto Küsel]) the Arbeitsdienst [work assignment leader]; Balke (inmate no. 3 [Artur Balke]) the *oberkapo* [senior kapo] in the carpenters' shop; "Mateczka" (inmate no. 4 [Fritz Biessgen]), who was given the nickname "Mateczka" ["Mom"] for his attitude towards us in the kitchen; Bock (inmate no. 5 [Hans Bock]), "Tata" ["Daddy"] in the krankenbau [hospital]; Konrad (inmate no. 18 [Konrad Lang]); Jonny (inmate no. 19 [Jonny (*sic*) Lechenich]), began to help us, completely unaware of and not suspecting the existence of any kind of organization.

Specific members would approach them with supposedly personal matters or for a friend and they, whenever possible, would go out of their way to help us. Otto, by issuing specific kommando postings; Balke by getting a significant number of our people into the carpenters' shop indoors; Mateczka by serving "seconds" (of soup from the kitchen) to especially exhausted members; Bock by smoothing the way in the hospital; Jonny, who as a kapo on the *landwirtschaftskommando*

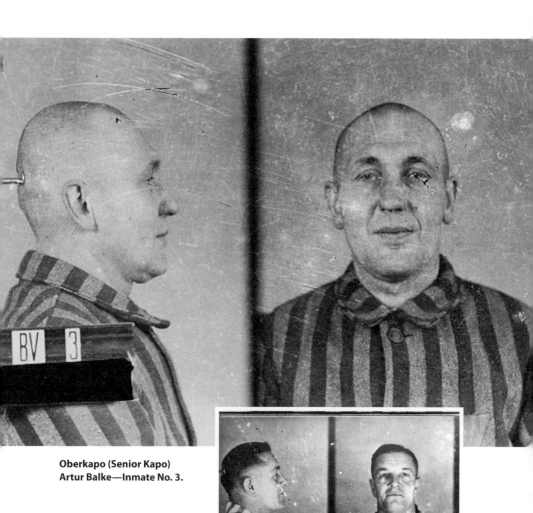

Oberkapo (Senior Kapo)
Artur Balke—Inmate No. 3.

"Mateczka" Fritz Biessgen—Inmate No. 4.

ABM

ABM

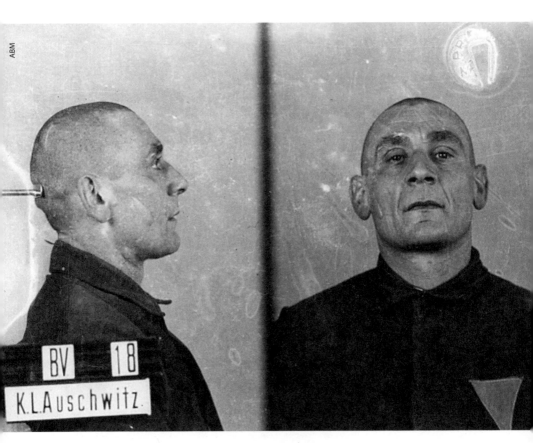

**Konrad Lang—Inmate No. 18.**

[farming kommando] initially did not prevent and later helped us get in touch with the outside world through contacts with our organization on the outside and working with 13 "Zofia" [Zofia Szczerbowska] (in Stare Stawy), he must inevitably have sensed that something was going on.

He did not betray us and from the moment that he received a bench beating from the camp authorities for supposedly "failing to notice" that inmates were being tossed additional food by the local population (loaves of bread)—the authorities never suspected anything more—he became a firm friend.

Thus was I putting together and "knitting," having what for conditions at that time was an exceptional amount of time convalescing during February of '41 in the hospital on Block 15 (old numbering system).

That lasted until the 7th of March.

Suddenly a couple of events coincided.

On the 6th of March, I was summoned to the *erkennungsdienst* [the records office] on Block 18 (old numbering system) where we had originally all had our pictures taken.

I was shown my own photograph and was asked whether I knew the inmates who had had their pictures taken immediately before and immediately after me. I said that I did not.

The SS man sneered, saying that it was highly suspicious that I did not recognize people I had arrived with.

He then looked at my picture closely and claimed that it bore little resemblance to me and that this too was very suspicious.

Indeed, I had tried as they were taking my picture to look unnatural and puff out my cheeks. I replied that I had a kidney complaint which led to puffiness.

That same 6th of March Sławek [Sławek Szpakowski]

informed me that he was to be released from the camp the next day and would be going to Warsaw.

Always the optimist, he announced that he would wait for me in Warsaw.

He was released without going into quarantine; that's how it was then.

He had been released thanks to the efforts of his wife and the intervention of the Swedish Consulate. At the same time that evening I learnt from Dr. 2 [Władysław Dering] that I was to be summoned the next day to the main schreibstube [office] and it was common knowledge how that usually turned out.

I did not know why and racked my brains trying to work out what they wanted.

I had no record.

It just crossed my mind that Westrych might have either intentionally or through carelessness "burnt" me by saying that I was in the camp under a false identity.

Westrych had in fact been released from the camp barely a fortnight before.

Perhaps before leaving he had "confessed" his secret.

In that case my fate was sealed.

Dr. 2 [Władysław Dering] was very worried about me and taught me how to fake an illness which was very common at the time in the krankenbau [hospital]—meningitis—which might spare me questioning.

He tried to find out what was going on from one of the SS (who had formerly been an NCO in the Polish Army)[25] and asked that they not beat his friend (me), for I was sick.

Dr. 2 [Władysław Dering] was already slowly consolidating his position in the hospital, he was valued as a good doctor

---

[25] He would likely have been a Polish citizen of German descent whom the Nazis had conscripted during the Occupation. Translator's note.

and had a few contacts among the SS, whom he sometimes advised.

The morning of the 7th of March, my number was called out at roll call with an instruction to go to the main schreibstube.

There were several of us.

They lined us up to one side.

The whole block gave us a look which said that we would not be coming back.

They were not far wrong.

When the gong sounded for arbeitskommando and everyone ran off to their work details, we were marched off to Block 9 (old numbering system).

In the corridor in front of the main schreibstube the numbers of all those brought over were called out and checked; there were about twenty of us from different blocks.

They stood me to one side by myself.

"What could be going on?" I wondered. "Why am I not with the others?"

They pointed at me and something was said to an SS man, which I did not hear.

"Here's a fine one," appeared to be their attitude.

However, things turned out somewhat better than I had imagined.

The others all marched off to the political department, and I was led to the erkennungsdienst [the records office].

"That's better," I thought.

On the way I began to understand the reason for this summons and became calmer with every step.

All the häftlings had to write letters to their families and only to the address that they had given upon their arrival.

Just after being brought to Auschwitz we had been interrogated at night.

We were all woken up. We were told to talk (it was on Block 17a), and asked with an odd smirk for an address to which notification would be sent in the event of an accident befalling us—as if death came here only as a result of accidents.

Every fortnight a letter was to be sent to that very address, so that just in case there would be access to an inmate's family.

I gave my sister-in-law's address in Warsaw, through which my family, about which the camp authorities must not learn, would be able to get news of me.

My sister-in-law [Eleonora Ostrowska] was given as one of my friends, I was pretending to be single and with no family apart from my mother.

I had written only once to the address provided, in November, saying where I was. I had written no more letters, so that in the future my "friend" would not be held responsible for any stunts I might pull here.

I thus wanted to sever all contact with people outside that would have been visible to the German authorities.

I was escorted by an SS man into a wooden hut where at one end (the furthest from the door) was the *blockführerstube* [SS guardroom] and at the other the *postzensurstelle* [mail censorship office].

Here, there were over a dozen SS men sitting at desks.

As I was brought in they all looked up and then continued censoring letters.

The SS man walking behind me reported my arrival.

Whereupon one of them called out to me: "Ah! Mein lieber Mann [Ah! My dear sir] . . . Why are you not writing letters?"

I replied: "I am."

"So, you're lying too! What do you mean you're writing? We keep a record of all outgoing correspondence."

"I do write, but my letters are returned. I can prove it."

"Returned? And he has...proof??? Well I never...he has proof!"

Several SS men surrounded me, jeering.

"What sort of proof?"

"I have letters which I was writing regularly and which, I don't know why, were returned to me." I spoke as if I was upset that my letters were being unfairly returned.

"Where are these letters?"

"On Block 15."

"Hans, take him over to the block to get these letters, but if he can't find them...," he turned to me, "Ich sehe Schwarz für dich! [You'll be in for it!]"

I did indeed have such letters on the block.

Foreseeing just this kind of inquiry, I had been writing every fortnight the required letter beginning with the standard opening: "Ich bin gesund und es geht mir gut [I am fine and doing well]" without which, as the block chiefs announced, the letter would not get past the censor (even if an inmate was dying, if he wanted to write to his family again he had to include those two phrases). The family would no doubt realize from his handwriting how things really were and the state of his health.

Since by and large everyone wanted to write to their loved ones, perhaps some did it just for personal reasons or to ask for money, letters were generally written.

However, I had observed that the letters returned to inmates which had not passed the censor, or had annoyed the SS, had on the envelope a little green tick, or sometimes the words "zurück [returned]" on them.

I had obtained a couple of these envelopes with the characteristic markings from my comrades and using a similar pencil, supplied by Cavalry Captain 3 [Jerzy de Virion], I had made markings on my envelopes and not handed them in for collection on a "letter-writing Sunday."

I had carefully hidden these letters.

Heading off to the block with the SS man for these letters (7th March) at the gate I met Sławek who was being led out to freedom by an SS man.

In Room 7 in Block 15 (old numbering system) I gathered the letters. My comrades in the room seeing an SS man waiting for me and some letters were sure that this had to be a political matter and that they would never see me again.

I was now welcomed back to the postzensurstelle with interest.

Six or seven of my letters were handed over by my SS escort to the office manager and several SS men gathered round.

"So the letters do exist."

I obviously must have made the green pencil marks quite well.

In any case, it would not have crossed their minds that an inmate was conscientiously writing letters and not sending them.

They began to study the contents. There was nothing there—they were pretty terse.

"Aha, this must mean that you were not writing to the address you provided!!"

I retorted that I assumed that the letters must have been returned by some kind of mistake, since I was writing to the address provided.

They checked. It must have been right.

"Aha . . . so who is this Mrs. E.O. you are writing to?"

"A friend."

"A friend," with a sneering laugh. "Why don't you write to your mother? You indicated that you have a mother."

(I had indeed indicated that, although my mother had been dead for two years. I had wanted to draw as little attention to myself as possible, to be a bird with few ties to the earth, I wanted to suggest that I had a loved one out there, but I did not want to give the address of living people.)

"Oh yes," I replied "I have a mother, but she is abroad. Wilno is, after all, abroad, so I don't know whether I can write there."

The SS men slowly returned to their work.

Interest in my case began slowly to die down.

"Well then," pronounced the office manager like Solomon "your letters keep being returned, because you're not writing to your mother, although you've got one, and you're writing to some friend. You must petition the Lagerkommandant [Camp Commandant] in writing to allow you to make a change of address and state that you want to write to Mrs. E.O. You must send your petition using official channels through your block chief."

And thus ended my business with the postzensurstelle.

The following day, I hurried to write my petition on Block 3, where the block chief Koprowiak for a long time could not understand why I had hitherto been writing to Mrs. E.O. and that I was now politely asking the Commandant to change the address to this same Mrs. E.O.'s address.

However, before I even ended up on Block 3 the following day, a surprise awaited me on Block 15 that same day—7th March.

I was the only one of those whose numbers had been called out to return to Block 15.

With a bullet, the executioner Palitzsch had put an end to my comrades' final journey to the yard at Block 13 via the political department.

I returned from the postzensurstelle to the sick block at the precise moment when a panel was on the ward examining the patients; anyone not running a temperature was being kicked out into the camp, and sent back to work and to the blocks where they had been before coming to the hospital.

Now suddenly a "patient" walks in fully dressed from "taking a stroll" around the camp.

I took a few blows to the stomach and the head and was immediately booted out of the hospital...

Therefore, the following day I was writing my petition on Block 3a.

However, the petition was not the issue.

The issue was how to get onto an indoor kommando.

Westrych had gone. The small carpenters' shop on Block 9 (old numbering system) had been closed down. The large one, which Oberkapo Balke [Artur Balke] ran and was expanding, was at Industriehof I.

I needed to wangle myself indoors immediately. My convalescence was over, but to go to work immediately in the open in the frost would be too hard on me.

By now each kommando took careful note of the prison numbers of its members, so just getting oneself onto an unsuitable kommando could lead later to problems of "absenteeism," if one wanted to move to a better work detail.

So my comrades came to the rescue.

A few members of our organization were working in the large carpenters' shop at Industriehof I and one of them, Antek (14) [Antoni Woźniak] was even a master craftsman. Czesiek (9) [Czesław Wąsowski] was by now also working there.

Antek (14) [Antoni Woźniak] took me to Balke's office and introduced me as a good carpenter.

To the question what did I know I replied, following Antek's instructions, that I was good with machinery.

It so happened that machines were being brought in and installed in the shop.

Balke agreed.

For the time being he left me in the storerooms, which were run by Władek Kupiec.

The work was hardly onerous.

Władek Kupiec was an exceptionally fine fellow and a good comrade. He and five of his brothers were there.[26]

I now also met a couple of chums, one of them was called Witold (15) [Witold Szymkowiak], the other Pilecki (16) [Jan Pilecki].[27]

After a few days working in the carpenters' shop I set up a second "five" with Władek (17) [Władysław Kupiec], Bolek (18) [Bolesław Kupiec], Witold (15) [Witold Szymkowiak], Tadek (19) [Tadeusz Słowiaczek], Antek (14) [Antoni Woźniak], Janek (20) [Jan Kupiec], Tadek (21) [Tadeusz Pietrzykowski], Antek (22) [Antoni Rosa].[28]

After a few weeks working there I heard people saying that Colonel 23 [Aleksander Stawarz] and Lieutenant Colonel 24 [Karol Kumuniecki] were planning a camp revolt: Lieutenant Colonel 24 [Karol Kumuniecki] with the fit inmates would head for Katowice, while Colonel 23 [Aleksander Stawarz] would remain for the time being in the camp with the sick.

Owing to this plan's naiveté and the possibility that similar projects might be given away by other inmates, I avoided

---

[26] Three of the six Kupiec brothers (Antoni, Jan and Władysław) survived the camp; three (Bolesław, Józef and Karol) did not. Translator's note.

[27] No relation to the author. Translator's note.

[28] In Pilecki's autumn 1943 report (*Raport W*), neither Jan Kupiec nor Antoni Woźniak are mentioned, whereas Mikołaj Skornowicz is included. Translator's note.

discussing the organization with these officers and, initially, I avoided bringing in senior officers who were in the camp under their real names (with the exception of Colonel 1 [Władysław Surmacki] whom I trusted completely) for the simple reason that if suspicions were aroused, officers who were known to the camp authorities could be locked in the bunker and tortured and would be hard-pressed to remain silent.

That is how it was during the initial phases of my organizational work. Later, things were different.

In April and May of '41 the great transports of Poles arrived—prisoners from the Pawiak [Prison].

A great number of my friends arrived.

I now set up my third "five" into which I bring my former second-in-command in Warsaw, "Czesław III" (25) [Stefan Bielecki]; Stasiek (26) [Stanisław Maringe]; Jurek (27) [Jerzy Poraziński]; Szczepan (28) [Szczepan Rzeczkowski); Włodek (29) [Włodzimierz Makaliński]; Geniek (30) [Eugeniusz Triebling].[29]

The organization is now growing by leaps and bounds.

However, the camp machinery is speeding up the killing process.

The transports from Warsaw were at the camp's "sharp end" and were being beaten as we had been and were dying in droves, daily decimated by the cold and the beatings.

Starting in the spring of 1941 the camp novelty was the orchestra.

The Camp Commandant liked music, which led to an orchestra being formed of good musicians, of which there was no shortage in the camp, or indeed of any other trade.

---

[29] In his autumn 1943 report (*Raport W*), Pilecki has Wincenty Gawron, Stanisław Gutkiewicz and Stanisław Stawiszyński, instead of Stefan Bielecki, Stanisław Maringe, Jerzy Poraziński and Szczepan Rzeczkowski. Translator's note.

Working in the orchestra was a good "job," so that anyone who had an instrument at home, had it quickly sent and signed up for the orchestra which, under the baton of Franz [Franciszek Nierychło] (a real bastard) who before had been kitchen kapo, played all manner of compositions.

It really was a fine orchestra.

It was the Commandant's pride.

If a specialist on a particular instrument was lacking, he was easily found on "civvy street" and brought to the camp.

Not only the Commandant, but also the inspection teams which would stop by the camp from time to time, were delighted with the orchestra.

The orchestra played for us four times a day.

In the morning as we left for work, when we returned for lunch, after lunch when we went back to work and as we were returning for evening roll call.

The orchestra's "stage" was in front of Block 9 (old numbering system) near the gate past which all the kommandos marched.

One really felt the full horror of this scene when the details were returning from work.

The advancing columns dragged along the ground the bodies of their comrades who had been killed at work.

Some of the corpses were frightful.

To the strains of rousing marches, played in quick time, sounding more like polkas or Polish dances than marches, the staggering shapes of beaten inmates, exhausted by work, returned.

The ranks tried hard to walk in step, dragging the dead bodies of their comrades whose bare bellies had usually been bouncing along the ground for several kilometers over frozen ground, mud and stones, which had pulled off part of their clothing.

The columns representing the depths of human misery were surrounded by a ring of whippers-in belaboring the ranks with clubs and forcing them to march in time to the cheerful music.

Anyone out of step was clubbed over the head and a moment later was being dragged along by his mates.

Everyone was escorted by a double ring of armed "heroes" wearing German army uniforms.

In front of the gate, in addition to the armed security detachments, stood a group of "supermen"—the camp's senior ranks—NCOs (on whom in the future one will be able if necessary to put the blame for everything: "what can you expect of simpletons?").

All of them were jovial, and with radiant faces they proudly watched the dying, despised race of *untermenschen* ["subhumans"].

That is how the kommandos working in the fields returned.

There were very few "old numbers" among them.

Either they had already left "up the chimney," or they had managed to get inside.

For the most part the kommandos were composed of zugangs.

The "hundreds" of those who worked in the workshops returned differently: they were strong, fit and walked in dressed ranks with a spring in their step.

The grins of pleasure disappeared from the faces of the gang by the gate. They usually turned away unwillingly. However, for the time being they needed the workshops.

More than one SS man was having some necessary item made to order for him "on the side" in the workshops, unbeknownst to the authorities.

Even these senior ranks standing there were having jobs done for them, hiding them from the others.

Every one of them was afraid to report these things to higher authority.

Killing people was different: the more one did, the more highly was one regarded.

These were the very things which, as I have said, took place "not on this earth."

What do you mean? Culture... the 20th century... whoever heard of killing people?

In any case, you can't get away with things like that on earth.

Supposedly (though it is the 20th century with such a high level of culture) these people from a great culture...somehow sneak a war through... even justifying it by necessity.

Aha... suddenly even war... when discussed by civilized people, becomes "inevitable and necessary."

Agreed, but hitherto, recognizing the veil drawn over the need to murder one group in the best interests of another, mutual killing was left to some offshoot of society: the military.

Yes, unfortunately that is how it must have once been. But now that's in the past, which was more beautiful than our times.

What can humankind say now—that very humankind which wants to demonstrate cultural and personal progress and rank the 20th century much higher than centuries past?

Can we from the 20th century look our ancestors in the eye and... laughably... prove that we have attained a higher cultural plane?

For these days an armed group destroys not some enemy army, the "cloak" of the past having been cast aside, but whole defenseless nations and societies using the latest technical inventions. Civilization's progress—yes! Cultural progress???—don't make me laugh.

We have strayed, my friends, we have strayed dreadfully.

What's worse is that there are no words to describe it...

I would like to say that we have become animals...but no, we are a whole level of hell worse than animals!

I have every right to say all this, especially in light of what I have seen and what began to happen a year later at Auschwitz.

The difference between "to be" and "not to be" was so enormous, so greatly did the conditions vary for those who worked indoors in stables, stores or workshops from the mass who were being finished off in the most varied ways in the open air.

The former were recognized to be necessary; the rest paid with their lives for the need, for the requirement, to finish off as many people as possible in this grinder.

There had to be a price, a justification for this distinction.

The price was a skill, or ingenuity in place of a skill.

The camp was self-sufficient.

Crops were sown; livestock (horses, cows and pigs) were kept.

There was an abattoir turning animal meat into items fit for human consumption.

USHMM/ IPN

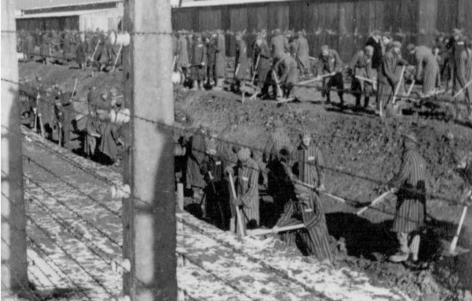

Yad Vashem/ Otto Dov Kulka

**The majority of inmates have to endure endless hours of backbreaking work outdoors...**

Yad Vashem/ Otto Dov Kulka

Yad Vashem/ Otto Dov Kulka

**... and in all weather. The lucky ones worked on indoor kommandos—such as the locksmiths, bakers, tanners, woodcarvers, or those in the hospital, kitchens or stables.**

Not far from the abattoir stood a crematorium where human meat was turned into ash, which then fertilized the fields—the only use for this meat.

The best indoor job was in the pigsty, where the swill was far more plentiful and rich than what was in the pots in the kitchen for the häftlings.

The pigs were fed the remains of the "supermen's" unfinished meals.

Those inmates whom fortune had chosen to be swineherds ate part of this fine food, taking it away from their charges—the pigs.

In the stables for the horses the inmates had other opportunities.

I was invited several times from the carpenters' shop by my friend 31 [Karol Świętorzecki] to the nearby stables, where I would go with my tools supposedly to repair something, thus justifying my presence there to any passing SS man.

My friend would greet me with a real feast.

He would give me a mess tin filled with black sugar, which after rinsing with water—to separate out the salt—turned almost white. We would add wheat bran to this. After mixing this, I would eat it as if it were the finest cake.

Then it would seem to me that I had never before eaten anything so tasty, nor would I, should I ever succeed in returning to freedom.

My friend also had milk which he took from the portion provided for the stallion.

However, one had to take great care not to be "found out."

Just coming without a specific reason and repair job assignment from a kapo was forbidden.

My friend 31 [Karol Świętorzecki] had set up a cell of our organization amongst the stable staff.

On the 15th of May, my friend was released thanks to his mother's efforts and left for Warsaw, taking my report on our work.

Much later, my friend 32 [Leszek Cenzartowicz], established with my help in the stables, kept his exhausted body alive milking mares with foal and drinking their milk.

There was also a tannery, where some of the fellows took advantage of the conditions by cutting off the skin of pigs delivered for tanning, shrinking them in their current shape and cooking a "wonderful soup" from the scraps of skin.

In the summer of '41, for the first time I ate dog meat, unaware of what it was, provided by friends in the tannery.

I later did so knowingly.

The instinct to retain one's energy made anything fit to eat, tasty.

My friend 21 [Tadeusz Pietrzykowski], who worked with the calves, secretly supplied me with raw bran which had been so poorly cleaned that once upon a time my own calves would probably have refused to eat it, and I would put it in the soup which was brought to us in the carpenters' shop, wondering whether to put in two spoonfuls or one—we were *kommandiert* [ordered to stay at work], so we did not go to the camp for lunch or midday roll call and were counted in the shop.

When my friend 21 [Tadeusz Pietrzykowski] managed sometimes to bring more bran, I would simply put a handful in my mouth and slowly, after chewing it as much as possible, swallow it raw in small pieces together with the chaff.

So it turns out that everything is possible and that everything can taste good.

Nothing affected me, maybe because I have always had an exceptionally strong stomach.

I was no expert carpenter and I had to make up for this with ingenuity.

Initially supported by friends (impossible to do for very long), I then had to face up to the challenges of carpentry.

So I learnt how to sharpen tools.

Clearly most carpenters would assume that I had mastered that a long time before.

In addition to Oberkapo Balke, there were a couple of kapos and a number of master craftsmen in front of whom one had to pretend to be a competent carpenter.

Under the direction of Władek and a few other friends, I learnt to saw, plane, smear board ends with paste and glue boards into tabletops

However, the main work was done—with the eyes.

At Auschwitz, one's ears and eyes worked the most, whatever the position or trade.

One had to be on the lookout so that a momentary rest could be taken when an overseer—a kapo—was not watching.

But if a supervisor's gaze running over the shop and its people rests on you, or you are in this gentleman's field of vision even just in the corner of his eye, then, my friend, you had better be working or cleverly pretending to do so.

You can't stand around or rest, even if you have been working away before in this gentleman's absence.

If you really had been doing that you would have been careless.

Beware! Arbeit macht frei! You read that several times a day over the gate.

You can leave this place "up the chimney," if you wear yourself out.

You can be clubbed if you happen to be taking a breather when one of the supervisors is watching.

Obviously it was different for a first-rate craftsman, who already had a fine reputation.

He did not have to pretend.

Others, even if they were really good carpenters, had to be careful.

There were several hundred slots in the shop—and thousands were dying in the camp.

New real craftsmen were clamoring to get into the shop.

"Butterfingers" were removed—and died in the open.

Hence out of necessity I was slowly becoming a carpenter. I could make quite decent joints and I did finishing work.

I managed to get my friends, who had arrived from Warsaw (April–May of '41) and whom I had brought into the organization, indoor jobs.

I got 25 [Stefan Bielecki] and 26 [Stanisław Maringe] into the *fahrbereitschaft* [motor pool] with the help of our member 33 [Stanisław Kocjan] who ran that kommando like his own.

I got 27 [Jerzy Poraziński] into the hospital as a nurse, with the help of Dr. 2 [Władysław Dering].

I got 34 [name unknown] into the hospital as a secretary, with the help of Second Lieutenant 4 [Alfred Stössel], and so on.

In the spring of '41, I went around zugang Blocks 11 and 12 (old numbering system), where new fellows were brought in, I went around often looking for friends, picking out fellows for work, getting them indoors, saving them.

One day there, I met the Czetwertyński family all together: Ludwik, the owner of Żołudek and his two sons, as well as his brother from Suchowola. I also met my friend from the resistance movement in '39—Officer Cadet 35 [Remigiusz Niewiarowski].

A few days later I also met two colleagues from work in Warsaw: 36 [Stanisław Arct] and 37 [name unknown].

I watched everyone carefully, for one could never tell how

a fellow might behave after having passed through Aleja Szucha[30] and the Pawiak in Warsaw.

Some were exhausted; some were broken.

Not everyone was suited to our organization or to new underground work.

Major 38 [Chmielewski], who had worked with us in Warsaw using the nom de guerre "Sęp II," on seeing me for the first time on the parade ground at Auschwitz in the summer of '41 delightedly rushed over calling out loudly "Ah, so you're here, the Warsaw Gestapo chopped my a— into little pieces asking what had happened to Witold... Have you been here long?... You do have an old number... How did you manage it?... But I saw you two months ago in Warsaw... That's what I told them at Aleja Szucha," he shouted in the presence of a dozen or so of my friends, blowing my cover, for here I was Tomasz.

Fortunately, there were no rogues among us.

As for how I had managed to be in Warsaw two months before... it appeared to me simply that, after being beaten at Aleja Szucha, he had gone slightly soft in the head.

It turned out much later that there was a completely different reason.[31]

Out of the dozen or so of my old colleagues who arrived over the course of these months, 25 [Stefan Bielecki] and 29 [Włodzimierz Makaliński] were the most useful to me in my work and I trusted them almost as much as I trusted myself.

Standing in the corner of a room in the zugang blocks and watching these people who had just arrived from the outside world and who still had, so to speak, the dust of Warsaw on them, one felt slightly odd.

---

[30] Gestapo headquarters in Warsaw. Translator's note.

[31] Which we never learn. Translator's note.

As if one had more than one person inside.

One of these people wanted to feel sorry for himself and longed for the outside world, were it not for the shame he felt at such a thought.

However, another was stronger, and it was he who felt within him the joy of victory over impulses and the trivia to which people become attached in the real world, but which were of no value here.

The third one watched with a kind of pity, but not in the worst sense of that word, but with a certain inner, friendly smile, indulgently looking at these new arrivals who were still addressing each other formally using professional titles and military ranks.

Good Lord! How quickly you will have to shed all that; the sooner the better.

Here, the first order of business was finishing off the intelligentsia, because that was what the camp authorities had been instructed to do, but also because if an intellectual, unsuited to a manual craft in the workshops, failed to get into the camp's reservoir of intellectuals—the baubüro [construction site office], the schreibstube [office], the hospital, the effektenkammer [storeroom for inmates' personal belongings] and the *bekleidungskammer* [clothing storeroom]—he died, for he contributed nothing here, since an intellectual, even one possessing great knowledge, was unfortunately sometimes lacking in practical skills.

Furthermore, he was more delicate, unused to physical labor and any old food.

It is sad, but if I want to present a true picture of the camp, I cannot ignore this.

Anyone reading this who thinks that I am out to "blacken" the intelligentsia is wrong.

I believe that I could be considered one of them, but that does not mean that I am not to write the bitter truth.

A high percentage of the intellectuals brought to the camp had few survival skills. They did not realize that they needed to conceal their professional pedigrees for the time being as well as possible beneath a flexible approach, seeking a way to scrabble for their lives in this stony, harsh concentration camp soil.

Professional courtesy was out; they needed to come to grips with the conditions.

Engineers could not demand to work in an office, nor doctors to work in the hospital; they had to content themselves with the slightest "hole" through which they could wiggle out of a zugang block to find some work which the camp authorities found useful and which was not an affront to a Pole's honor.

There was no "puffing up" because one was a lawyer, which was of absolutely no consequence here.

One had above all to be on good terms with every Pole, if one was not a bastard, and take advantage of any kind of help and repay it in kind.

For here the only way to live was cooperating in friendship and work... helping one another.

But how many did not understand that!

How many egoists there were about whom one could say: "he neither seeks the wave, nor it him."[32] Such people had to die. We had too little and so many to save.

Furthermore, the willpower was lacking not to eat everything one could not digest, and not all our intellectuals had strong stomachs.

---

[32] A quotation from Adam Mickiewicz's poem "Oda do Młodości" ("Ode to Youth"). Translator's note.

"Stupid, f— intellectual," was the most insulting epithet in the camp.

From the spring of '41 the camp population gained the word "*muselmann*," for that is what the German authorities called an inmate who, nearing the end, was weak and could barely walk—and the word caught on.

In the words of a camp ditty:

"...muselmänner...flapping like a banner..."

This was a being on the dividing line between life and...the crematorium chimney.

It was very difficult for him to regain his strength, he usually ended up in the hospital or on the *schonungsblock* [the so-called convalescence block] (Block 14 using the old numbering system; Block 19 in the new system) where several hundred of these wraiths could benefit from the camp authorities' mercy and stand all day in rows in the corridors doing nothing; but this standing also finished them off.

The mortality rate in this block was enormous.

In July of '41, as I was passing a group of a dozen or so young boys, aged 16 or 17, brought straight from their school desks for singing patriotic songs, one of them, 39 [Kazimierz Radwański], rushed over to me shouting: "Uncle!" Blown again.

However, I was pleased, obviously not that he was there, but at getting some family news.

A few weeks later, in the carpenters' shop, in the machine shop, someone's eyes bored into mine and without blinking stared at me carefully.

I held their gaze.

A short man, an inmate, a Pole, came over and asked me if I was XY, giving my real name.

I told him he was wrong. But he would not be put off, assuring me that there was nothing to fear.

A few weeks later, he was sworn in and was working for us: 40 [Tadeusz Szydlik].

He was working in the carpentry machine shop.

I swelled our ranks in the carpenters' shop by swearing in three brave Poles: 41 [Stanisław Stawiszyński], 42 [Tadeusz Lech] and 43 [Antoni Koszczyński].

Shortly afterwards, 44 [Wincenty Gawron], 45 [Stanisław Gutkiewicz] and 46 [Wiktor Śniegucki] joined us.

I was managing by now to cope in the carpenters' shop.

Fate decreed that my work and profile as a "sort of carpenter" did not bother the kapos.

Once only, as I was preparing boards for gluing on my own, Oberkapo Balke stood a few paces behind and watched me for a moment, of which I was unaware; he then called over Kapo Walter and pointing to me said slowly, enunciating the words: "Wer ist das? [Who's that?]," but they moved on leaving me to my work.

I was told this by some of my friends next to whose work stations the kapos had been standing.

He apparently was aware that I was not a carpenter.

In fact Balke was an interesting person. Tall, handsome and with an intelligent appearance, he was rather stiff and cold.

On Sundays, when they tormented us with the so-called *blocksperre* [confinement to blocks] until noon, we were locked in for various uniform inspections, then Balke would appear and order all carpenters onto the parade ground where he paraded us, rearranged us and formed us up in twenties, assigning "twenty" leaders and kept us on the parade ground in the sun, with the orchestra playing until blocksperre was over. Then he would cheerfully dismiss us with a smile and let us return to our blocks.

Our camp was continually growing.

Not the actual head count of inmates, of whom there were at that time always about 5,000–6,000.

The running total, of course, came to over 20,000 inmates, but over 10,000 had vanished into the crematorium.

The camp was growing in another way; it was building.

In addition to the eight blocks on the parade ground (which led to a change of numbering throughout the camp) and the fact that they were extending the camp in the direction of Industriehof I, branches were being rapidly built in the main camp—the so-called *stammlager*. One was at so-called "Buna," 8 kilometers to the east of the camp, where they were working on a factory for making artificial rubber; another branch of our stammlager was the newly created camp of Birkenau (Brzezinka), named after a little birch wood. It was also called "Rajsko," which had nothing to do with the village of Rajsko (Birkenau was several kilometers to the west; the village of Rajsko was to the south); the name was simply ironic.[33]

Droves of people were dying on the building sites at both subcamps.

Every day hundreds of inmates marched out to Buna before morning roll call. They got up much earlier than we did and returned several hours after we had finished our workday.

Barracks were being built at Birkenau—wooden and still virginally new ones.

Only later would nightmarish things take place at Birkenau-Rajsko.

Framers and carpenters were needed to build the barracks

---

[33] The name Rajsko was a camp pun on the Polish word for paradise—*raj*. Hereafter Pilecki often uses Rajsko for Birkenau. Translator's note.

and, in the absence of a large number of framers, carpenters were brought in at the start.

That meant working in the open air, in the rain and later the snow, urged on by the kapos' clubs, since orders were to build this hell in Rajsko as quickly as possible.

Carpenters from our shop were to be sent there—to die.

Balke had to supply these carpenters. He did it unwillingly. He took his time choosing.

This was a difficult time for the carpenters and apparently also for him.

Most of the carpenters who went to build the barracks in the open air (about a third of all the carpenters went) died there: they caught cold or simply collapsed from exhaustion.

Therefore, he assigned the worst craftsmen.

He would look at me carefully as if thinking: "assign him or not?"

And somehow he would continue down the line of standing carpenters awaiting their fate, leaving me in the shop.

A minute percentage of people in Auschwitz were released.

They were usually fellows from Warsaw street round-ups with no records whose families bought them out, using a variety of intermediaries who had got in on this act, and sometimes fell afoul of blackmailers or charlatans. Or by families with their own connections at foreign consulates, or even at Aleja Szucha.

In the autumn of '40 about 70–80 people from the Warsaw transports were released.

In the course of '41, releases were very rare, merely a handful in all before the autumn (several dozen in all) until in the autumn of '41 about 200 inmates were sent to the "freedom" block (set aside for this purpose), where they were "quarantined" before leaving the camp.

That means they were given better food to make them more presentable, they were not beaten, and those bearing the marks of beatings or injuries were kept in the hospital for these to heal and in order to convalesce, so as not to leave with evidence of the treatment meted out to inmates at Auschwitz.

However, taking into account that those arriving at the camp in November 1941 were given camp numbers over 25,000, what did over three hundred releases mean?

Every released inmate, after getting into his civilian clothes (from the bags in the effektenkammer in which his things had been hanging), had to go either alone, or with a group of other fellows being released, through the little wooden hut (where the postzensurstelle [mail censorship office] was also located) where an SS man would say goodbye, making it quite plain that that, once free, he was to say not a word about the camp at Auschwitz.

If anyone were to ask what it was like in Auschwitz, the inmate was to reply: "Go and find out for yourself!" (a naive suggestion).

And, if the German authorities learned that one of those released had failed to keep his mouth shut, he would rapidly find himself back at Auschwitz (this was more convincing, and former inmates of Auschwitz really did stay silent as the grave).

The game which I was now playing in Auschwitz was dangerous.

This sentence does not really convey the reality; in fact, I had gone far beyond what people in the real world would consider dangerous, simply passing through the wires into the camp was beyond dangerous.

Indeed, the work I had begun completely absorbed me, and since it was beginning to pick up speed in line with my plan, I really began to worry that my family might buy me out, like some of the other fellows, and interrupt the game I was playing, for I also had no record and had been brought in from a round-up.

So, unable to reveal my work, I wrote to my family that everything was just fine, that they should not raise my case and that I wanted to stay on. Fate would decide whether I would get out and so on.

I received in return a reply that Janek W. [Jan Włodarkiewicz], whose conscience troubled him when he learnt where I was, kept asking everyone: "Why did he go?" However, he stayed true and told the family when they asked for help in buying me out that he didn't have the money for it.

I discovered a way to send letters to my family writing in Polish.

A young friend of mine 47 [name unknown], going to work in the town, had managed to make contact with the locals through whom I sent two letters to my family.

My letters were sent on to [Home Army] High Command.

In addition to those initial colleagues from Warsaw I have mentioned, I met here in Auschwitz at the beginning of '41 Stach 48 [Stanisław Ozimek], who was shipped out to the quarry, and in the summer of '41 Janek 49 [Jan Dangel] who was sick and whom we managed to get on a transport to Dachau, which was a much better camp than Auschwitz.

A number of escape attempts led the camp authorities to decide to apply collective responsibility and (starting in the spring of '41) ten inmates were shot for each successful escapee.[34]

The selection of ten men to die for one escapee was a difficult moment for the camp and especially for the block where the selection was being made.

*At that time we, as an organization, took a clear position against escapes.*

*We organized no escapes and opposed any thought of them, as evidence of extreme egoism, until there were major changes in this area.*

*For the time being all escapes were lone ventures having nothing to do with our organization.*

A "death selection" was held immediately following the roll call at which an escapee's absence had been discovered.

The Camp Commandant and his retinue arrived in front of the block in which the escapee had been living, now standing in ten ranks, and walking down a rank he would point to inmates who appealed to him or who maybe did not.

This rank would then take "five paces forward" and the whole retinue walked down the next rank.

Some ranks had several people picked; others had none.

Those who looked death bravely in the eye were usually not chosen.

Not everyone could take the tension and sometimes someone would run forward, behind the inspecting team's back, to the rank already inspected; these types were usually spotted and taken off to their death.

It once happened that a young inmate was chosen, whereupon an old man, a priest, stepped out of the ranks

---

[34] Prisoners selected to die for an escape often were not shot, but sent to the bunker to be starved to death. A truly terrible punishment. Translator's note.

and asked the Camp Commandant to take him and release the young man.

This was a powerful moment and the block froze in amazement.

The Commandant agreed.

The heroic priest went to his death and the other inmate returned to the ranks.[35]

The political department was hard at work—leading to shootings for "outside" cases.

The camp authorities were especially pleased when they managed to assemble a largish group of Poles to be shot on days which had been formerly celebrated on the outside, in Poland.

Almost as a matter of course we had a larger "cull" on the 3rd of May[36] and the 11th of November,[37] and once, as a bonus, we had a group of Poles shot on the 19th of March.[38]

When I had been in the "outside world" and longing for some creative work with a chisel, or a bit of carving, I had thought to myself: well, since I just never seem to have the time for this, they might as well put me in jail.

Fortune has always shone on me and it must have been listening in.

Now I was locked up, so I needed to try my hand at carving, about which I knew absolutely nothing.

The carpentry department had a carving shop.

---

[35] This was the famous case of Father Maksymilian Kolbe, who took the place of Franciszek Gajowniczek, who had a family. Afterwards, the camp authorities more or less left Gajowniczek alone and he survived. Translator's note.

[36] Commemorates the ratification of the Polish Constitution on the 3rd of May 1791. Translator's note.

[37] Polish Independence Day, dating from the 11th of November 1918. Translator's note.

[38] Marshal Józef Piłsudski's name day. Translator's note.

With the exception of a couple of professionally trained painters such as 44 [Wincenty Gawron] and 45 [Stanisław Gutkiewicz], everyone working there was a woodcarver, most of them from the Polish mountains.

With the help of 44 [Wincenty Gawron] and 45 [Stanisław Gutkiewicz] I got into the carving shop.

My transfer was easier, given that the carving shop was a subunit of the carpenters' shop where I had been working for several months.

The head of the shop was a fine fellow: 52 [Tadeusz Myszkowski].

I arrived there (1 Nov. '41) and made a couple of drawings of paper knives.

I was told: "That's fine... on paper, but now please do it in wood."

So I began work as a permanent member of the carving shop.

During my first week I carved three knives.

The first knife was really an opportunity for me to get used to holding and using the tools, the second was a little better and as for the third—52 [Tadeusz Myszkowski] showed it to the woodcarvers saying: "That's how you carve a knife!"

So the work went fine.

On one side sat 42 [Tadeusz Lech]—a first-rate fellow and always cheerful—and on the other my friend 45 [Stanisław Gutkiewicz].

On the morning of 11 Nov. '41, comrade 42 [Tadeusz Lech] came over and said: "I've had a strange dream, I feel that they're going to 'top' me today. Perhaps it's nothing, but at least I can take comfort in dying on the 11th of November."

Half an hour later, at morning roll call, his name was read out together with a number of others.

He said goodbye to me warmly, asking me to tell his mother that he had died in good spirits.

A few hours later he was dead.

The division of labor was such that news regularly received by us from the outside world by means of an established route was disseminated in the camp by a cell composed of three of our members.

One of them, our unforgettable "Wernyhora"[39] 50 [Jan Mielcarek], would continually make optimistic predictions at every intersection surrounded by a crowd of inmates.

He was in great demand and much liked.

The organization grew.

During my time in the carving shop I brought a couple of friends into our ranks: 53 [Józef Chramiec] and 54 [Stefan Gaik], followed by 55 [Mieczysław Wagner], 56 [Zbigniew Różak], 57 [Edward Ciesielski], 58 [Andrzej Marduła].

After being personally recruited by me, each "five" would fan out amongst the prison body to various kommandos, through its own efforts building branches based on the profile of a new candidate.

Everything was built exclusively on mutual trust.

Tackling the issue of the leadership of each group connected to me, I decided to rely on specific leaders, junior and senior, in each case simply taking into account a given leader's personal attributes.

There was no other way to handle it.

---

[39] A legendary Cossack bard and mystic, who figures in the play *Wesele* by Stanisław Wyspiański. Translator's note.

All "outside" suggestions had to be ignored completely.

It was irrelevant who had been what in the past, but it was very important to have in each leadership position a "real man," who, if the time came, would lead people not by virtue of some title, since no one knew it; he had to be someone who had hitherto kept his mouth shut and, if the time came, would be able to inspire the others, and so had to be someone who was clearly brave and whom the lads would willingly follow.

Not only did he have to be brave, but he had to distinguish himself by his inner strength and tact.

This minor detail, when one was molding and selecting people, often brought in those who had positions of authority in the camp.

A room supervisor sworn in by us would then try to be helpful, serving "seconds" and keeping up the strength of our members needing nourishment whom we would send him, even keeping some of them in his room.

But if someone who came wanting to get on the right side of a room supervisor could not behave, did not have the tact or the strength of character to resist holding out his own bowl for "seconds" for himself, then our work came to naught.

It was another matter if the candidate, after a couple of conversations with the room supervisor, had the strength of character not to mention food, even if his guts were screaming; the room supervisor would raise the subject, then the food he got in coming there would not get in the way of setting up a network.

Unfortunately, there were a few who coming on organizational matters to a room supervisor who was a recent acquaintance would hold out their bowl for "seconds" for themselves.

In such cases, our work could not prosper.

The room supervisor would "sort out" such visitors with a bowl of soup and that would be the end of it.

# 1941...

The outbreak of the German–Bolshevik war [in June 1941], apart from filling us with joy at this long-expected news, for the time being brought few changes in the camp.

A few of the SS men left for the front. They were replaced by other, older men.

Only in August 1941 did this new war affect us, like everything else, with a terrible resonance.

The first Bolshevik prisoners, for the time being just officers, were brought in and after seven hundred of them were locked into one room on Block 13 (Block 11 in the new numbering system) and packed in so tightly that none of them could sit, the room was sealed (we did not yet have gas chambers).

That same evening a group of German soldiers led by an officer arrived.

The German team entered the room and, after donning gas masks, threw in a few gas canisters and observed the effects.

Our comrades working as pflegers [nurses] who the following day had to clear out the corpses said that it was a terrible sight.

The men had been so tightly packed that even in death they could not fall over and they hung, leaning against each other, their arms so intertwined that it was hard to separate the bodies.

They must have been Bolshevik senior ranks judging by the uniforms, from different formations, in which they were gassed.

This was the first effort there at gassing using Prussic acid.

The first person who came to tell me the news was 19 [Tadeusz Słowiaczek].

He was very distressed by this and his mind quickly jumped to the conclusion that such an attempt would lead to others, perhaps using inmates.

At the time this still seemed improbable.

Meanwhile, the camp was again deloused (the summer of '41), after which all the carpenters were assigned to the same block: Block 3, on the ground floor.

We were given bunks, since almost the whole camp, block by block, was being issued bunks.

This was another opportunity for whippers-in and the SS men to have fun.

The bunks had to be made more neatly than at officer school and so there was more harassment, more beatings.

Then (in September) some of the carpenters (including me) were moved to Block 12 (new numbering system), and in October to Block 25 (new numbering system, formerly Block 17).

It was there, living that November on Block 25, that going out in the morning in front of the block before roll call and fidgeting a little from the biting wind cutting my face with alternating rain or freezing snow, I was struck by a sight which amazed me.

I saw, about 200 paces away on the other side of the double wire fence, columns of "hundreds" of completely naked people, arranged in the usual camp style in twenty "fives," who were being urged on by German soldiers' rifle butts.

I counted eight "hundreds," but the head of the column was already jammed in the building's doorway and several hundred might have already entered before my arrival.

The building they were entering was the crematorium.

These were Bolshevik prisoners of war.

As I later learnt, there were more than a thousand of them.

In June 1941 more than 4.5 million German and other Axis troops invaded the Soviet Union—their former ally—along an 1,800-mile front.

An estimated 3 million Soviet soldiers were taken prisoner by the rapidly advancing German forces.

Pilecki reports that the first Soviet POWs were brought to Auschwitz in August 1941.

Block 11, where the first Soviet POWs were gassed during the testing of Zyklon B, which was used later in the mass extermination of the Jews.

Bundesarchiv Bild 192-360/ Francisco Boix

ABM/ Lidia Foryciarz

Apparently people can be naive till the day they die.

I assumed at the time that they were issuing these prisoners of war underwear and clothes, but did not know why they were using for that purpose the crematorium and the precious work time in that factory, where our fellows, working three shifts and round the clock, could not keep up with burning the remains of our fellow inmates.

It turned out, however, that they had been taken there specifically to save time.

The doors were shut.

One or two canisters of gas were dropped in from above and then the twitching corpses were quickly thrown onto the heated grates.

They were burnt for the simple reason that accommodation had not been prepared at Auschwitz for the POWs sent there, and the orders had been to finish them off as quickly as possible.

A fence was hastily erected within the camp, which was squeezed, allocating nine blocks to Bolshevik prisoners of war.

The administrative offices of a death camp were also set up.

It was announced in the blocks that anyone who spoke Russian could get a job as a room supervisor or even a kapo in the POW camp.

As an organization, our attitude was one of scorn towards this idea and towards those willing to offer their services in the murdering of prisoners of war, recognizing that the authorities were only too happy to have Poles do their dirty work for them.

The fence was quickly finished and the camp for the Bolsheviks was ready.

Over the internal gate in the fence between our camps a sign was hung with a large notice: "Kriegsgefangenenlager" ["Prisoner of War Camp"].

It later emerged that the German kapos and SS men quickly and efficiently murdered the Bolshevik POWs, as they had murdered us, since the 11,400 prisoners whom they brought in at the end of 1941 (I got the number from the main schreibstube [office]) were very quickly finished off over the course of a few winter months.

With the exception of a few dozen who accepted the hideous task of finishing off their own comrades and then Poles and other nationalities in the Birkenau camp, and with the exception of a few hundred who accepted a job as partisans and whom the German authorities put in uniform, trained and fed and who were to be used as partisans behind Bolshevik lines.

They lived in barracks near the little town of Oświęcim [Auschwitz].

The rest were finished off at work with an exceptional effort by means of beatings, hunger and freezing.

Sometimes in the evening or the morning they were kept for hours in front of the blocks in their underwear or naked.

This was accompanied by Germans laughing that people from Siberia were not afraid of the cold.

We could hear the screams of people freezing to death.

At this time in our camp things became a little more relaxed and there was a reduced emphasis on finishing us off, for all the rage and energy going into beatings and murdering was directed at the Bolshevik camp.

The rail which had been struck in the early days of the camp's existence, giving off the sound of a "gong" (for all roll calls and parades), was replaced by a bell hung between posts by the kitchen.

The bell had been brought here from some church.

On it was the inscription: "Jesus, Mary, Joseph."

After a time the bell cracked.

The inmates said that it had been unable to take the camp scenes.

Another one was brought. This too soon cracked.

Whereupon a third one was brought (the churches still had bells) and it was used carefully. It lasted until the end.

Thus a church bell sometimes aroused many emotions.

When at times we stood at evening roll call, the evening could have been beautiful were it not for the continual spirit of murder hovering over us.

The setting sun would illuminate the sky and clouds with beautiful colors and then the camp siren would start its terrifying wailing, warning all the sentries that they could not come down from the towers of the outer postenkette [security perimeter], since one or more inmates were missing.

It was an ominous warning to us that there would be a "death selection" of ten inmates, or at any rate a "punishment parade" at which the numbing frost would slip deep into us.

Or some other time, as we stood like a guard of honor for a victim who, his hands bound, was waiting by the gallows and was in a moment to hang in the noose... suddenly... then... in the general hush the calm, unruffled sound of a bell drifted in. It was tolling in some church.

How close it was to our hearts and in its proximity... and yet so distant and unobtainable... for there... in the outside world... people were ringing it.

They lived, prayed, sinned; but what did their sins count when compared to the offenses here?

From the summer (of '41) a custom was introduced, supposedly to regulate admissions to the krankenbau [hospital] for inmates who were feeling so weak in the morning that they could not go to work, while everyone was running to their work columns to the sound of the morning bell signalling "arbeitskommando formieren"; then the weak, sick muselmänner would go to stand in a small group in the courtyard by the kitchen, where they were inspected by pflegers [nurses] and the Lagerkapo [discipline kapo], sometimes by the Lagerältester [Head Inmate], who assessed their strength by shoving them.

Some of them were sent to the hospital, some went to the schonungsblock [convalescence block], some of them, however, despite their exhaustion were packed off to "fives" in kommandos working in the fields and sent off at a brisk pace to a certain death at work.

Those in the schonungsblock and hospital usually did not last much longer.

When I moved to Block 25 (November of '41)[40] I met and got to know better my future friend 59 [Henryk Bartosiewicz].

He was a brave and cheerful fellow.

I was setting up a new, fourth "five," which not only 59 [Henryk Bartosiewcz], but also 60 [Stanisław Kazuba] and 61 [Konstanty Piekarski] joined.

At this time two senior officers, Colonel 62 [Jan Karcz] and Lieutenant Colonel 63 [Jerzy Zalewski], were brought to the camp along with some other fellows.

I suggested that Colonel 62 [Jan Karcz] join the organization and he agreed and started to work with us.

---

[40] Earlier in this Report, Pilecki said that he had moved to Block 25 in October. Translator's note.

I had made the first exception, since, as I have already mentioned, I had hitherto avoided senior officers who were in the camp under their own names.

However, the organization was growing, and some of the fellows intimated that perhaps my reason for avoiding senior officers was excessive ambition—and an opportunity to settle this matter arose, for 59 [Henryk Bartosiewicz] had discovered Colonel 64 [Kazimierz Rawicz], who was there under a false name and pretending to be a civilian through and through, so I suggested that Colonel 64 [Kazimierz Rawicz] endorse our organization and that I would serve under him.

Colonel 64 [Kazimierz Rawicz] approved of the approach I had been using and we continued to work together.

At this time I brought in 65 [name unknown] and 66 [name unknown], and with the help of 59 [Henryk Bartosiewicz], 67 [Czesław Darkowski], and 68 [Mieczysław Januszewski] who shortly thereafter, on becoming an arbeitsdienst [work assign-ment leader], began to provide us with valuable assistance.

I eventually saw the day, of which at one time I had been able only to dream hopelessly, when we set up a political cell in our organization which comprised fellows who worked together very well, but who in the real world had been at each others' throats in Parliament.

No. 69 [Roman Rybarski]—right wing; 70 [Stanisław Dubois]—left wing; 71 [Jan Mosdorf]—right wing; 72 [Konstanty Jagiełło]—left wing; 73 [Piotr Kownacki]—right wing; 74 [Kiliański]—left wing, 75 [Stefan Niebudek]—right wing and so on: a long list of former political party men.

So one had to show Poles daily a mountain of Polish corpses in order for them to reconcile and to decide that beyond their differences and the adversarial attitudes they had adopted towards one another in the real world, there was a greater reality: agreement and a joint front against a common enemy, of whom after all we had always had not a few.

Thus the opportunity for agreement and a common front always was and always had been there, in contrast to what we Poles had been doing in the real world: endless litigiousness and wrangling in Parliament.

From a number of friends of Colonel 64 [Kazimierz Rawicz], I swore in 76 [Bernard Świerczyna] and 77 [Zbigniew Ruszczyński], and then I brought in 78 [name unknown] and 79 [name unknown].

In November 1941 oberkapo Balke left the carpenters' shop and was replaced by oberkapo Konrad, who was well disposed and polite towards the Polish carpenters.

He loved the art and carvings of the mountain wood-carvers.

He convinced the authorities to detach all the woodcarvers, with the addition of the eight best carpenters selected from among several hundred, who were specialists at making fine jewelry boxes, inlays and other marvels of woodcarving, and he moved this artistic élite from working at Industriehof I to a place near the town on the site of a large tannery with a factory chimney, surrounded by a wooden fence with four watchtowers.

A great number of specialist kommandos were located here: the tailors, the locksmiths, the painters, the blacksmiths, stables with a few horses, as well as the "aristocrats" of the specialist brotherhood—the well-placed tanners.

Amongst this artistic brotherhood was a group, a real woodcarving shop, since our kommando was for the most part composed of woodcarvers.

For instance, in this small group Professor Dunikowski worked, together with Janek Machnowski and his friend

Fusek, who both kept out an eye out for the professor; Wicek Gawron was also for a short time assigned there.

Every kommando had its kapo.

All this was under the iron hand of Oberkapo Erik [Erik Grönke]—a consummate bastard and his assistant, the crazy kapo Walter.

We—the woodcarving-cum-carpentry-cum-artistic kommando that the carpentry oberkapo Konrad had wanted—joined this collection of different trades.

But Konrad had not taken into account certain dark sides to moving to the *lederfabrik* [tannery].

This was Oberkapo Erik's domain and he recognized no other oberkapos.

Two personality types clashed: Konrad—an honest lover of art, but naive and openly fond of Poles; and the devious, cunning and evil Erik—someone even the SS feared, for he had some shady arrangements with the Camp Commandant and he behaved in the tannery as if he were on his own property, running things and sometimes hosting the Commandant, with whom he had some business dealings in finished leather.

Needless to say, Konrad lost.

Our workshops were located in two rooms in the factory.

Beyond several walls, in the tannery proper, was a tank into which hot water was poured.

The tank was so large that one could even swim a few strokes in it.

Once, taking advantage of having friends in the tannery, I took a bath and felt as I had once felt as a free man.

It had been a long time since my skin had experienced a warm bath.

All this was done on the side.

Who would have imagined that a häftling in Auschwitz could take a hot bath?

Could one say that one had been for a swim? It was inconceivable.

One day, Konrad took a bath in the tank unbothered by the fact that he was doing so together with a häftling—a Pole.

For that matter, no one feared him, for he was never mean.

But some bastard saw it and a first *meldung* [report] about Konrad was sent.

In December (1941) we were kommandiert [ordered to stay at work] in the evenings and we worked (not attending evening roll call) until 22:00 hours (10 p.m.).

We had a great deal of work producing custom-made toys for the children of some of our German "higher-ups."

One evening, a kapo—one of Erik's confidants—arrived together with an SS man and they convinced Konrad to go into town.

Konrad—an inmate yearning for the company of free people—agreed and, together with the escorting SS man, they set off for the town.

An hour later, just before our departure from the tannery for camp, Konrad appeared in our room, drunk.

Another kapo and SS man, different ones, came in right behind him. They were not the ones who had been in town with him.

They witnessed Konrad patting some of his favorite craftsmen on the head, saying that some should be kapos because they were excellent workers, and "appointing" a number of men "twenty" leaders and kapos.

That was enough: he was locked up in the bunker for a long time.

Thus did Erik rid himself of an oberkapo in his fiefdom.

Because the authorities now began to sort out individual inmates' accommodations, trying to house them by kommando, I was moved from Block 12 together with a group of other inmates who worked at the lederfabrik [tannery], or as it was still officially called the *bekleidungswerkstätte* [clothing workshop], to Block 25 (as I have already mentioned).

The bunks with which the blocks were being equipped one by one were wooden and stacked one on top of the other on three levels.

They had not yet got around to installing bunks in Block 25.

We slept side by side, about 240 of us to a room, tightly packed, our feet "tucked in" in camp jargon, and on one side.

At night (just as a year before) people walked on each other's heads, stomachs, aching feet when going to the lavatory and on their return found nowhere to sleep.

This is not the most pleasant memory, but since I am writing everything, then I shall mention it too.

Owing to some failure in camp organization, during the winter as early as December (of '41) turnips were brought in on freight cars and stored in mounds, after being carried from a railroad siding about three kilometers from the camp.

The farm kommandos provided too few men, while other ones with zugangs being finished off in the fields were too weak, and so stronger people from the workshops were used, Sundays being set aside for the task.

I usually avoided this work, managing with Dr. 2's [Władysław Dering's] help to be summoned to the hospital for a fake X-ray, or a test or something or other.

However, one Sunday the sun was shining and the weather was fine.

I went off with the others.

Together with a friend, Zygmunt Kostecki, I carried the turnips in baskets, or wheelbarrows.

The kapos and SS men checked that the wheelbarrows were filled right up, which we were doing.

Then, in loading up the rest of the turnips which had been dumped there, we filled up only half of our wheelbarrows and, as it was time to return to barracks and the "hundreds" were beginning to form up, the unterkapo who was loading our wheelbarrows decided that it was too late to go somewhere else to fill up the wheelbarrows and told us to take what we had.

There was an SS man standing on the parade ground through which we were carrying the turnips who, spotting from some distance that our wheelbarrows were not full, ran over and beat me on the arms.

We stopped, he assaulted me with his club, shouting for some reason: "Du polnischer Offizier [you Polish officer]" and beating me about the head and face with the club he was holding.

It must be a nervous tic, but at moments like that (there have been a few) I pull a face which looks a bit like a smile, which enraged him and he hit me on the head with his club even harder.

This could not have gone on for long, but at such times a great many thoughts run through a man's brain.

The thought "You can beat all you like, but you won't . . . " came to me; it was a saying which had been around since some uprising or other. . . and now I really did smile.

I must have been stunned, for I did not feel any great pain.

The SS man stared and growled: "Du lächender Teufel [You laughing devil]."

I don't know how things would have gone had it not been for the camp siren, which turned his mind to other things: someone had escaped.

My friends later told me that I'd been lucky.

My head and face were swollen for a fortnight.

I was beaten again, much later, in the tannery.

Fellows were smoking in the lavatory, for there was no smoking at work. Kapo Walter burst in like a tiger.

I had not been smoking, but was just leaving.

He dashed over: "Who's been smoking?"

I said nothing and unwittingly had some sort of smile on my face.

"Was? Gefällt es dir nicht? [What? Don't you like it?]"

(I have no idea what I was supposed to like or not like.)

Walter was a fiend and could knock down a man with a single blow.

I then received a great number of blows to the head and fell down several times. However, as 59 [Henryk Bartosiewicz] and 61 [Konstanty Piekarski] told me, I kept getting back on my feet in front of him with that smiling grimace of mine on my face.

Walter left me alone, for the Camp Commandant had arrived and Erik was absent.

Meanwhile, far away in the outside world in Warsaw, I was promoted.

For setting up the TAP [Tajna Armia Polska—The Secret Polish Army]; for integrating it into the KZN [Konfederacja

Zbrojna Narodu—The Nation's Armed Alliance];[41] for ignoring my own ambition and, the moment I had seen General Sikorski's authorization, working towards integrating all formations into the ZWZ [Związek Walki Zbrojnej—The Union for Armed Combat], which had been the first cause of my disagreement with 82 [Jan Włodarkiewicz] and, who knows, maybe the reason I had had to leave Warsaw.

And yet Janek W. [Włodarkiewicz] had recommended me and, according to "Bohdan" 85 [Zygmunt Bohdanowski], had stayed on the case and had told him that my promotion meant more to him than his own.

Colonel "Grot" [Stefan Rowecki][42] promoted a number of us from the KZN.

No. 82 [Jan Włodarkiewicz] and 85 [Zygmunt Bohdanowski] became lieutenant colonels.

Thus I had finally become a first lieutenant under my real name (in other words, I had reverted to 1935).

If all these issues from the outside world had not seemed trivial in this hell, then I might have felt bitter about them.

When it came to good jobs in Auschwitz, then after the pflegers [nurses]—not of people but of pigs, the so-called *tierpflegers* [animal or veterinary nurses]—and the musicians, who in addition to playing in the orchestra were usually room supervisors, a good job was that of barber.

---

41 Pilecki conflates the Konfederacja Zbrojna (The Armed Confederation—KZ) with the Konfederacja Narodu (The Confederation of the Nation—KN). Translator's note.

42 Lieutenant General Stefan "Grot" Rowecki commanded the Polish Home Army (the Armia Krajowa, or AK) until his arrest by the Gestapo in June 1943. He was executed in Sachsenhausen concentration camp by the Germans in August 1944. Translator's note.

A photo of three-tiered
bunks in a barracks taken
by the construction
management of the
SS (Waffen SS und Polizei
Bauleitung) in 1941.

Barrack room shortly
after liberation by
Soviet forces, 1945.

Yad Vashem/ Stanisław Mucha

**A group of soldiers from the Polish Underground Home Army (Armia Krajowa, or AK).**

Usually people tried to combine these two positions: shaving and room supervisor.

But even if a barber was not a supervisor, he did quite well for himself.

There were barbers who only shaved the SS men, but each block also had a number of barbers whose sole job was to shave the whole block every week.

It was a häftling's responsibility to cut his hair and shave, but the barbers did it.

The block chiefs and room supervisors were responsible for an unshaven inmate or hair that was too long.

The barbers had more than enough food from the block chief, the kapos and room supervisors living on that block.

One evening in December '41, I was standing talking with Colonel 1 [Władysław Surmacki] and Dr. 2 [Władysław Dering] by Block 21 (new numbering system) when we beheld the sight of a group of naked people, visibly steaming, coming out of Block 26 (new numbering system).

There were about a hundred of them.

This was a transport of Poles who had been sent to be finished off quickly.

After taking long (about half-hour) hot showers—they had willingly washed in the hot water suspecting nothing—they were made to stand naked in the snow and frost and kept there.

We had to go to our blocks, while they froze.

They gave a muffled groan, or rather an animal wail.

They were kept out there for several hours.

When people were finished off like that or in other ways, or large numbers were shot together, the krankenbau [hospital] received a list with their numbers and, when submitting the list of deaths that day in the hospital to the main schreibstube [office], had to add 50 numbers daily to the list as having died from heart failure, TB, typhus or some other "natural" cause.

In this way 1941 drew to a close.

My second Christmas in Auschwitz came, together with another parcel from home—of clothes (there were no food parcels at that time).

On Block 25, where the block supervisor 80 [Alfred Włodarczyk] turned out to be sympathetic to our work, in room 7 where the supervisor was 59 [Henryk Bartosiewicz] we put up a Christmas tree with a Polish eagle hanging secretly on it.

The room was decorated really tastefully by 44 [Wincenty Gawron] and 45 [Stanisław Gutkiewicz], with a bit of help from me.

On Christmas Eve some of the representatives of our political cell said a few words.

Could Dubois have listened with pleasure in the outside world to Rybarski and then have warmly shaken his hand and vice versa?

How moving such a picture of agreement would have been in Poland, and how impossible.

And yet here in our room in Auschwitz both of them willingly spoke.

What a metamorphosis!

Through 81 [Alojz Pohl], a Volksdeutsche—a Silesian—who actually worked with us, I was informed that the [camp] political department was planning a new operation, which might seriously threaten me personally.

By now there were very few of us "old numbers."

This was particularly obvious when money was being paid out.

Money, sent to us by our families, was paid out monthly in the amount of 30 marks, or 15 marks twice.

Larger sums remained in our accounts.

The monthly allowance was later raised to 40 marks.

The money could be spent in the camp canteen, where one could obtain everything that could harm us the most: cigarettes, saccharine, mustard, sometimes a (marinated) vinegar salad.

Everyone was required to line up by numbers to receive their allowance.

Sometimes everyone was ordered in, even those who had received no money, to sign their accounts.

It was then that one could easily count the numbers from the highest to the lowest and see in each "hundred" how many of us were still alive...

The gaps in the "hundreds" were enormous, especially in the transports from Warsaw.

Perhaps because the transports before us had taken the indoor jobs, while we had been finished off in the open air.

Perhaps because, as the Silesians said, people from Warsaw were not tough.

Perhaps because others were more "in" with the camp authorities.

Suffice it to say that some of the "hundreds" from Warsaw transports now had only two people.

There were six of us in our "hundred."

There were "hundreds" with a comparatively large number living—eight—and there were those no longer represented by a single soul.

It was then that the political department hit on the idea of checking the personal details of everyone still living, starting with the lowest numbers which, given our reduced number, was not difficult.

Maybe someone was hiding under a false name (such as me).

In order to start such "birds," the political department was sending letters to specific parishes asking for the details of specific inmates from their records.

To the parishes where the inmates had been born, or which they had provided during their interrogations.

In order to get an idea of how I stood, we need to go back to 1940, to Warsaw.

Our population in Warsaw had very willingly provided help to people in the underground movement, especially during its initial phases when people had not yet been terrified by dreadful descriptions of concentration camps, or of the Aleja Szucha.

Later, finding "safe houses" would be harder, but at first honest Polish families willingly provided their own work and accommodation for the underground movement.

In the initial phase I had several flats and sets of personal papers in all sorts of names and with different addresses.

At that time it was still possible to go out leaving one's papers at home.

Therefore, I did not carry an identity card, and if I was stopped, I used the name associated with our currently "cleanest" accommodation and where I had one of my cards.

One of the flats out of which I was working belonged to Mrs. 83 [Helena Pawłowska].

One day, Mrs. 83 [Helena Pawłowska] told me that she had some identity papers made out in the real name of one of our officers, 84 [Tomasz Serafiński], who had left on resistance business in another sector before the papers had been finished.

Since there were work papers as well as an identity card, I agreed to Mrs. 83's [Helena Pawłowska's] suggestion to use these papers after changing the photograph.

When I set off for the round-up, I took that document with me, since the name was, as I rightly surmised, not yet "burnt."

So I had with me the papers of a man (84 [Tomasz Serafiński]), who was living somewhere in the outside world.

However, the papers made no mention of his mother's maiden name.

When we were interrogated that night at Auschwitz, just after being brought to the camp, I made up a mother's name, since I had had to give one.

So now the situation was anything but clear.

When my number came up, as it would over the next few months, and the political department sent off an inquiry to the parish in the town of Z [Bochnia] for my (or rather Mr. 84's [Tomasz Serafiński's]) details from the register, the mother's maiden name would not tally with the one I had given.

So they would summon me and ask me who I was—and that would be that.

By a fortunate coincidence, some fellows from a round-up, several hundred (as I have already mentioned), were "in quarantine" and were shortly to leave for Warsaw.

I send details of my situation to my sister-in-law, Mrs. E.O. [Eleonora Ostrowska] through released inmate 14 [Antoni Woźniak], indicating what maiden name I had given here.

A number of fellows are leaving, some of them members of our organization, and in addition to 14 [Antoni Woźniak], there is also 9 [Czesław Wąsowski].

Colonel 1 [Władysław Surmacki] is also headed for the "freedom" block, since he has been released from the camp owing to the efforts of a former college friend from Berlin, who now is a senior officer in the German Army.

I send a report through Colonel 1 [Władysław Surmacki] to Warsaw about our organization's work here.

I also send a great deal of information through 86 [Aleksander Paliński], who has been in the camp for the sole reason that he has the same name as some colonel.

In order to paint a full picture of the camp at this time (obviously things I have seen myself, for I am in no position to describe everything one hears from fellows working in other kommandos), one must include so-called "Seidler week."

Every evening at roll call for a week in December (of '41) we endured the régime of Seidler [Fritz Seidler], a real sadist who was standing in for the Lagerführer [Camp Head].

It was a week of especially unpleasant weather. The wind and the rain, together with freezing snow, seemed to slice through not only our clothes, but also our bodies. We were frozen right through. At night there was frost.

Seidler decided to take advantage of this to finish off the strength and the lives of as many häftlings as possible.

Daily, from the gong for evening roll call 15 minutes before 18:00 (6:00 p.m.), we stood fighting the frost in our cold clothes until 21:00 (9:00 p.m.), when we were released from punishment parade just before the bedtime gong.

We then quickly gulped down a cold dinner, which at that time we were given in the evening, and rushed through those 15 minutes to get everything done before bed.

These punishment parades lasted for a week, for supposedly every day that week someone was missing at roll call, which was pure invention on Seidler's part.

For they ended when he ceased temporarily taking Palitzsch's evening roll call.

Yet that week had cost us a great deal of energy and health, and many weaker fellows—their lives.

Death notices were sent to families through the main schreibstube [office] only on the political department's clear instructions, for news of an inmate's death getting out into the real world was not always convenient for the German police authorities, and also because investigation of some matter might still be continuing and others, held in some prison, could be threatened that they were holding inmate X, who was telling them the "whole truth."

Thus ended 1941.

The year 1942 began, which, as far as Auschwitz was concerned, was *the most dreadful*; as far as our organization's work in the camp—*the most interesting* and the one in which we achieved the most.

It so happens that, owing to a lack of time caused by my new decision,[43] I must write almost in shorthand.

There was a sudden profound change in attitude towards Jews.

To everyone's astonishment, the remaining Jews were pulled out of the Penal Company and, together with new Jewish arrivals, zugangs, were placed in good conditions in indoor jobs: in the sock storeroom, the potato shed and the vegetable storeroom.

---

[43] Pilecki is referring here to his decision to return to Poland in 1945. Translator's note.

They even became more important than us.

They did not suspect that this was a terrible, devious scheme.

The issue was their letters home in which for several months they wrote that they were working in workshops and that conditions were just fine.

That these workshops were located in Auschwitz—why, the name of this small town meant nothing to Jews in France, Czechoslovakia, Holland, Greece, or wherever those letters went.

When even Poles in Poland knew little about Auschwitz and were still rather naive about someone's time there.

Our Polish Jews were usually finished off at Treblinka or Majdanek.

Jews from almost the whole of Europe were brought here— to Auschwitz.

After a few months of writing letters about the good conditions which they were enjoying, the Jews were suddenly rounded up from their jobs and quickly "finished off."

Meanwhile, Jews arrived daily by the thousand from the whole of Europe and were sent straight to Birkenau, where the construction of camp huts (like those built in the initial phase) had been completed.

The attitude towards priests had also changed some time before, but for another reason.

On the basis of some Vatican influence on the German authorities, by way of their ally Italy, priests were sent to Dachau. The first time, at the start of 1941, and the second such transport of priests from Auschwitz to Dachau left in July 1942.

At Dachau priests apparently had quite reasonable conditions, compared to those here. In the interval between those two transports I came to know in Auschwitz a few very brave priests, including Father 87 [Zygmunt Ruszczak] who was our organization's chaplain.

We held mass and confession away from prying eyes. We received communion hosts from clergy on the outside through contacts among local civilians.

The beginning of 1942 saw the rest of the Bolshevik prisoners of war finished off.

The pace of murdering increased.

The blocks were needed for other things.

A new nightmare was about to begin here.

The corpses of Bolsheviks, killed at work on building sites and digging ditches in the Birkenau area, were brought to roll call on carts.

At every roll call there were several fully laden carts.

Some of the prisoners simply froze to death, since they lacked the energy to work and thus warm themselves up a bit.

One day, there was a revolt during work. The Bolsheviks attacked the kapos and the SS.

The revolt was put down bloodily and the whole unit shot.

The corpses to be counted by the authorities at roll call were brought in on carts in several waves.

After they had all been finished off (February '42), with the exception of the few hundred whom I mentioned earlier, the fence between our camp and the POW camp was quickly dismantled.

Meanwhile, a fence was being built in another direction and for another reason.

Ten blocks to house women were fenced off from us by a large wall made of concrete blocks.

This was a first.

In its initial phase the camp had also worked on Sundays,

then Sundays were supposedly free, with the caveat that blocks had so-called blocksperre [confinement to blocks] until lunch.

Now, to reduce our ability to get together and organize, two more hours of our Sunday free time were withdrawn.

After lunch, between 13:00 hours and 15:00 hours, a häftling had to undress and sleep.

Block supervisors checked the rooms.

This block sleeping time was checked by the Lagerältester [Head Inmate] or the Lagerkapo [discipline kapo], since an inmate who did not sleep was after all (irony of ironies) failing to conserve energy which was needed by the Third Reich and thus was a "saboteur."

On the 18th of January (of '42) 45 inmates were locked up for the night in the "black hole" owing to a lack of space in the overcrowded bunkers.

A little later that evening, in the cellars of Block 11 (new numbering system) a loud hammering on the door was heard as well as shouts for the duty SS man to open the door.

They came from the 45 who were suffocating and, using their teeth, fists and knives, they fought for access to the door where a little air came in through the cracks.

In the morning, out of the 45 locked up alive the previous evening, there were 21 corpses who had been suffocated or killed in the struggle. Of the remaining 24 barely on their feet, 9 were taken to hospital more dead than alive and the remaining 15 were sent to the Penal Company for having failed to die in the "black hole."

They included Konrad, the former carpenters' shop oberkapo.

A witness of this dreadful scene was Kapo "Jonny" [Jonny (*sic*) Lechenich] doing time in the stehbunker [standing bunker] for what the authorities called "dealings" with Poles.

In February (of '42), the political department received a letter from the party authorities in Berlin forbidding collective responsibility and the shooting of 10 inmates for a single escape.

Supposedly, this had led to similar reprisals in some [Allied] camp for Germans.[44]

At around the same time, an order was officially read out forbidding the beating of inmates (it would be interesting to know whether that was as a result of our reports).

Thereafter, there were no great reprisals against the remaining inmates for escapes.

Thus, the idea of escape took on a new lease of life and our organization began to gear up and prepare to send reports to Warsaw by means of organized escapes.

The Bolsheviks had left behind lice and a terrible strain of Siberian typhus for which large numbers of our fellows began to sicken.

The typhus swept the camp, creating havoc.

The authorities rubbed their hands, calmly watching this ally finish off häftlings.

We then began to cultivate typhus-infected lice in the krankenbau [hospital] laboratory and release them onto the coats of SS men at every parade or inspection of our blocks.

A mailbox was hung outside Block 15 and it was announced in every block that letters, either signed or unsigned, with information on overheard conversations should be left in the box.

A häftling would be commended for any information of use to the authorities.

---

[44] This translator is unaware of either the Americans or the British ever using such methods. The Soviets were another matter. Translator's note.

They meant to take measures against our organization's work.

Anonymous tips and denunciations poured in.

Then, with the help of Captain 88 [Tadeusz Dziedzic], we would open the box every evening and review the reports in it, before Palitzsch opened it at 22:00 hours.

We destroyed the ones that were unhelpful or dangerous for us, and we would leave denunciations of harmful individuals.

A paper war began.

We were ordered to sing German songs in our blocks and on the way to work.

Several times the whole camp had to sing during roll call parade.

In Rajsko-Birkenau, gas chambers were being hastily built and some were already complete.

What I had once been afraid of—bringing into the organization officers who were in Auschwitz under their real names—had its raison d'être. For if there had been any suspicions that an organization existed, they would first of all have picked up the officers.

One day, they took Colonel 62 [Jan Karcz] and locked him into a bunker prison cell, taking him off daily to the political department for interrogation from which he would return pale and barely able to stay on his feet.

I began to fear problems.

One evening over a fortnight later, Colonel 62 [Jan Karcz] came over to me and comrade 59 [Henryk Bartosiewicz] and said: "Congratulate me, they've let me out. They wanted to know whether there was any organization in the camp," and he turned to me to say goodbye, for the bed gong had sounded and said: "Don't worry, I haven't said a word. I'll tell you the rest tomorrow."

# 1942...

**The dimly lit interior of a gas chamber.**

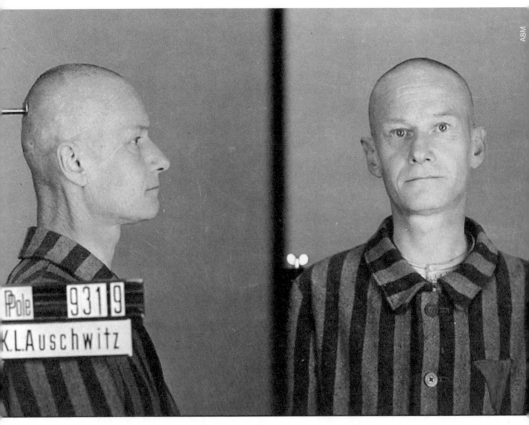

Colonel Kazimierz Rawicz (Pilecki's comrade—code no. Colonel 64)—Inmate No. 9319.

But the next morning they took off Colonel 62 [Jan Karcz] and moved him to Rajsko, apparently so that he could not tell us anything.

Colonel 62 [Jan Karcz] was a brave man.

Over one hundred Czechs were brought in. They were all intellectuals, from the "Sokół" [Falcon] organization.

They put them in our room (Block 25, Room 7).

They began to finish them off in short order.

On behalf of our organization I got in touch with their representative 89 [Karel Stransky] (he is alive and living in Prague).

After receiving Colonel 64's [Kazimierz Rawicz's] agreement, I take my friend First Lieutenant 29 [Włodzimierz Makaliński], whom I trusted greatly, around all our organization's cells in the camp.

I'm doing it in case anything should happen to me.

First Lieutenant 29 [Włodzimierz Makaliński] reports to Colonel 64 [Kazimierz Rawicz] that we have visited 42 cells.

One morning a group of Silesians (about 70 or 80) are moved from our stammlager [main camp] Auschwitz to Birkenau (there was a rumour that they were to be finished off), including my friend 45 [Stanisław Gutkiewicz].

He had been greatly worried the previous evening and, sensing something, his whole body shook during the night.

He asked me to send news of him to his wife and little boy Dyzma.

He never returned from Rajsko.

Every one of these Silesians was finished off.

Some of them had been there from the camp's beginning and felt that they were going to survive.

The remaining Silesians in the camp now clearly began to show an interest in working against the Germans.

One morning, visiting some workmates, I was in Block 5 (new numbering system), and running quickly to roll call through the now empty corridors I came face to face with Bloody Aloiz who, recognizing me although more than a year had passed, stopped and shouted in some surprise and yet with what seemed to me an odd pleasure: "Was? Du lebst noch? [What? You're still alive?]". . . he grabbed my hand and shook it.

What was I to do? I did not pull away. He was an odd man.

Of the bloodthirsty types from the early days, of which he was one, a number were no longer alive.

The camp authorities began to try to show the camp in a slightly better light for visiting inspection teams (which included a number of gentlemen in civilian suits).

They were shown new blocks and only ones with bunks.

That day the kitchen would produce a good lunch.

The orchestra was in fine form.

Only the healthy and strong kommandos, the workshop types, returned to camp from work.

The rest of the kommandos, the zugangs and other miserable-looking fellows, waited outside for the inspection team to leave, taking with it a completely unrealistic impression of the camp. When, needing to show the camp in a better light, the sight of some of the tyrants from the early days was no longer appropriate, the authorities decided to move a number of kapos to another camp, including Krankenmann and Sigrod.

After loading them into freight cars at the station, the SS men supervising the inmates let the häftlings know that they would have nothing against the inmates taking their revenge on Krankenmann.

That was all the inmates needed; they scrambled into the

cars and hanged Krankenmann and Sigrod with their own belts.

The SS men turned away for a moment and did not intervene.

Thus did the murderers perish. Every witness to the killings sanctioned by the camp authorities was inconvenient, even if it was a kapo and a German.

So these two were witnesses no more.

Our organization continued to grow.

Together with my friend 59 [Henryk Bartosiewicz], we recruited Colonel 23 [Aleksander Stawarz], Lieutenant Colonel 24 [Karol Kumuniecki], as well as some new people: 90 [name unknown], 91 [Stanisław Polkowski], 92 [Wacław Weszke], 93 [name unknown], 94 [name unknown], 95 [name unknown].

That marvelous human being, 44 [Wincenty Gawron], helped a great number of fellows, giving them his own food while he painted a portrait of someone in authority, receiving food as payment.

A transport from Warsaw (March of '42) again brought in a great number of friends as well as information about what was going on.

Major 85 [Zygmunt Bohdanowski] arrived, as well as that fine man 96 [Tadeusz Stulgiński], who had endured a record number of beatings at the Aleja Szucha and the Pawiak.

I learnt from them that Colonel 1 [Władysław Surmacki] had been rearrested and was in the Pawiak.

Colonel 1 [Władysław Surmacki] had told 96 [Tadeusz Stulgiński] to get in touch with me.

I got 97 [Jan Machnowski], who had already joined our organization, to get him into his kommando.

We were also building up in two other directions, bringing

in 98 [name unknown] and 99 [name unknown] from the baubüro [construction site office], and 100 [name unknown] and 101 [Witold Kosztowny] from the hospital.

Meanwhile Professor 69 [Roman Rybarski] died.

As if on pillars, our organization reposed on two departments: the Krankenbau [hospital] and the Arbeitsdienst [work assignment office].

If one of our fellows had to be saved from a zugang transport and given an indoor job, or someone had to be got out of a kommando where he was beginning to "flag" or kept attracting some bastard's attention, or we had to set up our network in some kommando, then we would go off to see Dr. 2 [Władysław Dering] saying: "Dziunko, so and so will come to see you tomorrow and you must admit him to the hospital for a time." (Or we arranged it with Dr. 102 [Rudolf Diem]).

And when it happened (in a kapo's mind a häftling was already a dead man, for very few people returned from the hospital alive), then we would go off to 68 [Mieczysław Januszewski] saying "Give us a card for so and so for such and such kommando," or sometimes we would go off to 103 [name unknown] with equally good results and it was all fixed.

In this way we prepared too for 25's [Stefan Bielecki's] and 44's [Wincenty Gawron's] escape.

Both were first-class people and both were in the camp for arms possession. Their cases were clear-cut and they would definitely be shot. The only question was how soon their cases would catch the eye of Grabner in the political department.

By some miracle they were still alive.

No. 44 [Wincenty Gawron] painted portraits of SS men and it was possible that his case was being delayed, but things could not continue like that for long.

Using the method described above, in February of '42 we got 25 [Stefan Bielecki] moved to the Harmense kommando, to the fish ponds. The inmates worked at the ponds several miles from the camp and lived there.

Much later, in May, comrade 44 [Wincenty Gawron] went there; and the very day he arrived, bringing from me for 25 [Stefan Bielecki] the instruction not to wait for me but to "move out," both of them "did a runner," escaping from a hut through the window and taking my report to Warsaw.

In Erik Grönke's empire, the tannery, the kommando of woodcarvers and selected carpenters went through a crisis after Konrad had been bundled off to the bunker.

At this difficult time Tadek Myszkowski was standing in for the kapo.

Instead of the gentle gaze of Konrad, the art lover, we now had Erik's wild-cat, piercing eyes.

Soon wanting to destroy what Konrad had put together, calling the woodcarvers' existence a luxury, he scrapped the woodcarving shop and had us making spoons.

He gave us as kapo "Hulajnoga" ["Scooter"]—a nasty idiot.

He ordered the carpenters making artistic jewelry boxes to produce cupboards and very simple objects.

In the spoon shop we started off making 5 spoons a day each, then 7 and finally 12.

At that time former member of Parliament 104 [Józef Putek] was working there.

I then brought into the organization 105 [Edward Berlin]; 106 [name unknown]; 107 [name unknown]; a former soldier in my resistance group (from '39)—108 [Stanisław Dobrowolski]; as well as Second Lieutenant 109 [name unknown]; 110 [Andrzej Makowski-Gąsienica]; and 111 [name unknown].

Amongst those painting the toys which we made (where Colonel 62 [Jan Karcz] had been working for a short time, before going to the bunker), Officer Cadet 112 [Stanisław Jaster] joined us, recommended to me by Captain 8 [Ferdynand Trojnicki] who had been released.

We had taken over all the kommandos, but there was one we could not penetrate.

Finally, in February ('42), having been kommandiert [ordered to stay at work] I returned late to the camp, and when I reached the block I learnt from 61 [Konstanty Piekarski] that 68 [Mieczysław Januszewski] had been around. The *funkstelle* [the SS garrison's radio room] needed two cartographer-draftsmen, and that he, 61 [Konstanty Piekarski], had given his own number and that of our former commanding officer, 113 [Sokołowski].

Within a day or two it turned out that 113's [Sokołowski's] hands shook, so we had him transferred to the SS potato kommando where he was guaranteed good food, and I got myself into the funkstelle in his stead (after squaring this in the woodcarving shop with 52 [Tadeusz Myszkowski]).

I worked with 61 [Konstanty Piekarski] in the funkstelle on maps for a few weeks and, after taking stock of the situation, since training courses were held there in addition to the normal work on the SS radio station, with the help of 77 [Zbigniew Ruszczyński], I managed to get hold of some valves and other parts, for which we had been hunting fruitlessly for months.

Using spare parts to which our häftlings had access.

The result was that after seven months we had our own transmitter, which Second Lieutenant 4 [Alfred Stössel] worked on in an area which the SS men entered most unwillingly.

Until, in the autumn (of '42), one of our fellows' big mouth was the cause of us having to dismantle the radio station.

We broadcast details, repeated by other stations, on the number of zugangs and deaths in the camp, and the inmates' state and their conditions.

The authorities were going nuts, searching, ripping up floors in the workshops in Industriehof I and in the warehouses.

We broadcast infrequently, at different times and it was hard to catch us.

The authorities gave up searching in the main camp, and concentrated on the outside areas near the town of Oświęcim [Auschwitz]. They reasoned that our ability to provide detailed information on the camp came from our contact with an outside organization via civilian workers. They searched the *gemeinschaftslager* [the camp for civilian forced laborers].

There was indeed contact with the civilian population.

The route from us led through the civilian population (amongst whom there were members of our organization on the outside) in Brzeszcze.

The route also led through the gemeinschaftslager by way of those who worked for us as ostensibly our superiors, and then led to Buna, also by way of civilian workers.

In this way I sent out to the "free world" a whole stack of German cipher keys, the so-called *verkehrsabkürzungen*, also sneaked out of the funkstelle.

From the free world we received medicine, anti-typhus shots; on the one hand we had Dr. 2 [Władysław Dering] working on this, and on the other my friend 59 [Henryk Bartosiewicz].

My friend 59 [Henryk Bartosiewicz] was an interesting fellow.

He did everything "with a smile" and things just worked out for him.

He was always rescuing and feeding a few fellows in his room and in the tannery, to put them back on their feet so that they could cope on their own.

He was forever rescuing someone by bringing him into the tannery.

He never did things by halves, acting bravely and with a certain pushiness where others would have held back.

Large, broad-shouldered, with a smiling face and a big heart.

When Heinrich Himmler arrived with some commission, 59 [Henryk Bartosiewicz] was block supervisor on Block 6 (old numbering system) and was instructed on how to report to Himmler, before whom all trembled. So when the great day came and Himmler entered the room, 59 [Henryk Bartosiewicz] stood before him and ... said nothing ... and then laughed and Himmler also laughed.

Perhaps what saved him was the fact that Himmler was accompanied by two civilian gentlemen and that perhaps such gentle treatment of a häftling was good publicity.

Yet another time, 59 [Henryk Bartosiewicz], seeing through the tannery window an inspection team in the courtyard which was inspecting the warehouses and which was heading for the door leading into the great hall where the tanners were working, grabbed a rubber hose and, ostensibly cleaning up for the team, he began spraying the walls and floors and intentionally and thoroughly hosed down the team, composed of German officers, then he dropped the hose as if horrified and again he got away with it.

As the columns entered the camp, grim thoughts on the inmates' minds, suddenly 59 [Henryk Bartosiewicz] in a carrying voice could be heard issuing commands in Polish and counting loudly: "One ... two ... three ..."

# 1942...

**USHMM/ IPN**

**During a tour of the Auschwitz III building site, Reichsführer-SS Heinrich Himmler extends his hand in greeting to the engineers supervising the construction.**

Inmates' orchestra.

Inmates' orchestra during a Sunday concert for the
SS men in Auschwitz.

No doubt, he also had his faults, but then who doesn't?

In any event, he always had a great many supporters around him and he could have impressed and led a great many.

The final releases of 1942 were in March and a couple of fellows in the orchestra were released, since the Commandant who, as I mentioned, loved music, had got the authorities in Berlin to agree to a couple of members of the orchestra being released each year.

It had been announced to the orchestra that anyone who tried to play really well would be released and so the orchestra played beautifully. The Commandant was intoxicated with music.

Every year, those who were the least needed in the orchestra were released.

After March there were no more releases throughout the whole of 1942, given the unwanted existence in the outside world of any witnesses of Auschwitz, or especially of what began to take place in Auschwitz in 1942.

Finally, the first women—prostitutes and criminals—were brought from German prisons to Auschwitz, to a part of the camp whose barracks were separated from us by a high wall, and they were appointed as the training cadre for the women who were shortly to be brought there—honest women, "political criminals."

In Rajsko, the first daily gassings of people began in the gas chambers which were now ready.

On the 16th of March[45] (of '42), 120 Polish women were brought in.

They smiled at the inmates who were entering the camp in columns.

---

[45] In the original typed Report, Pilecki wrote the 19th and then amended it by hand to the 16th. Other edited versions have the 19th. Translator's note.

After interrogations and maybe some special torturing, which no one could confirm, that same evening wagons took to the crematorium a number of bloody corpses in pieces, with severed heads, hands, breasts.

The old crematorium was unable to burn the bodies from our central camp and also the bodies from Rajsko. (The chimney built in 1940 had cracked and collapsed from the constant heat of the bodies. A new one was built.)

So the bodies were buried in wide pits using kommandos composed of Jews to do the work.

Two new crematoria with electric ovens were being hastily constructed in Rajsko-Birkenau.

The plans were drawn up in the baubüro [construction site office].

In the words of the fellows in the baubüro, each crematorium would have eight stations, each of which could take two bodies.

Electric incineration would take three minutes.

The plans were sent off to Berlin.

After approval, they returned with instructions to complete the work initially by the 1st of February, then the deadline was moved to the 1st of March and in March they were ready.

Now the factory began to work at full steam.

An order came down to destroy all signs of previous killings. So began the work of digging up all the bodies buried in ditches, of which there were tens of thousands.

The bodies were already decomposing. A terrible stench surrounded these great opened communal graves.

Those working on some of the older ones had to wear gas masks.

The size of this job from hell was enormous.

# 1942...

Over a thousand a day from the new transports were gassed. The corpses were burnt in the new crematoria.

Cranes were used to bring up the bodies from the pits and they dug their metal talons into the disintegrating corpses.

In places small fountains of stinking pus spurted.

The body parts torn from the piles of corpses by the cranes and dug up by hand were taken to huge piles where wood and the remains of human beings were stacked alternately.

These piles were then lit and sometimes the petrol was not spared...

The piles then burned day and night for two and a half months, spreading around Auschwitz the stench of burning meat and human bones.

The kommandos assigned to this task were composed exclusively of Jews and lived for only two weeks. They were then gassed and their corpses were burnt by other newly arrived Jews, formed into new kommandos, unaware that they were to live for only two weeks and hoped to survive longer.

The beautiful horse chestnuts and apple trees bloomed...

It was above all at this time of the year, the spring, when one felt one's imprisonment most keenly.

When marching along the gray road towards the tannery in a column raising clouds of dust, one saw the beautiful red light of the dawn shining on the white flowers in the orchards and on the trees by the roadside, or on the return journey we would encounter young couples out walking, breathing in the beauty of springtime, or women peacefully pushing their children in prams—then the thought uncomfortably bouncing around one's brain would arise ... swirling around, stubbornly seeking some solution to the insoluble question:

Were we all... people?

Those walking amongst the flowers and those heading for the gas chambers?

Those constantly marching alongside us with their bayonets… and we—for some years now the damned?

They brought in the first large female transports and put them in the segregated blocks (Nos. 1–10, new numbering system).

Shortly thereafter female transports began to arrive one after another.

German, Jewish, Polish women arrived.

They were all entrusted to the care of criminal elements: prostitutes and common criminals.

With the exception of the Germans, they all had their heads and body hair shaved.

This was done by our male barbers.

The interest of the barbers, starved of female company, changed quickly to exhaustion as their eyes' earlier unrequited desires were now overloaded with distaste.

The women were in the same circumstances as the male inmates.

They did not experience the same killing methods as in the first year, for in the men's camp the methods had already changed. Yet they too were finished off in the open air by the rain, the cold, the work to which they were unaccustomed, the lack of rest and the roll call parades.

We daily encountered the same columns of women whom we would pass heading off to work in different directions.

We recognized a number of profiles, heads and pretty little faces.

Initially holding up well, the girls quickly lost the sparkle in their eyes, their smiles and the spring in their step.

Some of them continued to smile, but more sorrowfully.

**Construction of the roof of Gas Chamber III—Auschwitz-Birkenau.**

Crematorium IV
under construction—
Auschwitz-Birkenau.

Incinerators in Crematorium III—Auschwitz-Birkenau.

Their faces grew gray, animal hunger began to stare out of their eyes, they were turning into that camp phenomenon: muselmänner.

We more often began to notice the lack of familiar faces in their "fives."

The columns of women heading out to be finished off at work were also escorted by "people resembling human beings," dressed in the heroic uniforms of German soldiers, together with a whole pack of dogs.

In the fields two, or sometimes just one, "hero" with a few dogs guarded hundreds of women.

They were weakened and could only dream of escaping.

From the spring (of '42) we were surprised by the sight of all the muselmänner, still standing around as before in a group by the kitchen for inspection, being freely admitted to the krankenbau [hospital].

After that no one stood around in a group; everyone went straight to the krankenbau on Block 28 (new numbering system) where they were freely admitted with no fuss.

Things are looking up, the inmates said to one another. There are no beatings. People are admitted to the hospital and so on.

Indeed. In some of the hospital wards several patients lay on a single bed, yet they were still freely admitted.

Only an SS man named Klehr would go there daily and take down the numbers of the weakest inmates.

The word was that they would probably get an extra helping to keep them going.

The numbers noted down were later read out and those häftlings were sent to Block 20 (new numbering system).

Soon thereafter these numbers could be seen in the daily pile of corpses lying in front of the hospital (every inmate admitted to the hospital had a large number written on the skin on his chest with a chemical pen so that there would be no problem with identification after death when the daily list of those killed and those who had died was drawn up.)

They were being finished off with phenol—a new method.

Thus did the image of Auschwitz change radically.

No longer did one see (at least not within the confines of the stammlager [main camp] itself) heads being crushed by spades, people killed by having boards hammered into their intestines, or an inmate lying helpless having his chest crushed, his ribs cracked by the heavy boots of degenerate butchers jumping with their whole weight on his chest.

Now quietly and calmly the inmates whose numbers had been taken down in the krankenbau by a German (SS) doctor, undressed and stood completely naked on the corridor of Block 20 (new numbering system) calmly awaiting their turn.

They entered the waschraum [washroom] singly through a curtain and were placed on a chair, two executioners pulled back their shoulders pushing forward their chest, and the SS man Klehr gave them a phenol injection with a long needle straight into the heart.

At first the injection was made intravenously, but the victim lived too long—several minutes—so in order to save time the system was changed and the injection was made straight into the heart and the inmate lived much less— a few seconds.

The still-twitching body was pushed into the toilet behind a wall and the next number entered.

Yes, this was a much more intelligent method of murder, but still terrible in its secretiveness.

Everyone standing in the corridor knew what awaited them.

Passing the queue one saw friends and said: "Greetings Jaś or Staś, today it's your turn, tomorrow it could be me!"

They were not necessarily very ill or even exhausted.

Some of them ended up there only because Klehr did not like them, and their number then stayed on the "needle list"—there was no way out.

Now, there were different butchers from those in the camp's early days, but I daresay they could still be called degenerates.

Klehr murdered with the needle with great concentration, a deranged expression on his face and a sadistic smile, making a tick on the wall after every murder.

In my time there he extended the list of those killed by him to 14,000 and daily boasted about this with great satisfaction, like a hunter describing his successes.

An inmate, Pańszczyk [Mieczysław Pańszczyk], to his eternal shame, volunteered to give his fellows injections into the heart and killed quite a few less, about 4,000.

Klehr had an incident.

One day, after taking care of everyone in the queue for an injection, he entered as usual the toilet where the dying häftlings were dumped to admire his handiwork for the day, when one of the "corpses" came to life (there must have been an error and he had received too little phenol), stood up and started to stagger over the other corpses like a drunk towards Klehr saying: "Du hast mir zu wenig gegeben, gib mir noch etwas!... [You didn't give me enough, let me have a little more!]"

Klehr went white, but not panicking, rushed at him—the executioner's apparently cultured mask slipping—pulled out his pistol and without shooting, not wishing to make a noise, he finished off his victim by hitting him over the head with the butt.

The krankenbau room orderlies gave a daily report on the number of deaths on their wards.

There was an incident (I know of at least one, there could have been more) when an orderly made a mistake, giving a living man's number instead of a dead man's.

The report went to the main schreibstube [office].

For fear of being removed from his post and for his own peace of mind, this criminal told the sick man, a zugang who did not even understand what was going on, to get up and stand in the queue for one of Klehr's injections.

One extra person made no difference to Klehr.

Thus did the orderly correct his mistake, for the man who died in his ward and the other who got one of Klehr's "shots" were now both well and truly dead, and the report was accurate, for the number of the man on the ward who had died had been added to it.

However, we did have a great number of orderlies in the hospital who were very good Poles.

We twice needed numbers altered and this was carried out easily and without harming anyone.

During the high death rate from typhus, when great numbers of corpses were thrown out daily from a number of blocks, two of our people were admitted to hospital as serious cases; we saved them by writing their numbers on corpses with similar numbers, taking care too that the dead men did not have any serious unfinished business with the political department.

Thus, also equipped with changed personal details (provided by colleagues in the schreibstube), we managed to get them into Birkenau straight from the hospital.

There they were completely unknown, new numbers, zugangs, their trail ran cold and the plan worked.

Our organization continued to expand.

I proposed to Colonel 64 [Kazimierz Rawicz] that he nominate my friend Bohdan, Major 85 [Zygmunt Bohdanowski] as overall military commander in the event of action, since in Warsaw in 1940 I had considered him for a similar post in the underground.

Colonel 64 [Kazimierz Rawicz] willingly agreed.

Bohdan knew the area, for some years before he had commanded a battery of the 5th Horse Artillery Regiment there.

I decided then, and Colonel 64 [Kazimierz Rawicz] approved the idea, to develop a plan of eventual action based on four key objectives which we had identified.

This was due to the fact that in order to take over the camp in accordance with our work's eventual aim, we needed to prepare detachments along parallel lines. One system for a workday operation. Another one for nighttime or days off when we were in our blocks, and this for the reason that we still were not living in blocks as complete kommandos. Thus there was one set of contacts, links and commanders during the workday, another on the blocks.

Therefore, the plan had to be based on an outline of essential objectives which required individual preparation.

It was then that the need to fill four command positions emerged.

I proposed Captain[46] 60 [Stanisław Kazuba] for one of them, Captain 114 [Tadeusz Paolone] for the second one; Second Lieutenant 61 [Konstanty Piekarski] recommended First Lieutenant 115 [name unknown] for the third one and Captain 116 [Zygmunt Pawłowicz—in the camp as Julian Trzęsimiech]

---

[46] Some sources give his rank as Colonel. In Pilecki's original it was Captain. Translator's note.

for the fourth one. Colonel 64 [Kazimierz Rawicz] and Major 85 [Zygmunt Bohdanowski] agreed with us.

Eventually, with the help of comrade 59 [Henryk Bartosiewicz] and after long discussions on the need for agreement, and the essential requirement to be able to stay silent even if one of us ended up in the bunker and was interrogated by the butchers of the political department, Colonel 23 [Aleksander Stawarz] and Lieutenant Colonel 24 [Karol Kumuniecki] join us.

A first-rate Silesian Pole and my friend, 76 [Bernard Świerczyna], is working very effectively in his area, supplying us with clothing, uniforms, sheets and blankets from his storerooms.

Providing work for a number of our lads, including a friend from our time in Warsaw, First Lieutenant 117 [Eugeniusz Zaturski], and 39 [Pilecki's nephew, Kazimierz Radwański].

No. 118 [name unknown] and Cavalry Sergeant 119 [Jan Miksa] join our organization.

One of our former Warsaw comrades, Dr. 120 [Zygmunt Zakrzewski], arrives in a transport from Kraków.

At this time a bomb factory was discovered near Kraków.

These people were brought in and quickly finished off.

Dr. 120 [Zygmunt Zakrzewski] somehow managed to survive and was sent off to another camp.

From time to time the camp authorities would try to infiltrate informers. A Volksdeutsche pretending to be a Pole, who had agreed to work with Grabner and wanted to discover if we were up to something, was "outed" by our fellows who came into contact with the SS, before or just after his arrival.

Such a gentleman received from us a few drops of artfully administered croton oil from the hospital, leading shortly to such stomach pains that he had to rush off to the krankenbau for some medicine.

People there had been warned of the bastard's arrival (his number having been taken down) and he was again given a few drops of croton oil in some inoffensive medicine.

After a couple of days he was so weak that he went back to the krankenbau, where he was given a supposedly essential injection, which would have been harmless had it not been made with a rusty needle.

However, in two cases the matter had a little more spice to it.

In the first one, when such a gentleman was already in the krankenbau, he was given a chest X-ray which "showed" that he had well-developed TB (the X-ray was of someone else's lungs).

The next day he was pointed out as tubercular to Klehr doing his rounds.

That was enough; he took down his number.

The gentleman knew nothing of this, but when he was led off to the "needle" he began to go wild, using Grabner's name.

Klehr, on hearing the name, turned white, lost his temper, hit him in the face and quickly "finished him off" so that other malcontents could not throw Grabner's name about.

The second incident was almost identical, with the difference that it involved a newcomer to the camp who, going to the needle, knew nothing and did not threaten anyone with Grabner. To his own surprise he was "finished off" with the needle.

However, shortly thereafter there was a great fuss when Grabner, having not heard from them for some time and looking for them, established that they had already gone up in "a puff of smoke" through the chimney some time before and that furthermore they had been finished off by his own man—Klehr.

There was an inquiry in the hospital as to how these two had been taken care of so quickly.

Thereafter Klehr, before using the needle, had to send a list of his victims to Grabner who would check it carefully to ensure that none of his people was on it.

Thus Easter came around.

I continued to live in Room 7 on Block 25.

I compared the numbers in the room with those at Christmas (as one always did in Auschwitz) to see how many of the lads were no longer alive.

Typhus was taking a terrible toll on us. Everyone was sick and only a few of us older fellows were still hanging on.

Anyone going in for typhus rarely returned.

But "our" specially reared lice were doing their job and typhus hit the SS barracks and the epidemic grew.

The doctors were having difficulty dealing with the Siberian typhus, as were SS bodies. The SS men suffered serious losses. They were sent to hospital in Katowice, where they usually died.

In June, a transport left Auschwitz for Mauthausen.

Colonel 64 [Kazimierz Rawicz] was on it (although he could have avoided it) and he intended, as he told us, to escape en route (which did not happen).

Officer Cadet 15 [Witold Szymkowiak], Cavalry Sergeant 119 [Jan Miksa] and Second Lieutenant 67 [Czesław Darkowski] were also on it.

Before leaving, Colonel 64 [Kazimierz Rawicz] suggested to me that I should recommend Colonel 121 [Juliusz Gilewicz] to take his place, which I did.

Colonel 121 [Juliusz Gilewicz] agreed and joined us and we continued to work well.

Colonel[47] 122 [Teofil Dziama] also joined us.

It was at this time that Colonel 23 [Aleksander Stawarz] and former member of Parliament 70 [Stanisław Dubois] were shot.

After building the first two electric-fired crematoria in Birkenau, construction of two similar ones began.

Meanwhile the first ones were now working at capacity.

And the transports kept coming and coming.

Some were brought to us, to the camp where they were processed, each häftling receiving a number, which was now higher than 40,000, but the vast majority of the transports went straight to Birkenau in Rajsko where people, without being processed, were quickly turned into smoke and ash.

During this period about 1,000 people were burnt every day.

Who was going into the jaws of death and why?

They were Jews from France, Czechoslovakia, Holland and other European countries. They had travelled alone, without an escort until a dozen or so kilometers from Auschwitz, when the railroad cars were surrounded and finally shunted onto a siding at Birkenau in Rajsko.

Why had they been on these trains?

I was able to have several conversations with Jews from France and once with a rare transport from Poland. They were Jews from Białystok and Grodno.

From what they all said, it appeared that official advertisements in various towns and countries under German control assured them that only those Jews who went to work in the Third Reich would live, so they were going to work in the

---

[47] Strictly speaking, he was a Lieutenant Colonel. Translator's note.

Third Reich. They were also encouraged by letters from Jews in Auschwitz, and doubtless other camps, that they were working in good conditions and were thriving.

They had been allowed to take whatever hand luggage they could carry.

So they had taken one or two suitcases in which they tried to take all their earthly possessions, selling real estate and other items and buying small valuable items, such as diamonds, gold, gold dollars and such like.

The freight trains carrying daily about a thousand people ended their journey on a siding in Rajsko.

The trains rolled up to a ramp and their contents were unloaded.

One wonders what the SS men were actually thinking.

There were a great many women and children in the wagons. Sometimes the children were in cradles. They were all to end their lives here together.

They were being brought like a herd of animals—to the slaughter!

For the time being unaware of anything, the passengers followed orders and got out onto the ramp.

In order to avoid any unpleasant incidents they were treated relatively politely.

They were instructed to put their food onto one pile and all their belongings onto another. They were told that their belongings would be returned to them. The first anxiety arose amongst the passengers: would their belongings not disappear, would they find them again, would their suitcases not be switched and so on?

They were then split into groups. Men and boys over thirteen went to one group. Women and children (boys under thirteen) to another. Under the pretext of the need for a bath,

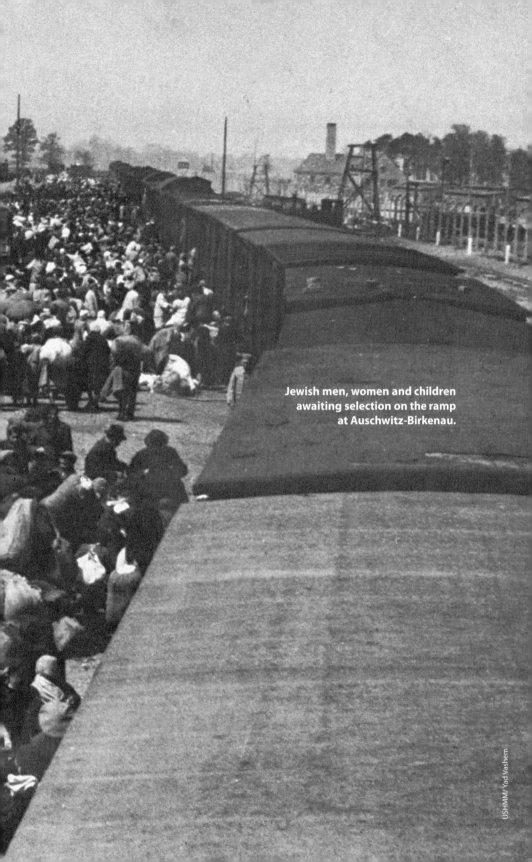

Jewish men, women and children awaiting selection on the ramp at Auschwitz-Birkenau.

**To the left—selected to die.**

# 1942...

To the right—selected to live... for now.

**Zyklon B, the cyanide-based pesticide used by the Nazi Germans to kill between 1.1 million and 1.5 million people, mainly European Jews, in the gas chambers of Auschwitz.**

they were also told to undress in their different groups, retaining some pretense of modesty.

Both groups also arranged their clothes in two great heaps, supposedly to be disinfected; now people were clearly anxious that their clothes and underwear might be switched.

Then, in hundreds, women and children separately from the men, they went off to huts which were supposedly showers, but were gas chambers. The outside windows were fakes and inside there was a wall.

After the tight-fitting doors were shut, mass murder was committed inside.

From a balcony arcade an SS man in a gas mask dropped gas in on top of the crowd beneath him.

Two types of gas were employed: in bottles which were broken, or in cakes which, after opening sealed canisters and being dropped in by an SS man wearing rubber gloves, turned into a gas which filled the gas chamber, quickly killing the people inside.

This lasted several minutes. They waited for about ten minutes. Then they ventilated: doors on the side away from the ramp were opened and Jewish kommandos carried out the still warm bodies on wheelbarrows and carts to the nearby crematoria where the corpses were quickly burnt.

Meanwhile, the next hundreds were heading for the gas chambers.

Later, technical improvements were introduced to this human slaughter, after which the process was even faster and more efficient.

Everything that these people had left behind: mountains of food, suitcases, clothes, underwear, were actually supposed to be burnt too, but only in theory.

In reality, the underwear and clothes were sent, after being disinfected, to the bekleidungskammer [clothing storeroom] and the shoes went to the tannery to be sorted into pairs.

The suitcases were taken to the tannery to be burnt.

But the SS men and kapos picked out the best for themselves from the piles in Birkenau and on the way to the tannery, saying that Auschwitz had become "Canada."[48]

This term caught on and henceforth anything left over after the people had been gassed, was called "Canada."

Thus there was an edible "Canada" from which various hitherto unavailable delicacies found their way into the camp: figs, dates, lemons, oranges, chocolate, Dutch cheeses, butter, sugar, cakes and so on.

In theory, it was forbidden to have products from "Canada," let alone bring them into the camp.

There were constant checks at the gates.

Anyone caught with something from "Canada" went to the bunker and rarely returned.

However, the level of risk in life in Auschwitz differed from that in the outside world, and it was always so great that it was nothing to risk one's life for some pleasing trifle.

A new state of mind, developed here, almost demanded a little pleasure—purchased at great risk.

So we continually tried to get hold of whatever food we could sneak out from nearby "Canada."

Returning from work to the camp we went through the checks at the gate in a high state of tension.

There was another "Canada" for underwear, clothes and footwear.

It was not long before we saw kapos and SS men wearing

---

[48] The country Canada was seen as a symbol of wealth. Translator's note.

# 1942...

Inmates in the Aufräumungskommando (salvage kommando) sort through a mound of personal belongings confiscated from an arriving transport of Jews.

Jewish women who have been selected for death, watch as trucks loaded with their confiscated personal property drive past on the way to the "Canada" warehouses.

A truck full of confiscated possessions is unloaded at the "Canada" warehouses, as inmates in the Aufräumungskommando (salvage kommando) sort through the roof-high haul.

"Canada" offers rich pickings for both the SS personnel as well as some privileged inmates of the Aufräumungskommando (salvage kommando).

the finest garments, often from the French capital. Silk shirts, similar pants, as well as expensive shoes.

In addition, they had soaps, the finest perfumes, razor blades, shaving brushes and ladies' cosmetics.

It is difficult to establish everything that a well-heeled woman or man would have brought with them.

"Organizing" something from "Canada" was, with a few exceptions, an almost universal goal, and for some the main daily focus.

The SS men rooted around in the suitcases and wallets, looking for gold, money, diamonds.

Auschwitz soon became the source of a steady trickle of diamonds and gold.

Soon the German field police could be seen on the roads checking everyone and also stopping military vehicles.

When it came to going through belongings, the SS men and the kapos had nowhere near as much ingenuity as häftlings, who occasionally came across a diamond in the heel of a shoe, in the lining of a suitcase or a handbag, in toothpaste, in a tube of cream, shoe polish and in the most unlikely places.

They did this secretly and only when conditions were right for them to find items which had belonged to gassed people.

The SS men were also secretive amongst themselves about this, for the Camp Commandant himself would drive over to see Erik at the tannery, to which came truckloads of suitcases filled with expensive belongings that had already been sorted: watches, perfume, money and so on, and so he must have been turning a blind eye to the behavior of his SS subordinates, himself afraid of being turned in.

Those häftlings who had access to any of the "Canadas" quickly became a privileged class in the camp.

They traded in everything, but it would be wrong to suggest

that the camp was in chaos and that the influence of gold led to some kind of more easygoing régime.

Despite the closer relations between us and the guards, death was still the main punishment and so trading was done in secret without any obvious outward signs.

The jasmine was in full bloom with a beautiful fragrance when a first-rate fellow, Senior Uhlan 123 [Stefan Stępień], was shot (rather murdered with a shot to the back of the head).

I can still see in my mind's eye a brave man with a cheerful face.

Shortly afterwards, one of my dearest friends, a gallant officer of the 13th Uhlans, First Lieutenant 29 [Włodzimierz Makaliński], was shot in the same way.

He left me in his will information on the hiding places from 1939 of the colors of two Uhlan regiments: the 4th and the 13th.

I send another report to Warsaw through Officer Cadet 112 [Stanisław Jaster] who, with three of his friends, has carried out a superb escape from the camp.

Some time ago I saw the film *10 z Pawiaka* [*10 from the Pawiak Prison*].

I venture to suggest that the escape of four inmates from Auschwitz in the finest car there, the Camp Commandant's, dressed in SS uniforms, against the background of that hell, could make a truly fine subject for a film.

The *hauptwache* [main gate guard] presented arms.

Lagerführer Aumeier [Hans Aumeier], hastening on horseback from Buna for evening roll call, met the car en route. He dutifully saluted, somewhat surprised that the driver was taking the car over a disused grade crossing.

The car quickly backed up and crossed the tracks at another spot.

He put it down to vodka and the driver's weak head.

They kept their nerve and the escape succeeded.

The Lagerführer arrived back at Auschwitz in time for roll call, when everyone was already standing with their blocks in dressed ranks.

Now the fun really began!

He was informed that four inmates were missing from roll call and, worse still, that they had taken the Commandant's car.

This took place in the blockführerstube [SS guardroom].

Aumeier went almost crazy, tearing out his hair. He was shouting that he had met them.

Then he threw his cap in despair on the ground and... suddenly burst out laughing.

There were no reprisals, no shootings and no long punishment parades.

That policy dated from February of '42.

The football matches which had been held on the parade ground in '41, now, in '42, were quite out of the question owing to the new construction.

The one sport in which teams of German kapos competed against the Poles was boxing.

Just as in football, despite the differences in food and work, the Poles always licked the Germans at boxing.

A boxing match was the one opportunity to punch a kapo in the face, which the Polish häftling did with the greatest satisfaction accompanied by the spectators' general joyful cries.

We had several quite good boxers among us. From my work in the organization I knew only 21 [Tadeusz Pietrzykowski], who always won his bouts, giving some thug a pasting.

Inmates caught trying to escape were hanged publicly and ostentatiously.

This was an improvement though; they were not killed with a club or speared with a piece of wood.

Only after a time in the bunker was the victim hanged on a wheeled gallows near the kitchen during evening roll call, when all the inmates were drawn up on the parade ground.

Furthermore, he was hanged by those who in the next round would themselves be hanged by their successors.

This was done to increase the cruelty.

Once, during such a hanging, we were read an order in which the Camp Commandant solemnly informed the häftlings that an inmate could even be released for good behavior and effective work. Therefore, no foolish attempts to escape should be made, since that led, as we could see right now, to an ignominious death by hanging.

Somehow the order did not "hit the spot." No one believed in release. Our eyes had seen too many murders for their owners to be set free.

Furthermore, reading it out at such a harrowing moment was oh so very German.

The wave of humanitarian methods of killing— a testament to our tormentors' culture—produced the quite open dispatch of inmates from the hospital blocks to the gas chamber.

When, several days in succession, so many people were admitted to the hospital that there was no room and they were even lying three to a bed, Klehr's appetite for the needle had been satisfied and the hospital was still packed, then the sick were taken in trucks to the gas chambers in Birkenau.

Initially, this was done with a certain amount of shame, taking the inmates at night, late in the evening or in the early morning so that no one could see.

Then, slowly, as the whole camp learnt of this practice and the authorities stopped feeling ashamed of the "sick tourists," they took the "sick tourists" off to the gas in broad daylight.

Sometimes this was done during roll call when a reinforced guard detail and the barrels of their guns stared coldly at us from the watch towers.

More than one inmate, being driven to the gas and recognizing a friend in the ranks, would call out:

"'Bye, Jaś. Take care!..." He would wave his cap or hand and ride on "in fine spirits."

Everyone in the camp knew where they were going. So why was that fellow so pleased?

I daresay that he had already seen so much and suffered so much that he did not imagine anything worse after death.

One day, 41 [Stanisław Stawiszyński] ran up to me in camp saying that he had recognized (had clearly seen) Colonel 62 [Jan Karcz] amongst those brought in from Birkenau to be shot.

The information was confirmed. Colonel 62 [Jan Karcz], a gallant officer, lost his life.

I gave these several dozen pages in which I described scenes from Auschwitz to several friends to read.

They stated that I sometimes repeated myself. That's possible—partly from a lack of time to reread everything one more time, but also because this great "mill" grinding people into dust, or, if you prefer, a "steamroller" crushing human transports, revolved around one and the same axis, whose name was—destruction.

Yet fragments of individual scenes from camp, repeated daily—over three hundred of them in a year—on another day but in similar fashion showed, sporadically or regularly, the same side of the steamroller in all its detail... and if one watched this for almost a thousand days... Well then? If people living comfortably in the outside world make a minimal effort to read these pages and focus a few times on a single image? Especially if it is illuminated from the other side!

Perhaps it is better, at least to a small extent, that those reading along with us join us in thought, which is as different as are two and a thousand, for we were ordered a thousand times to look and no one could get bored.

There was no time there for English "spleen"!

And yet I want to repeat myself again.

It was hard to look at the columns of women, worn out by work, dragging themselves across the mud.

Their faces have become gray... their clothes muddied... They move along, holding up the weak "muselmänner."

There are still a few whose strong spirit supports their own and others' muscles.

There are eyes which continue to look boldly around trying to dress their ranks.

I don't know whether it was harder to look at those who returned in the evening tired from work or at those who in the morning, with a whole day before them, headed off to the fields, supposedly having rested, holding up their weaker comrades.

One saw faces and physiques which were unprepared for, and unsuited to, hard work in the fields.

One saw too our country lasses, supposedly accustomed to hard work, worn out just as much as the "ladies."

They were all marched on foot for kilometers to work, whether the weather was fine or rainy.

When the women sank into the mud, the "heroes" riding alongside them on horseback with dogs, cowboys, herded them like sheep or cattle, shouting and smoking cigarettes.

By now we had a real Tower of Babel in the camp. Many languages were spoken. For in addition to the Poles, Germans, Bolsheviks and Czechs, a few Belgians, Yugoslavs and Bulgarians, French and Dutch were brought in, as well as some Norwegians and finally Greeks.

I remember that the French received numbers above forty-five thousand.

They lasted less than anyone else. Unsuited for work or friendship. Sickly weaklings and foolishly stubborn.

The SS men would pull out of the ranks of arriving Jewish transports, waiting in their hundreds for their "bath" in the gas chamber, some of the young girls, saving them from death.

Apparently admiring the naked form, they would pick out every day several of the best looking.

If after a few days a girl continued to be able to save her life, paying for it with her beauty or some other form of cunning, she might sometimes be assigned to the schreibstube [office], or the sick room, or the camp offices.

However, there were few slots and many beauties.

The SS men would in the same manner pull out some of the young Jewish men from the hundreds going to the gas chambers.

They were processed normally. They came onto our blocks and to various kommandos.

This was another way of dealing with the remaining Jews in the world.

I have already mentioned that for a time the Jews, assigned for a short spell to indoor work, had written letters, sending them to their families saying they were happy here and they wrote alongside us, in other words twice a month, on Sundays.

Now, on the blocks where the Jews were living, SS men would show up from time to time, usually on a weekday. (We continued to write our letters on Sundays.) Coming in the evenings, the SS men would round up all the Jews living on that block and order them to sit at the same table.

They gave out standard camp letter forms and ordered them to write to their families, their relatives and if they didn't have any, to their friends.

They stood over them waiting for them to finish.

Then they would collect the letters themselves, sending them to various European countries.

If any of these hapless Jews had even thought of writing that he was unhappy... Everyone wrote that they were fine...

When our camp Jews had completed correctly their task of reassuring all the other hapless Jews in other countries and became "a useless burden to the camp," they were then finished off as quickly as possible by being transferred to hard work somewhere in Birkenau, or sometimes even straight to the Penal Company.

In the Penal Company, meanwhile, they were as always— finished off.

There was a Jew there, widely known as "the Strangler."[49] He had a daily quota of at least a dozen Jews to finish off. It depended on the Penal Company's overall strength.

On any given day an unpleasant death awaited the Jews destined for elimination from their powerfully built fellow-Jew, "the Strangler."

Every half an hour, more frequently or sometimes less, depending on the size of the queue for death, "the Strangler" ordered his selected prey to lie down on the ground on his back (he quickly and efficiently laid out anyone resisting), then he would place the handle of a spade on the lying man's neck and would then jump on the handle using his whole body weight. The handle crushed the throat. "The Strangler" would rock, shifting his weight from the left then back to the right-hand side.

The poor Jew under the spade croaked, kicked his legs, died. The thug sometimes told his victim not to fear and that death would come quickly.

In the Penal Company, "the Strangler" and the Jews assigned to him to be finished off were treated as a sort of autonomous sub-kommando of death.

In fact, the Penal Company, which had a majority of Poles, lived and died apart, accepting the same death in another fashion.

That summer, a large number of inmates were suddenly transferred to the Penal Company at the same time.

---

[49] His name was Izak Gąska. Translator's note.

This instruction came down from the political department, where a review of the files had established that these inmates' cases "on the outside" had been proved.

Among my friends and members of our organization in the camp the following were transferred to the Penal Company in Rajsko: Officer Cadet Platoon Sergeant 26 [Stanisław Maringe], First Lieutenant 27 [Jerzy Poraziński], Captain 124 [Tadeusz Chrościcki] (the father) and 125 [Tadeusz Lucjan Chrościcki] (the son).

Some time later I received a rather recklessly sent card from First Lieutenant 27 [Jerzy Poraziński] which, however, made it to me and in which he wrote... "I inform you that since we must soon become nothing but puffs of smoke, we shall try our luck tomorrow during work... We have little chance of success... Bid my family farewell, and if you can and if you are still alive, tell them that if I die, I do so fighting..."

The following day before nightfall the news came that that evening, at the signal announcing the end of work at Rajsko, the inmates of the Penal Company had all made a dash for it, trying to escape.

Whether it had been poorly organized or maybe someone had betrayed them and then everyone would have had to be warned, or perhaps conditions were too difficult, suffice it to say that the SS killed just about all the inmates, about 70 of them. German kapos efficiently helped the SS in the catching and killing.

Supposedly they had spared a few.

It was also said that over a dozen had got away. Supposedly some had swum the Vistula. However, the information was very contradictory. Three years later, though, I did learn from Romek G. that out of that group, 125 [Tadeusz Lucjan

Chrościcki] (the son of my Warsaw colleague) had somehow managed to avoid death then.

We knew that just as our inmates had once suffered on the blocks from lice, so in the women's camp, in the blocks isolated from ours, there was a great infestation of fleas.

We could not understand where it had come from, nor how these insects made such a gender distinction between the inmates. It turned out later that some kommandos from the women's camp had worked in flea-infested buildings and had brought the creatures back with them.

The insects, finding themselves now in good conditions, made themselves at home, chasing away the previous white tenants.

Shortly thereafter, the women were transferred from us and from blocks in the main camp to Rajsko-Birkenau, where they died in terrible conditions in wooden huts.

There was a lack of running water and lavatories in these blocks.

Some of them slept on the ground, for the blocks made from planks had no floors.

They floundered in mud above their ankles, for there were no drains or roads.

In the morning they remained in their hundreds on the parade ground, having no more strength for work. Downcast, these numb martyrs no longer looked like women.

They soon benefited from the camp authorities' "mercy," going by the hundred to the gas chambers.

Over two thousand beings, once women, were gassed.

A huge number of fleas remained on the blocks vacated by the women.

The carpenters who went to these blocks in order to make repairs to the windows or doors before male kommandos were moved back in, spoke of the terrible work in this kingdom of "brunettes," which jumped around the empty blocks in whole swarms.

Hungry, they rushed at the new arrivals, small dots, biting one after the other.

Nothing helped, not tying one's trouser legs at the ankle nor one's sleeves at the cuffs, so the carpenters immediately tore off their clothes putting them in some place free from fleas, and naked they would fight them off as animals grazing in the field beat off flies.

They swarmed all over the floor and if you looked at them in sunlight one got the impression of so many fountains.

By now we had lavatories and nice bathrooms in all the blocks in our camp. Drainage and running water were now the norm. Mechanical pumps worked in the cellars of three blocks supplying the whole camp with water.

A great many inmates had laid down their lives building all these improvements.

So now a zugang arrived in conditions different from those in which we had once been kept and in which we had also been "finished off" by the lack of washing facilities and the lack of a quiet moment in some lavatory.

Now someone was responsible for tidiness—a post which was the envy of many. He would sit in the lavatory eating his soup, he always had seconds, and it bothered him not a whit that his dining room was unusual. He would calmly carry on eating, shouting at the häftlings to go about their business in the beautiful lavatory faster.

The women who were moved from the kinds of conditions we had in the blocks in '42 to the primitive conditions of Rajsko, felt this all the more.

After the women had been moved, the high fence which had been built in the spring to separate us from the other sex remained until the whole camp was deloused.

However, the fleas somehow coped with the fence. Not all of them, but apparently the more enterprising amongst them, and after somehow making it over they rushed at our camp, finding plenty of nourishment on our blocks.

Meanwhile, developments in the spoon shop meant that one needed to start thinking about some other job, for we had turned out thousands of spoons and it was quite likely that our kommando would be disbanded.

Then, thanks to the influence of my friends 111 [name unknown], 19 [Tadeusz Słowiaczek] and 52 [Tadeusz Myszkowski], a place was found for me in the carpenters' shop, amongst the élite (once upon a time run by Konrad).

For the time being I worked with a master carpenter 111 [name unknown] in one workshop, but when 111 [name unknown] and 127 [name unknown] came down one after the other with typhus, I remained in a group of master craftsmen in the workshop on my own, having to pretend to be an expert and responsible for the shop's output.

There was a new kapo who, after the idiot Hulajnoga's [Scooter's] death (from typhus), had taken over the carpenters' kommando (in the tannery).

My position became difficult. I was given drawings for custom-made furniture, which I was supposed to produce on my own out of wood.

Although I did only twelve days on my own in that workshop, I have to admit that I was mentally exhausted.

I didn't want to come a cropper and yet I wasn't a professional. In any event I made a folding cupboard and although a first-rate craftsman 92 [Wacław Weszke] came to my shop to finish it off, I did for those twelve days successfully manage to impersonate a master carpenter for the fussy, but foolish, kapo.

By now I was not a complete novice at carpentry (the rest was down to ingenuity), but I greeted the arrival of 92 [Wacław Weszke] in my workshop, which he had chosen deliberately, with real delight.

Thereafter, I had more time to devote to setting up the "network" there, to coordinating our organization's work, meeting fellows in the tannery itself or on the pretext of picking out materials in the storeroom where planks were kept, conferring with 50 [Jan Mielcarek "Wernyhora"] and 106 [name unknown] on a pile of new straw mattresses reaching up to the ceiling. Through cracks in the roof we watched Erik's movements or the Commandant's, as if from a superb observation post.

Typhus continued to make its mark painfully, and delousing was carried out in the SS barracks.

People were sick on every block.

In our room (no. 7, Block 25), daily someone went off to the hospital sick with typhus.

By then we had one bunk for two of us.

The first of our crowd to come down was Officer Cadet 94 [name unknown], followed by Corporal 91 [Stanisław Polkowski], 71 [Jan Mosdorf], then 73 [Piotr Kownacki], 95 [name unknown], then 111 [name unknown] who was sharing a bunk with me, 93 [name unknown]—(then it becomes hard to remember who followed whom to the hospital). Just about everyone came down one after the other.

A great many never returned, riding the cart full of corpses to the crematorium.

Daily, one could see a couple of faces one knew amongst the bodies of häftlings tossed like wood onto the cart.

For the time being I did not come down with typhus.

Dr. 2 [Władysław Dering] appeared, suggesting that I inoculate myself against typhus; he had (secretly) obtained the vaccine from "outside"; however, I had to think what to do, since if I had already been infected by typhus-bearing lice (which was highly probable since I had been sharing a bunk with 111 [name unknown] who had already come down with it, and since from the initial infection to the first temperature usually took about a fortnight), then the vaccine was not to be administered, for it could lead to death.

However, coming to the conclusion that I had not been infected, I decided on the inoculation.

Out of our crowd of thirty lads standing at the head of our block at roll call, maybe seven or eight remained. The rest had died from typhus.

Out of our members the following died: brave Wernyhora 50 [Jan Mielcarek], 53 [Józef Chramiec], 54 [Stefan Gaik], 58 [Andrzej Marduła], 71 [Jan Mosdorf], 73 [Piotr Kownacki], 91 [Stanisław Polkowski], 94 [name unknown], 126 [Tadeusz Czechowski] and my much-missed friend 30 [Eugeniusz Triebling].

To be honest, can I write that someone was "much-missed"? I missed them all.

I tried so hard to save Captain 30 [Eugeniusz Triebling]. He was always cheerful, he kept up people's spirits with his sense of humor and "seconds" bowl; several people were always being kept alive near him.

Before the typhus he suddenly caught a blood infection,

which was cured: Dr. 2 [Władysław Dering] made a quick operation on his arm and removed the danger.

Then, a week later, he caught typhus, went to Block 28 where for a few days he would hospitably invite his friends to join him in eating delicacies brought in for him from "Canada," loudly calling out: "God has provided, good people have brought it, now you eat it up."

He had a high temperature, he kept talking and talking, he amusingly said that he must live, even if he were to have his head under his arm, but he would get out of Auschwitz, since he had endured terrible things in Hamburg and that he must see his Jasia. So saying he caught meningitis.

He was moved to Block 20. They made a spinal tap. He had good care, but there was nothing to be done.

He did leave Auschwitz, but only as smoke from the chimney.

He gave me a message: "Isjago." If anyone can make sense of it, please get in touch with me.

So (that summer of '42) saw many losses, but there were gains too.

It was then that new comrades joined our organization, although some of them had been in the camp for a long time: 128 [name unknown], 129 [Leon Kukiełka], 130 [name unknown], 131 [name unknown], 132 [name unknown], 133 [name unknown], 134 [name unknown], 135 [name unknown], 136 [name unknown], 137 [name unknown], 138 [name unknown], 139 [name unknown], 140 [name unknown], 141 [name unknown], 142 [name unknown], 143 [name unknown], 144 [name unknown].

I had been working for several weeks on a block, not going to the carpenters' shop at all, making the most of the friendly attitude towards me of block chief 80 [Alfred Włodarczyk], who had earlier come to my rescue at difficult moments.

He gave me some "creative" work to do on the block, justifying it to the authorities by the need for official signs on the block roster.

I painted scenes of camp life: "seconds of soup," "evening foot inspection with a beating on the 'bench.'"

Out of colored paper I made a kind of picture cut-out, or sticker.

It turned out quite well; even when Palitzsch for once stopped by the block a month later, when I had already left, and ordered all the pictures to be destroyed, breaking the glass into little pieces and even smashing the frames—he took my cut-out for himself.

A new delousing of the camp began.

One day, it was between the 20th and the 25th of August of '42, as always of late I had not gone to work and was sitting painting on the block. I suddenly saw vehicles carrying large numbers of SS men driving into the camp and up to the typhus block (Block 20—new numbering system).

The SS men quickly surrounded the block.

I have to admit that watching that scene for a moment my blood froze and then boiled. I imagined another reason for the SS actions. But what I was shortly to see, was also distressing.

The sick were pulled out and shoved into the vehicles.

Those who were unconscious and those who were now well, those convalescing having been ill a month earlier but who were still in quarantine, they were all packed into the vehicles and taken off to the gas chambers in several waves.

Everyone in Block 20 was taken away, including those who had recovered and who had stayed on for a few days' rest; the only exception were the pflegers, who could be recognized by their dress, since for several months all the hospital staff had been wearing clothes that were clearly distinguishable from ours. They were made of white linen with a red stripe painted across the back and a similar one on the trousers.

It was then that Dr. 2 [Władysław Dering] saved a number of Poles, telling them to change, a few at a time, into the pflegers' whites, presenting them to the commission of SS doctors as tending the sick.

It was eventually pointed out to him that there seemed to be an awful lot of nurses. But since at the end the real nurses, whom the SS men knew, were leaving, they somehow got away with it.

I saw an SS man throwing two small inmates into the vehicles. A little fellow, who was eight years old, asked the SS man to spare him and knelt on the ground. The SS man kicked him in the stomach and threw him into the vehicle like a puppy.

They were all finished off the same day in the gas chambers at Rajsko.

Then for two days the crematoria worked away, with new batches of inmates continually being brought in from the camp.

They did not stop at Block 20, they then took people from Block 28 and then from the wooden hut between Blocks 27 and 28, which had been built for the duration of the epidemic. Then they just picked people out of kommandos.

A commission roamed around picking people from normal blocks where the kommandos lived, taking off to the gas chambers all those who had swollen feet or some physical defect giving the appearance of a weak worker.

Then they set about the schonungsblock [convalescence block] and all the muselmänner in the camp, of whom there were in fact fewer, owing to the influence of "Canada."

However, what muselmänner there were, were taken off to

the gas chambers for "delousing." From the gas chambers they went by way of the crematorium up the chimney as smoke.

This new expression "de-lifing" caught on in the camp.

The piles of clothing and underwear remaining after the transports of people who came from the free world to give up their lives in the gas chambers, were also packed into separate gas chambers, hung up to be disinfected, in other words for real delousing. From this, any activity using gas, be it of objects or häftlings, was called "delousing."

A few days later, on the 30th of August, I had a temperature, my joints ached and my calves hurt if I put pressure on them. In other words, just about all the symptoms of typhus. All I needed was the headache, but I have never had a headache in my life and I don't know what it feels like. I think that I have inherited this from my father, who with some surprise used to say: "... a head that hurts must be really stupid..."

However, since the doctors and my friends said that, whether you like it or not, typhus must be accompanied by a headache, I waited a couple of days.

Fortunately, I was grateful to block supervisor 80 [Alfred Włodarczyk] for the opportunity to stay on the block and I did not go to work.

My temperature was over 39 degrees Celsius and I found it hard to stand upright at roll call.

However, I did not want to go to the krankenbau, for there was no certainty that they would not come again in their vehicles and would not take everyone off to the gas chambers, especially since the illness, with its compulsory quarantine, had to last for at least two months.

This was my second serious illness in Auschwitz.

In addition, I had had a temperature on a number of occasions during my time in the camp, exacerbated by a cold; in the outside world this might have turned into some kind of 'flu, but here, from sheer willpower, or maybe even nervous tension, I fought the illness by going to work.

Now, however, day after day, especially in the evening, I felt that I was not "getting over" this sickness and that I was running out of strength even to walk.

I don't know what would have happened if, just as the first time, delousing had not taken a hand, but in a different way.

I was worn out by the temperature which had lasted for several days.

The delousing had already gone through all the blocks and it was our turn next.

Despite my temperature rising to 40 degrees in the evening, I prepared myself for delousing, helping the room orderly, my friend 111 [name unknown] (who had made a good recovery from typhus). When the block went off to be deloused leaving only those checking the block, all of whom in half an hour had to go for delousing, then feeling very weak and remembering how difficult it had once been for me to go through delousing while running a temperature, I was not too keen on it.

There was only one way to avoid it: go to the hospital where again they might take everyone off to the gas chambers.

I was hesitating, but Dr. 2 [Władysław Dering] appeared and, seeing that I had a high temperature, he arranged all the formalities for me at unofficial speed, placing me in Block 28 (in the hospital) and pulling me out of Block 25 at the very last moment before roll call.

My temperature had reached 41 degrees and I was very weak—it was my turn to come down with typhus.

The absence of a headache had the advantage that I did not lose consciousness.

Perhaps my bout was less serious, owing to the typhus shot.

The first "raid" took place during the first night I spent on Block 28: a couple of aircraft illuminated the Rajsko camp and dropped two bombs.[50]

Perhaps they were trying to hit a crematorium, but in any case it was not a major operation.

However, it had a wonderful effect on us. We saw the confusion it caused amongst the SS. Two of the "guards" on the nearest towers abandoned their towers and ran along the wire fence as if they had lost their heads.

SS men ran from their barracks towards our camp in a chaotic mass, looking for one another.

Unfortunately it was a feeble raid and the only one on Auschwitz, at least during my time there.[51]

For two days my stay on Block 28 was "for observation."

There, comrade 100 [name unknown] gave me especially kind and attentive care, and spent his every free moment by my side or bringing me lemon or sugar.

Through him I was in touch with my workmates and could control the organization.

My rash, however, was so pronounced that they had to transfer me to Block 20 with its recent grim history.

While I was still on Block 28, Dr. 2 [Władysław Dering] had given me an injection which within a few hours had lowered my temperature from 40 degrees to a little over 37 degrees.

---

[50] Józef Garliński in *Oświęcim Walczący* (London: Odnowa, 1974), p. 172, footnote 120, believes this to have been a Soviet raid. Translator's note.

[51] On the 13th of September 1944, the Americans bombed the I.G. Farben works near the camp, killing fifteen SS men, forty inmates and thirty civilian workers. However, this attack was directed against an industrial installation and not the camp itself, and it was not intended to help camp inmates to escape. Translator's note.

So when he appeared the following morning with his syringe, I joked that if my temperature were now to drop from 37 degrees to 34 degrees, I would doubtless die, and so I refused any further injections.

My body has always reacted strongly to any medicine or shots.

Block 20, after the recent removal of all the patients to the gas chamber, was once again full.

Daily the corpses of typhus victims were tossed onto carts, like so many blocks of wood.

I don't know if I have already mentioned the fact that all the bodies taken to the crematorium were naked, no distinction being made as to their means of death: typhus, some other illness, Klehr's needle or a bullet from Palitzsch.

Here, on the typhus block, after the morning disposal of bodies, already by noon and definitely by evening, new naked, blue bodies lay in the corridor, piled one on top of the other, looking like some bloodbath of lean meat.

After an initial rather brusque brush with a fellow who worked here as a doctor, within a few hours I was favorably disposed towards him. Devoted, the man I had as my doctor, 145 [name unknown], thinking only of his patients, the whole day long took care of everything, ran around, bathed, fed, gave injections.

Another courageous doctor here was the kindhearted and also energetic Captain Dr. 146 [Henryk Suchnicki].

In addition, I also received care from comrade 100 [name unknown], from his friend 101 [Witold Kosztowny], who worked here as a nurse with his syringe, or drawing blood for analysis.

Amongst the block's staff was a member of our organization who worked in the storerooms, my young friend Edek 57

[Edward Ciesielski]. When I began to recover, he would bring me additional portions of pork fat and sugar.

In addition, Kazio 39 [Pilecki's nephew, Kazimierz Radwański], working with 76 [Bernard Świerczyna], provided me with a pillow and a blanket from "Canada."

Before the crisis passed, in this great mortuary of the half-living—where nearby someone was wheezing his final breath, someone else was dying, another was struggling out of bed only to fall over onto the floor, another was throwing off his blankets, or talking in a fever to his dear mother, shouting, cursing someone out, refusing to eat, or demanding water, in a fever and trying to jump out of the window, arguing with the doctor or asking for something—I lay thinking that I still had the strength to understand everything that was going on and take it calmly in my stride.

I was thinking that these experiences alone could make one fall ill, and that one could develop too an aversion to this human vale of tears, taking pity on the human body's imperfections; indeed, one could develop an aversion to sickness itself.

Hence there arose within me an overwhelming desire to leave, to regain my strength as soon as possible.

When the crisis had passed and I felt that I was strong enough to venture down the stairs to the lavatory (hitherto I had been using a rather primitive one for patients on the ward), it turned out that I was so weak that I had to cling to the wall.

It seemed odd to me that not only did I not have the strength to climb the stairs, but that going down was just as hard.

My strength returned, or so it seemed to me, very slowly.

During my period of weakness, on more than one occasion my friends had been ready to carry me up to the attic and conceal me in the event that there were plans to sweep everyone off to the gas chambers.

Klehr walked through the ward a number of times and with his basilisk stare would pick victims for "the needle."

Here I meet and bring into our organization 118 [name unknown], 146 [Henryk Suchnicki], 147 [name unknown], 148 [name unknown] and 149 [name unknown].

Dr. 145 [name unknown] gave his all in this post, which was so suitable for him, so that there was no need to set up or change anything—I just knew that I could rely on him.

From time to time Dr. 2 [Władysław Dering] would appear bringing me lemons and tomatoes, which he had obtained as usual "on the side."

I was on my feet pretty quickly. Going down into the yard during my period of quarantine I would talk to my friends through the grille separating the "plague-ridden" block.

Comrade 76 [Bernard Świerczyna] would come to discuss a new "branch" of the organization, which he had just set up; 61 [Konstanty Piekarski] with a plan to escape by tunnelling out of Block 28, suggested by 4 [Alfred Stössel] and begun with the help of 129 [Leon Kukiełka] and 130 [name unknown]; 59 [Henryk Bartosiewicz] with a proposition to amalgamate all new forces and then deploy them with permanently designated commanders for specific groups, which Colonel 121 [Juliusz Gilewicz] also wanted (when changes were made after the most recent delousing).

Then I prepared the following amalgamation and deployment plan:

Because the camp authorities, after the general delousing, assigned häftlings to blocks by kommando, there was no longer any need for the parallel plans for taking over the camp (i.e., at work and in the blocks in camp) and I made each block the basic unit.

Each block was a platoon, that is to say everyone who belonged to the organization living on that block, taking no account of their primary organizational affiliation, henceforth formed a skeleton platoon which, on the "outbreak," would expand depending on how many men they could encourage, trying immediately to neutralize the pro-German elements.

Block X—inmates on the ground floor, and Block Xa—those on the first floor, at once became a two-platoon company in one building with a company commander on the spot.

Several blocks/buildings formed a battalion.

I divided the whole camp into four battalions.

As overall military commander, I renominated Major 85 [Zygmunt Bohdanowski].

As commander of 1 Battalion, Major 150 [Edward Gött-Getyński] (Blocks 15, 17, 18).

As commander of 2 Battalion, Captain 60 [Stanisław Kazuba] (Blocks 16, 22, 23, 24).

As commander of 3 Battalion, Captain 114 [Tadeusz Paolone] (Blocks 19, 25, the kitchen, as well as the hospital staff from Blocks 20, 21, 28).

As commander of 4 Battalion, Captain 116 [Zygmunt Pawłowicz] (Blocks 4, 5, 6, 7, 8, 9 and 10).

I refrained from organizing the remaining blocks for technical reasons, since they had either recently been filled, such as Blocks 1 and 2, or were being used as storerooms, such as Blocks 3, 26 and 27, or were still under construction, such as Blocks 12, 13, 14, or the special block, 11.

Colonel 121 [Juliusz Gilewicz] approved the plan.

A couple of days later I left the hospital for the camp. My quarantine had been shortened by friendly doctors, who entered a (false) earlier admission date in the camp records.

It was the beginning of October 1942.

I went off to work among five "hundreds," as usual to the tannery, but not to the carpenters' kommando where I had been working before my illness, but to the tanners' kommando (the real tanners), thanks to comrade 59 [Henryk Bartosiewicz] who introduced me to the new tannery kapo "Mateczka" as a tanner who had been ill and was now returning to work.

Initially working in the tannery alongside Colonel 121 [Juliusz Gilewicz] on white materials, then, owing to the friendly disposition of 59 [Henryk Bartosiewicz] and 61 [Konstanty Piekarski], I moved to the drying room, where it was warm since there was a great iron stove there and for four months I pretended to be a tanner, learning this new trade.

Nothing much had changed in the huge tannery.

Daily, several vehicles would bring items left by the people who had been gassed, to be burnt in the tannery's great furnace. Shoes were not burnt.

Every day a vast number of all kinds of shoes—brown and black, men's and women's, children's in many different sizes— were thrown onto huge piles.

A kommando was formed to sort these shoes into pairs. Someone else took care of burning the other pile of suitcases, wallets, ladies' handbags, prams and various toys.

Colored wool, which the women had brought with them for knitting, was set aside. It was not burnt. Anyone who could, kept some for himself to make sweaters.

The great tannery furnace, with its factory chimney, devoured everything—the fuel was free and brought almost right to the door.

Those who were doing the burning were able to rummage around a bit in the suitcases.

Sometimes, someone from the tannery would dig into a pile of suitcases in front of the furnace, since it was difficult to take anything from them in the yard under the eye of Erik or Walter.

Again I saw how, in the desire to obtain gold or a precious stone, suitcases, handbags, briefcases were taken apart and shoes, creams and soaps were searched.

The only paper money taken were dollars.

Banknotes, mainly French francs, fluttered all over the yard, blown like autumn leaves by the wind. Nobody saved them, especially given the dangerous searches at the gate. They seemed to us to be quite useless. They were used only in the lavatory.

There was a time when the men from the tannery, "the aristocracy" of all the kommandos, never took less than 50,000 francs when going to the lavatory.

The current joke was that anyone taking any less might be seen as a miser.

The hardest thing of all is to write about oneself.

To a degree which surprised even me, I could walk past gold and precious stones with indifference.

Today, writing about it back in the real world, I am trying to work out exactly why.

The goods belonged really to no one, which is how the häftlings justified it to themselves.

At the time I was close to agreeing with this justification.

Yet above all I was unable to overcome a distaste for things which to my mind were stained with blood and in any event, even if I had overcome it, I saw no sense in it; why would I do it? Oddly enough, for me these objects had lost their value.

Moreover, I was at the time going through a phase, either under the influence of my experiences or the dictates of my faith, for I am and always have been a believer, when I knew that self-respect was of greater value to me than some stone.

Suffice it to say that if I had forced myself to take gold or jewels I would have been only too aware that I was slipping from the heights which I had so laboriously attained.

Furthermore, the first essential obstacle to looking for gold was the almost tangible feeling that I was doing myself great harm.

That is how I felt at the time, but who knows how I would behave were I once again to find myself in similar circumstances.

People reacted differently.

I didn't need any money at the time, but when much later I wanted to escape and money would be useful on the road, I approached an inmate named Romek suggesting that we escape together and asking whether he had any money, just in case. He told me that he would count up what he had collected and would give me an answer the next day. The following day he told that he had over a kilo of gold.

However, an escape with him did not work out. I made it out with fellows who did not have two pennies to rub together. But that would take place much later; for the time being, I had no plans to get out, waiting for the most interesting moment in the camp's life towards which our whole effort was geared.

For some months now we had been able to take over the camp on more or less a daily basis.

We awaited an order on the assumption that without one, although there would be fine and unexpected "fireworks" for the whole world and Poland, we could not act simply for our own benefit and that of Mr. X or Mr. Y. We could not try such an experiment without orders from [Home Army] High Command.

But our hands itched daily.

We understood well that such action would be confirmation of our centuries-old national weakness. A rush of ambition and eagerness, unrelated to the overall picture and possibly bringing great reprisals throughout Silesia.

Especially since, at the time, it was hard to foretell how things would turn out.

We still had great hope that we would be able to play a part as an organized element in an overall coordinated operation.

Our reports were sent for the attention of the [Home Army] Commander-in-Chief along those lines.

For fear of someone's thoughtless action on the outside we needed to avoid using any intermediaries when sending out our reports.

We were unclear how deeply German Intelligence had penetrated our networks, even those right at the top of the Underground Movement in Poland.

There was always the chance that if German Intelligence picked up on something, it would again "take out" the most energetic elements here in the camp.

It was then echoes of the pacification campaign in the Lublin region reached the camp.

First of all, one day among the belongings and the poorer worn-out shoes being burned we came across Polish country footwear, large and small, and then Polish peasant clothes, missals in Polish and simple, rustic rosaries.

A sort of tremor ran through our "fives." We began to hang

around in groups. Eyes became hard and fists clenched impatiently...

These were the belongings of Polish families who had been gassed in the gas chambers in Birkenau.

As a result of the pacification of the Lublin region (so our fellows in Rajsko told us) the people from several Polish villages had been brought here for gassing.

That is how things are and there is nothing one can do about it; when the belongings of people brought in from some other country were being burned, these shoes and suitcases had for months for us in the tannery been a terrible thing and an evil echo of crime—but now, when we saw the little shoes, a woman's blouse and a rosary in their midst, the thirst for revenge became stronger.

Young boys, aged between 10 and 14–15, had been picked out from these Lublin transports. They had been segregated and brought into the camp.

We thought that these boys would survive. But one day, when we learned that a team was to come to inspect the state of the camp and in order to avoid any problems and have to explain where such young inmates had come from, although there might have been other reasons, all these boys got the "needle" with phenol on Block 20.

We had already seen many mountains of corpses in the camp, but this one, composed of about two hundred little bodies, made an impression on us, on even the old inmates, increasing our heart rate...

A number of new members joined from the tannery: 151 [name unknown], 152 [name unknown], 153 [name unknown], 154 [name unknown], 155 [name unknown].

At the same time we set up an advisory planning cell which Colonels 24 [Karol Kumuniecki] and 122 [Teofil Dziama], and 156 [Stanisław Wierzbicki] joined.

In Auschwitz, we often saw one of the fellows getting a letter from home, in which a mother, father or wife implored him to sign the Volksliste [the German People's Register]— initially these were usually inmates with German-sounding names, or with German names on their mother's side, or with some family connection or other.

Then the authorities began to make it progressively easier, so that eventually no German-sounding name was needed, just the wish to erase one's Polish conscience, unless there were some higher considerations.

How often did one see, there in "hell," an honest peasant whose foreign-sounding name did not prevent him being worthy of the name Pole.

Someone who with emotion said: "Yes, I love my mother, my wife, my father, but I won't sign the list! I know that I'll die here... My wife writes: 'Jasiu dear, do sign'... No! Over my dead body! No one will be able in future to spit on my sense of being Polish, which though recent, is resolute."

So many such men in Auschwitz died...

...A fine death, for they held out to the end on the ramparts of their Polish conscience.

But will all our compatriots out there, free and with Polish names fight for their Polishness?

What was really needed was some kind of instrument which could check for a Polish conscience, which in different families had taken different paths over these last few years of war.

In the second half of October, our fellows noticed (41 [Stanisław Stawiszyński] came running up with the news) that two of the kapos with the worst reputations (in addition to finishing off inmates they sent denunciations to the political department and its head—Grabner) were wandering around the camp, as if looking for someone, and taking down some of the häftlings' numbers.

One afternoon, as I was hurrying down the main path from Block 22 to my comrades in the hospital area, I bumped into these two kapos by Block 16.

One had a notebook, the other came up to me with a fake smile and asked: "Wo läufst du? [Where are you off to in such a hurry?]"[52] as if for the sake of saying something, and he clearly pointed out my number to the other and then walked away. The other one looked at me and appeared to hesitate, but as they walked off, I too went on my way thinking that there had been a mistake.

On the 28th of October (of '42), at the morning roll call the *schreibers* [clerks] on various blocks began to call out inmates' numbers telling them to go to the erkennungsdienst [the records office] to have their photographs checked.

Altogether 240 or so häftlings were called out, exclusively Poles as we later established and mainly from Lublin, with about a quarter of them Poles having nothing to do with the Lublin transports, and were for the time being sent to Block 3, which already made us suspicious, since why not go at once to Block 26 containing the erkennungsdienst, the ostensible cause of their summons?

The bell for arbeitskommando summoned us and we then left the camp as usual, each kommando going its separate way to work.

All the kommandos were abuzz at work; for the moment, we did not know if the others were in any kind of danger.

Then the news came from somewhere that they were to be shot. Two hundred and forty lads, mainly real Lubliners,

---

[52] As used here, the correct German question should be: "Wohin läufst du?" Translator's note.

to whom had been added at random by Grabner's "dogs" going through the camp the numbers of those who stood out by virtue of their energy and eagerness.

We never discovered the real reason, perhaps it had just been the "whim" of those two thugs.

However, it was also called the "Lublin pacification," whose echoes had reverberated around the camp.

Brave 41 [Stanisław Stawiszyński] from Warsaw was among them, he who had first come with the news that numbers were being taken down.

For the time being we did not know if they were to be shot; we thought it might be only a rumor.

They had hitherto never shot such a large number of inmates at the same time. The mask of apparent passivity was a burden, when we were ready and eager for action. Those of us leading the organization were biting our fingernails, gearing up in the event of a showdown.

Had that group rebelled and put up a fight, we would all have sprung into action.

The revolt would have ignited the ranks and would have represented force majeure, thus untying our hands.

On the way back to camp our five "hundreds" of fit indoor workers passed the baubüro [construction site office] beneath which lay a reserve arms store.

In any event, it would not have been difficult; the lads were up for a fight. Everyone was always ready for death, but we would have made the bastards pay for it with blood.

There were only nine miserable little watchtowers and the hauptwache [main gate guard], as well as barely a dozen *gemeiners* [low-level SS men] who while escorting us carried their arms slung over their shoulders and unslung them only as they approached the camp on account of their superiors, so accustomed were they to our docility.

Had by some miracle just the one word flown in from Warsaw "action"... that day... to rescue the others...

But that was only a dream.

Did anyone even know? Did it even cross their mind? To be sure, with hindsight, one can see that this was just one fragment of the Polish nation's suffering.

Yet, how very hard it was on us when the news came that afternoon that all of them had been calmly and with no fuss shot.

Sometimes amongst ourselves, on the day of a "shooting," in the evening we would discuss how different men had gone to their death: had he gone bravely... or had he been afraid?

The lads murdered on the 28th of October of '42 had known what awaited them. They had been told at Block 3 that they were going to be shot and so they threw cards to their comrades who were not going to die asking them to be sent on to their families...

They had decided to die "cheerfully," so that they would be well spoken of that evening.

Let no one tell me that we Poles do not know how to die!

Those who witnessed it said that they would never forget the sight.

From Block 3, between Blocks 14 and 15, between the kitchen and Blocks 16, 17 and 18 and then straight on between the hospital blocks they proceeded in a column in fives, their heads held high, some of them even smiling.

There was no escort and they were followed by Palitzsch with his Luger in his belt and Bruno, both smoking and chatting idly.

All it would have taken was for the last five to have done an about-turn and both those thugs would have been no more.

So why did they not do it? Were they afraid? What was there to be afraid of at a moment like that when they were going to their deaths?

It looked like some kind of psychosis... but they did not do it, because they had their own reasons...

It had been announced by the authorities and confirmed by fellows who had recently been brought to the camp that the whole family would be held accountable for any games played by an inmate. It was known that the Germans were ruthless when it came to reprisals and wiped out families, displaying all manner of brutality. And who knew better than us what brutality looked like?

To see, or just to know, that one's mother, wife or children could find themselves in the conditions endured by the women in Rajsko, was enough to stifle any thought of rushing the swine.

The whole camp was another matter.

To take it over, destroy the files... Who would be held responsible? It would be hard to lay hands on tens of thousands of families at the same time.

After lengthy consideration, we followed orders, given the possibility of reprisals, given the need to coordinate operations.

Accustomed to death, with which we came into contact several times a day, the idea of our own death was easier than the thought of a terrible blow directed at our loved ones.

Not really their death, but the terrible experience which accompanies a hard, ruthless hand taking our dearest from this world, breaking them psychologically and throwing them into another world, into a hell through which not everyone makes an easy passage.

The thought of one's old mother or father struggling with what was left of their energy through mud somewhere, prodded and beaten with a club... for the sins of the son... or one's own children going to the gas chamber... because of their father... was much harder than to think of one's own death.

And even if there was someone for whom this was too high a standard, then he went on, led by his companions' example.

He was "ashamed"—no, that's too weak a word—he was unable to break out of that fine column, going so bravely to its death!

So on they went.

By the canteen (a wooden building on the square behind Block 21), still following the path between Blocks 21 and 27, the column appeared to stop... hesitated... almost went straight on, but that lasted only a single short moment, and then it turned ninety degrees left and headed for the gates of Block 11 and into the jaws of death.

Only after the gates had closed behind them and they were left on the block for several hours—they were to be shot in the afternoon—during this waiting for death, various doubts began to emerge and five of the lads tried to convince the others to take over the camp, to start the operation.

They barricaded the gates and something more serious might have happened had the Germans not reinforced the guards; all our kommandos were just waiting for a sign, but the protest against these killings did not spread beyond Block 11.

For apart from those five, the rest did not rise to the bait, and the Silesian, who was an orderly on that block, informed the SS men of the start of a revolt; Palitzsch appeared on the block with several other SS men and dealt with those inmates, shooting them first and leaving the rest for the afternoon.

Their achievement was to rise in our esteem for having died fighting: Captain Dr. 146 [Henryk Suchnicki], 129 [Leon Kukiełka] and three other fellows.

By the afternoon all of them were dead...

From our organization, in addition to the three whom I have already mentioned, that day the following fellows lost their lives: 41 [Stanisław Stawiszyński], 88 [Tadeusz Dziedzic], 105 [Edward Berlin], 108 [Stanisław Dobrowolski] and 146 [Henryk Suchnicki], but there were also others in the organization whom I don't mention, because I didn't know everyone personally—an impossibility in Underground work.

On our return to camp after work we scented in the air the smell of our comrades' blood.

Efforts had been made to take the bodies off to the crematorium before our return.

The road was soaked with the blood dripping from the carts carrying the bodies...

That evening the whole camp was affected grimly by the death of these latest victims.

Only then did I realize that I had myself almost been on that list of names read out that day and, recalling the two kapos taking down numbers, I did not know whether I had not been written down by the kapo with the notebook because I had not looked like a dangerous inmate, or whether Grabner had later made a selection among the excess numbers, rejecting those who had no "political" case against them.

They brought in a new transport from the Pawiak in Warsaw which included my friends and former colleagues in the TAP in Warsaw: 156 [Stanisław Wierzbicki], 157 [Czesław Sikora] and 158 [Zygmunt Ważyński].

They brought me some interesting news.

Comrade 156 [Stanisław Wierzbicki] told me how 25 [Stefan

Bielecki] had reached Warsaw from Auschwitz and how he, Wierzbicki, had later driven him in a car to his post in Minsk.

However, 158 [Zygmunt Ważyński] told me in detail that, on receiving the news from me delivered by Sergeant 14 [Antoni Woźniak] about the possibility of inconvenient information about me emerging from the parish register in Z [Bochnia], my sister-in-law Mrs. E.O. [Eleonora Ostrowska] had hurried around to see him. My honest friend 158 [Zygmunt Ważyński] that very same day had taken the train and gone to the little town of Z [Bochnia] where he went to see the parish priest 160 [Kuc] and explained the situation. The priest 160 [Kuc] wrote everything down in pencil in the register next to the owner of my camp alias and promised to take care of the matter. He must have done so, for there was no sign of any activity in my case in the political department.

Comrade 156 [Stanisław Wierzbicki] pointed out to me among the new arrivals Captain 159 [Stanisław Machowski] from [Home Army] High Command in Warsaw—he had been second-in-command in "Iwo II."

One of our members, 138 [name unknown], knew Captain 159 [Stanisław Machowski] personally, having once served under him, and now as block chief he easily took him under his wing (76 [Bernard Świerczyna] pulled in 156 [Stanisław Wierzbicki], as well as 117 [Eugeniusz Zaturski] already working there).

Henceforth the two TAP members worked and lived together.

Of the men I had once known in Warsaw from the TAP, the following passed through Auschwitz: 1 [Władysław Surmacki], 2 [Władysław Dering], 3 [Jerzy de Virion], 25 [Stefan Bielecki], 26 [Stanisław Maringe], 29 [Włodzimierz Makaliński], 34 [name unknown], 35 [Remigiusz Niewiarowski], 36 [Stanisław

Arct], 37 [name unknown], 38 [Chmielewski], 41 [Stanisław Stawiszyński], 48 [Stanisław Ozimek], 49 [Jan Dangel], 85 [Zygmunt Bohdanowski], 108 [Stanisław Dobrowolski], 117 [Eugeniusz Zaturski], 120 [Zygmunt Zakrzewski], 124 [Tadeusz Chrościcki], 125 [Tadeusz Lucjan Chrościcki], 131 [name unknown], 156 [Stanisław Wierzbicki], 157 [Czesław Sikora] and 158 [Zygmunt Ważyński].

Since 129 [Leon Kukiełka] had been shot and 130 [name unknown] had died of typhus, it was impossible to continue the tunnel from Block 28. The tunnel was not discovered, but 5 [Roman Zagner] was arrested on another matter.

Later that autumn (of '42) when block chiefs were roped in to bake potatoes, 4 [Alfred Stössel] also had a long walk to work in the potato fields. Lachmann, an SS man from the political department and unfamiliar with the case, came to get him on some matter, but when he found that 4 [Alfred Stössel] was not there, Lachmann turned around and went away.

The lads quickly put two and two together and rushed into the room which 4 [Alfred Stössel], as the block chief for Block 28, had to himself, and removed anything which might have made things difficult for him.

Someone must have spilt the beans...

Lachmann got only as far as the gate and, as if struck by something, turned back and made a thorough search of 4's [Alfred Stössel's] room, but by now he found nothing.

However, he waited and as soon as 4 [Alfred Stössel] returned from work that evening, Lachman "arrested" him, led him off to the bunker, and 4 [Alfred Stössel] never returned to Block 28.

He was interrogated on Block 11, in the bunkers and in the political department.

Although lately 4 [Alfred Stössel] had had an unfortunate obsession, to give him his due he stood up bravely to the torture and interrogation in the bunkers and said not a word, although he knew a great deal.

Things went no further.

He was fortunate to come down with typhus and was moved from the bunker to the typhus block.

One needs to experience for oneself how relative things are to understand that just as life beyond the wires represented freedom for inmates in the camp, so camp represented freedom for someone in the bunker.

To get out of the bunker then, even if one was sick and on the typhus block, was a substitute for the substitute of freedom.

But here too he had an SS man with him nearly all the time.

Lachmann was not giving up!

However, 4 [Alfred Stössel] was tough and had a strong will. One night, he stopped living.

My comrades whom I have mentioned and who had come in from Warsaw, 156 [Stanisław Wierzbicki], 157 [Czesław Sikora] and 158 [Zygmunt Ważyński], remarked that they had not expected to find the inmates' physical condition and morale in Auschwitz to be so good.

They said that they had known nothing about the brutality here, the "wall of tears," nor about the phenol or the gas chambers.

They themselves had not thought, and no one in Warsaw had seriously considered, that Auschwitz could represent an active asset; for the most part people felt that everyone there was a skeleton whom it was pointless and useless to rescue.

It was bitter listening to this while looking at the lads' brave faces.

So, fine people were going to their deaths here and losing their lives so as not to implicate anyone outside, while far weaker people than us were casually calling us skeletons.

What perseverance would be needed to continue to die in order to protect our chums "enjoying themselves" in freedom?

Yes, all the methods of destruction in the camp hit all of us too hard, and now this opinion from the outside with its continual, ignorant silence.

The four battalions' duties were divided up in such a way that each battalion was on duty for a week, which meant that it was responsible for immediate action in the event of an air raid or an arms drop.

It also was the recipient during its week of any items "organized" and supplied by 76 [Bernard Świerczyna], 77 [Zbigniew Ruszczyński], 90 [name unknown], 94 [name unknown] and 117 [Eugeniusz Zaturski], dividing food and clothing amongst the incomplete platoons.

Despite the prohibition (after all, what did a prohibition mean for häftlings?), and despite the death penalty, there was an enormous increase in the camp of dealing in gold and diamonds.

A kind of organization developed, since two inmates who wanted to barter—for instance sausage from the abattoir for gold—were already connected to each other, for if one of them was caught with the gold and then beaten in the bunker, he might well let slip who had given it to him and in exchange for what.

Arrests in the camp for having gold now became more frequent.

The SS men eagerly hunted down this new organization, for it provided them with a profit.

In any event, the gold "organization" was an excellent lightning rod for us.

Attempts to get on our trail usually were sidetracked and eventually led to the "gold organization" and then went quite cold, for the SS were so pleased with this new source of income that they did not want to exert themselves in another direction.

I have already written that we watched the zugangs carefully, for one never knew what some newly arrived fellow might do, but our older inmates also sprang some surprises.

For instance, through the carelessness of one of our comrades, the too well-informed 161 [Bolesław Kuczbara], a typical schizophrenic, one day painted two honorary "Orders of the Garter" for Colonel 121 [Juliusz Gilewicz] and 59 [Henryk Bartosiewicz] for their work in the independence movement.

He spared me, thanks to the latter's intervention.

And with his "certificates" rolled into a tube he crossed the parade ground during lunch to show off his work in the hospital.

He could have been stopped by an SS man, or some kapo, interested in what he was carrying and he could have endangered his comrades, not to mention a wider group.

He showed it to Dr. 2 [Władysław Dering] saying about me that only I had my head screwed on, etc., etc., which is why he had not painted me a "certificate."

Dr. 2 [Władysław Dering], with the help of Dr. 102 [Rudolf Diem], managed to wrest the "certificates" from him and destroy them.

However, 161 [Bolesław Kuczbara] was clever, and one dark evening I was summoned from Block 22 by comrade 61 [Konstanty Piekarski] who led me to an SS man. It turned out to be 161 [Bolesław Kuczbara] dressed in an SS uniform and greatcoat. He managed to use them shortly thereafter in an escape.

Christmas came—the third in Auschwitz.

I was living on Block 22, together with the whole bekleidungswerkstätte [clothing workshop] kommando.

How very different this Christmas was from the previous ones.

The inmates, as usual, received parcels from home for Christmas with sweaters, but the authorities had finally permitted, in addition to clothes parcels, the first food parcels to reach Auschwitz.

Thanks to "Canada," there was no longer hunger in the camp.

The parcels also improved this state of affairs.

The news of major reverses for the German Army raised inmates' morale and improved everyone's state of mind dramatically.

This atmosphere was improved by news of an escape (30 Dec. '42),[53] organized by the arbeitsdiensts [work assignment leaders] Mietek and Otto, 161 [Bolesław Kuczbara] and a fourth partner.

The cheekily organized escape—made easier by the fact that arbeitsdiensts were able to move between the inner and outer security perimeters, and with the addition of 161's [Bolesław Kuczbara's] clever disguise as an SS man and involving an audacious departure in broad daylight on a

---

[53] They in fact escaped on the 29th. Translator's note.

horse-drawn cart outside the camp on a false pass, which the supposed SS man showed to a sentry from a distance—had the additional spice for all the camp inmates in that, on the basis of a discovered letter from Otto, the Lagerältester [Head Inmate] Bruno "inmate No. 1" and the camp brute, was locked up in the bunker by the authorities on New Year's Eve.

Bruno's enemy Otto had written in the letter—intentionally left in a coat on the cart, abandoned together with the horses, about a dozen or so kilometers from the camp—that it was a great shame that they could not take Bruno with them as agreed, for they were out of time and had to hurry and that Bruno could keep their joint stash of gold!

Known for their quick thinking, the authorities locked up the swine Bruno in the bunker where he stayed for three months. His conditions there were better than those of any other inmate. He was in a cell, but the camp was deprived of this thug forever, for he did not return to his former position but took the same one in Birkenau.

Meanwhile, the camp went wild with joy over Christmas, eating the parcels from our families and telling the latest Bruno joke...

Boxing matches and cultural evenings were held in the blocks. Ad hoc groups from the orchestra went around from block to block.

Everyone was so happy owing to the general situation, that older inmates shook their heads saying: "Well, well... there once was a camp called 'Auszwic' (Auschwitz), but it's gone... all that's left is its last syllable ... nothing but a 'witz.'"[54]

---

[54] This is a pun on the Polish word *wic* (meaning a joke, and pronounced "vits") which is the final syllable of the mock Polish word "Auszwic"—a Polish phonetic equivalent of Auschwitz. Translator's note.

Meanwhile, month by month the camp régime was becoming less harsh.

However, that in no way prevented us witnessing at that time some very painful scenes.

Returning from the tannery in our five "hundreds" just after New Year, I saw a small group of men and women standing in front of the crematorium (the old coal-fired one built right next to the camp). There were a dozen or so, young and old and of both sexes.

They were standing in front of the crematorium like a herd of cattle in front of an abattoir.

They knew why they were there...

Amongst them was a boy of about 10 who was looking for someone amongst our "hundreds" passing by... maybe a father... maybe a brother...

Approaching this group, one was afraid to meet the women's and children's eyes and see the contempt in them.

Here we were—strong, healthy men and five hundred of us, and there they were—soon to go to their deaths.

We were burning and seething inside, but no!—with some relief we saw as we passed that in their eyes was simply contempt—for death!

Going through the gate, we saw another little group up against the wall, their backs to the advancing columns and their hands raised.

Some would still endure interrogations before death, others would still go to the torments of Block 11 before the executioner Palitzsch did them the favor of a bullet in the back of the head and their bloody corpses were carried off in carts to the crematorium.

As we entered the gate the first little group of inmates was being herded into the crematorium.

Sometimes a bottle of gas was felt to be a waste for only a dozen or so people. They were stunned with rifle butts and pushed semi-conscious into the burning ovens.

From our block, Block 22, which was the closest to the crematorium, we sometimes heard, muffled by the walls, terrifying screams and the groans of people being tortured and quickly put to death.

Not everyone returning from work took our route.

Those who did not see the victims' faces went another way and were never free of the thought: maybe a mother... maybe a wife... maybe a daughter...

But a camp inmate's heart is hard. Half an hour later some were queuing to buy margarine or tobacco, ignoring the fact that they were standing next to a great heap of naked corpses piled one on top of the other, who had been "done in" that day with a phenol injection.

Sometimes someone stepped on an inert leg, already stiff and looked down: "Heavens, it's Stasio...what can you do? It was his turn today, maybe it'll be mine next week... "

And yet... the little boy's eyes looking at us searchingly... bothered me long into the night...

However, the "high spirits" in camp brought on by the Christmas atmosphere did lead to another painful episode.

Block 27, the uniform and clothing storeroom, was the workplace for the bekleidungskammer [clothing storeroom] kommando, composed almost entirely of Poles.

This was a "good" kommando, in other words it was an indoor job, with the additional bonus that its members—selflessly providing their friends with clothing, uniforms, blankets, shoes—also had an opportunity from inmates, well placed as block chiefs or workers in the abattoir or food storerooms, to obtain the means to make their lives more bearable by exchanging goods for food products.

In other words, it was a good billet, and with the help of 76 [Bernard Świerczyna] we managed to get a number of our fellows in there.

The feeling of a general lightening of tension in the camp and the absence in the camp of Bruno, who was locked up, led to some people taking security precautions too lightly.

Our fellows in Block 27 held a joint Christmas gathering at which 76 [Bernard Świerczyna] read aloud his own poem on a patriotic theme: a woman from Silesia had two sons, one was in the German Army, the other was an inmate in Auschwitz. While the inmate was escaping, the other son, a guard there, unbeknowingly shot his brother.

The poem was well written. The atmosphere was pleasant.

Result: the authorities decided that the Poles on Block 27 were having it too easy and the political department concluded that the Poles on Block 27 were organized.

On the 6th of January (of '43), SS men from the political department arrived at Block 27 during work. They formed up the whole kommando. They asked who was the colonel.

Colonel 24 [Karol Kumuniecki] initially refrained from replying. Whereupon Lachmann went up to him and pulled him out of the ranks (the whole business had already been planned by the political department).

Then they began to segregate people. They divided them into three groups. The Reichsdeutschen [German citizens] and Volksdeutschen formed one group, whom they left to continue working on the block. They divided all the remaining Poles into two groups, sending to the right a group of a dozen or so educated people, which included Colonel 24 [Karol Kumuniecki], Major 150 [Edward Gött-Getyński], Cavalry Captain 162 [Włodzimierz Koliński], Second Lieutenant 163 [Mieczysław Koliński] and lawyer 142 [name unknown];

and to the left those who in the eyes of the SS were less educated which included Major 85 [Zygmunt Bohdanowski] who was pretending to be a woodsman, Second Lieutenant 156 [Stanisław Wierzbicki] and a school pupil—my nephew 39 [Kazimierz Radwański].

They were kept on punishment parade for over a dozen hours in the frost.

Then the educated group was put in the bunker and the less educated were sent to the so-called Palitzsch *kiesgrube*.[55]

The first group was interrogated and tortured in the bunker, the object being to force them to admit that they were organized and to reveal what organization they represented.

The others, sent to be finished off at work in the frost, also appeared to be doomed. Yet a few of them managed to wangle themselves out of this kommando after a few months' of back-breaking work.

A couple of friends, 117 [Eugeniusz Zaturski] and 156 [Stanisław Wierzbicki], managed to do this a little too quickly.

They had been working together in the bekleidungskam-mer [clothing storeroom]. They had been living together in Block 3 in a separate room—the storeroom. Both fortunately managed that day (6 Jan. '43) not to be counted among the educated and thus avoided the bunker, and for the time being ended up in the Palitzsch kiesgrube.

Just after 156 [Stanisław Wierzbicki] had arrived from Warsaw a few months before, I had asked him how Warsaw was reacting to escapes from Auschwitz; he had replied that it was doing so in two ways: [Home Army] High Command was awarding the Virtuti Militari[56] (perhaps he thought that this might thus encourage me to escape), while the general

---

[55] A gravel pit in which members of the Penal Company worked. Translator's note.

[56] Poland's highest award for gallantry. Translator's note.

public, unaware that the policy of collective responsibility had been abandoned, considered escapes egoistic...

Now, when he himself was in a bind, he began to encourage me to escape with him.

I was not planning to leave at that stage, but he, poor fellow, never got to try...

Both of them were just a little too quick to land on their feet—they fell ill, after which they found themselves another, easier job.

They were not experienced "camp hands."

One day, when I thought that they were still in the hospital, I discovered that both of them had been shot (on 16 Feb. '43).

Lachmann had found them in another kommando and asked how they had got there; by the end of the day they were no longer alive.

Shortly thereafter, in March, they shot the whole educated group, which had been tortured in the bunker on account of the organization which a kapo, who had witnessed the unfortunate "joint Christmas gathering," had taken it into his head to imagine.

They had said nothing... GOOD MEN... these workmates of ours!

After the Poles had been thrown out of the bekleidungskammer [clothing storeroom] their places were taken by Ukrainians, who did not, however, suit the SS man running the kommando or the kapo as workers, and so some of the Poles began slowly to worm their way back in.

There was a break in supplies from this department.

However, other deliveries were working well. As Officer Cadet 90 [name unknown] calculated, just for Christmas alone (of '42) over 700 kg of meat products were brought in from the abattoir through the gate, despite the constant searches.

By the late autumn of '42, some unusual preparations were being made on Block 10.

All the inmates were removed, as well as some of the bunks. Wooden screens were installed on the windows outside, preventing anyone seeing in.

Some sort of equipment and apparatus was brought in.

Then some German professors started coming in the evening with students. Someone was brought in and work went on at night, then they either left in the morning or stayed for a few days.

I bumped into one of the professors during the day and he made a vile impression on me. His eyes were somehow loathsome.

For a time we could see nothing on this block and all we could do was speculate.

But they did need help from the pflegers from the camp hospital.

Initially they were cleaning, then they helped in other ways. They took two pflegers and happened to choose two who were in our organization.

Our lads eventually got into Block 10, which was perma- nently closed.

For a time that was of no help to us, since they were not let out of Block 10. However, one day one of them, 101 [Witold

Kosztowny], came to see me; he was terribly worried and said that he would not be able to stand it there for long and that he was reaching the end of his tether.

They were carrying out experiments there.

The doctors and medical students were carrying out experiments and, with so much human material available, they felt no sense of responsibility for it to anyone.

These guinea pigs' lives were in any event at the mercy of the deviants in the camp, so they would be killed in one way or another and would eventually end up as ashes.

So all sorts of sexual experiments were being carried out.

Men and women were being sterilized by a surgical procedure. Sexual organs of both sexes were exposed to some kind of radiation, which was supposed to kill their reproductive abilities. Subsequent tests were meant to show if the radiation had worked or not.

Sexual intercourse was not involved. There was a kommando of a few men who were to provide sperm which was immediately injected into the women.

The tests showed that after a few months the women whose organs had been subjected to radiation, again became pregnant. Then a far more powerful dose was employed, which burnt their sexual organs, and several dozen women died in terrible agony.

Women of all races were used in these experiments. Poles, Germans, Jews and later Gypsies were brought in from Birkenau. Several dozen young girls were brought from Greece and they died in these experiments. All of them, even after a successful experiment, were liquidated. Not a single man or woman emerged alive from Block 10.

Efforts were made to produce artificial male sperm, but they produced nothing but negative results.

Injecting the artificially produced substitute sperm brought on some kind of infection.

The women on whom these experiments were made were then finished off with phenol.

Seeing all this suffering, 101 [Witold Kosztowny] had for an "old hand" become exceptionally overwrought.

Another witness to what was going on in Block 10 was 57 [Edward Ciesielski] (both are alive and currently free).

Sometimes in the evening, there in Auschwitz, in our own crowd, we would say that it would be a miracle if anyone got out alive and that he would have difficulty getting on with people who had been living normal lives all this time.

For him, some of their concerns would simply be too insignificant.

He in his turn would not be understood by them...

But, if someone really did get out, then his duty would be to tell the world how real Poles were dying here.

Let him also tell how people, all people, were dying here... murdered by other people...

How odd this sounded in Christian terms: ... murdered by their fellow men, as was the case many centuries ago...

Therefore, I have already written that we had... taken such a wrong turning... but to... where? Where were we going... on this march of "progress"?

We received information through our channels from the political department that they were planning to send all the Poles (inmates) away for fear of incidents in the camp.

The authorities recognized that such a great concentration

of Poles—whose experiences alone had strengthened their resolve, turning them into individuals ready for anything—on Polish territory with local support outside, was a threat.

Should there be an airborne assault or an arms drop...

Neither we nor our Allies contemplated such a thing—or even conceived of it—so our enemies did.

For the time being they started to pull some of the Poles out of their kommandos, thus getting the kommandos used to doing without them.

Poles were always the best workers in every kommando.

The Germans said that they were as good as Germans, but that was not true.

They were ashamed to admit that the Poles were better.

At first, just those Poles whose appearance indicated that they had become "craftsmen" only in the camp were pulled out of the specialist kommandos.

About 150 of the 500 in the bekleidungswerkstätte [clothing workshop] were taken out.

Since I looked like an educated sort, I was among them. It was the 2nd of February (of '43).

For some reason this did not bother me at all. I felt that this change would not turn out badly for me.

The following day I was already in a basket-weaving kommando, taken on by my friends.

Indeed, there was now a custom that an "old number" was accepted into any kommando. He was now an elder in the prison world.

I worked there for only a day, not to the camp's benefit, but I did learn how to make shoes out of straw.

The next day I already had an excellent job in the newly formed "parcel" kommando.

Now that inmates were allowed to receive food parcels,

a growing number of truckloads of parcels was arriving daily. The authorities began to have their hands full. The allowance was one food parcel of up to 5 kg a week. On the assumption that it would be impossible to stem the flow of parcels, large parcels were banned, but no limit was put on the number of small parcels (up to 250 g each) that could be sent each week.

It then turned out that the authorities had blundered. An avalanche of small packages arrived every day.

Families, glad that they could help their loved ones in the camp, rushed off to send a small package every day, instead of one large parcel a week.

The result was the opposite of what the authorities had imagined. The volume of work involved in processing this vast number of deliveries and then distributing them to the inmates required a whole organization, a whole kommando into which I got myself.

We were allocated three small rooms on Block 3. One of the main rooms there was filled with packages.

The efficiency demanded of all camp kommandos required here too a major effort to clear the backlog, which was also in the inmates' interests, if it led to the speedy delivery of their packages.

The kommando operated in two shifts of 20 inmates each, and the parcel office worked around the clock.

I intentionally chose the night shift.

Given that parcels were being sorted around the clock, the main schreibstube [office] had to work at the same time as us day and night. A card was filled out for every package, and several hundred were sent every thirty minutes to the schreibstube, which put on the card in which block the given "number" (inmate) currently was living, or a cross was made to indicate that he was no longer alive. When the cards were returned, the parcels were sorted by block, shelves having been built, and the parcels whose cards were marked with a cross were put into a great pile in a corner of the room. There were a great number of packages addressed to fellows who had died.

In addition to those sent to inmates from Jewish, French and Czech transports, who for the most part had already been finished off, many Polish families sent packages too, unaware that the inmate had already died, since, as I have already mentioned, death notices were not always sent out, or the political department delayed sending them for months.

The SS men carried off the better parcels for those who had died, usually from France or Czechoslovakia and containing wine and fruit, by the basketload to their own mess.

The humbler parcels usually went to our kitchen, the *häftlingsküche*, where other food items, already picked over by the SS men, were brought in from "Canada." Everything was thrown into the cooking pots.

At this time we were eating sweet soups, which contained pieces of biscuits and cakes and seemingly smelt of perfume. In our room we once found what was left of some toilet soap, which had not quite dissolved.

The cooks would sometimes find at the bottom of the pots some gold item or even coins, which had been carefully hidden by their now-deceased owners in a piece of bread, a roll or a cake.

The men in the parcel office ate with a clear conscience the food packages of fellows who had died, usually handing out bread and soup to their hungrier mates on the block.

However, we had to be careful eating the packages of the dead. Only the *übermenschen* ["supermen"] were allowed to eat them; inmates were forbidden to do so on pain of death.

A search was once made of us inmates leaving work and seven häftlings were found to have white bread, butter and sugar, taken from dead men's packages, in their pockets. All seven were shot the same day.

An Austrian SS man ran the parcel department; really quite a decent sort for an SS man.

After a return to the previous system of a weekly 5 kg parcel, all sorts of packages would come, sometimes whole suitcases; the head of the parcel office did not demur and delivered them all to their addressees—he would make a fleeting inspection for lack of time, sometimes just cutting the string, but when a block chief, a German bastard, while distributing parcels in the block, took a handful of sweets from the parcel of a living inmate, the head of the parcel department reported him and the German block chief was shot the same day.

In this matter, there was justice...

I found another way to give my mates extra food.

I worked nights at the parcel office. The duty SS man would sit in front of me next to the warm stove and he would always doze off at about 2:00 a.m.

Behind me lay the great pile of parcels for dead fellows. There was also a separate small pile of better parcels ready to be eventually carted off to the SS mess.

Carrying, registering and moving parcels I took the smaller ones from this separate pile—the SS man was snoring away, I opened them, tore off the address, turned the paper inside out, wrapped it again, tied it up and wrote the address of one of my mates in the camp. I had the authority to repack poorly packed parcels. Some of them had their wrapping completely torn and were thus eminently suitable. Some I did not repack owing to the official stamps on them and simply stuck on a new address, written on another piece of paper. Such a parcel would take the normal route through the parcel office and reach the appropriate shelf.

The SS man had a comfortable job, since he slept at night and, relieved from duties during the day, he would take his bicycle to visit his wife who lived about 20 kilometers away. In other words, everyone was pleased with things as they stood. Over the course of a single night I tried to readdress eight parcels, two for each battalion, sometimes it was fewer and sometimes even more.

In the morning I would go around to see those fellows to whom I had sent "dead men's parcels" and warn them not to look surprised if they received an unexpected parcel.

Given my change of kommando I was moved to Block 6.

On the block and at work I met a couple of fellows whom I brought into our organization: Second Lieutenant 164 [Edmund Zabawski], Second Lieutenant 165 [Henryk Szklarz], and Platoon Sergeant 166 [name unknown].

Before the end of '42, Olek (Second Lieutenant 167 [Aleksander Bugajski]), was brought in on a transport from Kraków. I was told that he was a hero from the Montelupich Prison, that he had managed once to cheat death by escaping and that now he had two death sentences hanging over him, but because he was smart and somehow knew how to deal with the SS, he had been pretending to be a doctor and had apparently even been treating them, so he had managed to hide. But now they had brought him to Auschwitz, where they would certainly finish him off.

I got to know him and I liked his sense of humor.

I suggested to him a way out, which I had been preparing for myself.

The sewers.

Friends in the baubüro [construction site office] had brought me a map of the sewers clearly showing the best places to enter the system.

The German authorities usually only wised up when an inmate had used some particular escape route and then it was almost impossible to take the same route again.

Thus the proverb "For a Pole hindsight is the only accurate science"[57] should be applied to other nations too.

By giving Olek my escape route, I more or less ruled it out for myself, but I was not planning to leave just yet, while he was in grave danger.

I could use him to take out a report and I was counting on some fortunate circumstances for myself.

Meanwhile First Lieutenant 168 [Witold Wierusz] came to see me with a plan for escaping from his work kommando. He was a deputy kapo. The kapo was sick and so he had greater freedom of movement. He took his own kommando out on surveying work several kilometers from the camp.

I put him in touch with Second Lieutenant 167 [Aleksander Bugajski]; First Lieutenant 168's [Witold Wierusz's] plan suited him better, so 167 [Aleksander Bugajski] began to prepare to leave the camp by that route.

He transferred a little too suddenly from the parcel kommando where he was working to the surveyors' kommando where 168 [Witold Wierusz] worked.

In January (of '43)[58] seven of the lads got out by way of the SS kitchen during the night.

Seeing that hanging inmates caught escaping was no deterrent, the authorities tried a new approach. It was

---

[57] "Mądry Polak po szkodzie." Translator's note.

[58] Some sources place it in February 1943. Translator's note.

announced on every block that if an inmate escaped, his family would be put in the camp.

That hit us where it hurt.

No one wanted to endanger his family.

One day, after returning to camp we saw two women. One pleasant older woman and a pretty young one standing by a post with a sign, on which was written that our pal's ill-considered actions had condemned these two women to the camp.

This was by way of a reprisal for one of the fellows' escape.

Women were a sensitive issue with us.

At first the camp cursed the swine who had thus endangered his mother and fiancée while saving his own life, but then it turned out that the two women's numbers were around 30,000 whereas there were in fact over 50,000 women in the camp.

We concluded that they were two women who had been picked from the Rajsko camp and then told to stand for a few hours by the pole in our camp. An SS man stood nearby, preventing any kind of conversation.

Nevertheless, there was no certainty that they wouldn't bring in our families, and so a number of the lads decided not to attempt to escape.

No. 167 [Aleksander Bugajski] and 168 [Witold Wierusz] were preparing an attempt. Contact with Kraków had been made through the local population.

Clothes and female guides were to be waiting in several spots.

No. 167 [Aleksander Bugajski] also invited me to join him.

Discussing their method of escape with 168 [Witold Wierusz], I discovered that their plan had not been prepared in detail.

The inmates were to get the two SS men who went out surveying with them, and who despite orders went into the village for a vodka together, drunk and they would then tie them up. If they couldn't get them drunk, then they might have to do a "wet job."

At that, in the name of the organization, I formally protested.

In the name of the organization I could not agree to their escape plan, which could result in serious reprisals for the rest of the inmates.

The trick was to escape, but to do so in such a way that there were no major consequences for the rest of the camp.

They began to drug the SS men with a barbiturate.

From the krankenbau [hospital] they had managed to get hold of some barbiturate in powdered form to be administered in vodka—but when used on a few kapos, it did not produce decent results, since it failed to dissolve in the vodka and left a residue at the bottom of the glass.

They decided to administer the barbiturate in sweets.

Meanwhile nearly 20,000 gypsies were brought to Birkenau and left in a separate enclosure, for the time being with their whole families.

Then the men were taken away and finished off "Auschwitz style."

One day, some of the lads at Rajsko carried out an audacious escape, which we called "Diogenes's barrel."

On a dark, windy and rainy night, a dozen or so inmates got through the wire fence one by one by prizing apart the strands with poles and then inserting a normal barrel, minus its bottom, which had been used to carry food and which now served as insulation from the electric current and through which they crawled like cats through a muff.

A group of Gypsy women posing for German soldiers in a Warsaw park during 1940. Gypsies (Roma and Sinti) from Germany and throughout German-occupied territories were rounded up by the Germans, and killed or deported to Jewish ghettoes and to concentration camps.

**Gypsies interned at Belzec, one of the main Nazi German extermination camps along with Auschwitz-Birkenau, Treblinka, Sobibor, Majdanek and Chełmno.**

The authorities once again had to have gone wild and been beside themselves.

So many inconvenient witnesses to what was happening in Rajsko-Birkenau on the loose!

They decided to pull out every stop to catch the escapees. They brought in the Army to join the search and they searched for three days.

The camp was locked down, since there were no "posts," i.e., soldiers to escort the columns going to work.

The authorities took advantage of this lull to delouse the camp, which was accomplished in three days.

By coincidence, 167 [Aleksander Bugajski] and 168 [Witold Wierusz] were to have carried out their escape, which had been planned and agreed with an outside organization, the day after "Diogenes's barrel." Their inability to leave the camp made the escape out of the question. But there was more to come.

In the kommandos the supervisors and kapos, fearful of the authorities' rage, carried out searches of inmates. They checked their work, the roll and indeed anything with which someone else might find fault.

It was then that the supervisor and the kapo in the parcel department asked what had happened to Olek 167 [Aleksander Bugajski], who had been working there and who was no longer there; was he sick?

They ran off to the schreibstube [office] and discovered that Olek was now in another block and working in another kommando—and since he had transferred to another job and an outside one at that without informing them or getting a card from the arbeitsdienst [work assignment office], and since he had some serious business with the political department—they came to the conclusion that he must be planning an escape, so Olek was punished by a transfer to the Penal Company.

Just in case, I had been preparing an escape through the sewers for quite some time.

This was by no means easy. The network of sewers shown on the diagram from the baubüro [construction site office] ran in different directions, but for the most part consisted of pipes 40 to 60 cm in diameter. Only in three directions from the most convenient entry for me, near Block 12, were there branches with a 60 cm diameter on the vertical sections and 90 cm on the horizontal ones.

I tried once to get in and open the grate blocking entry into the sewers just beyond the manhole. But I was not the only one showing interest in this.

Some of the other lads were aware of this route too.

I reached an understanding with them; they were 110 [Andrzej Makowski-Gąsienica] and 118 [name unknown]. A couple of others also had their eye on the sewers.

The issue was who would make up his mind to use them.

When, before the most recent Christmas a group from the arbeitsdienst were to have got out, 61 [Konstanty Piekarski] was also burning to be away and I showed him this route, and possibly a couple of inmates might have used it on Christmas Eve, when predictably the guards' vigilance would be relaxed.

But on Christmas Eve itself, a second Christmas tree was put up right by the spot where they were to climb out, and the tree and the surrounding area were brightly lit.

When later I was working on the night shift in the parcel office there was a manhole nearby. It was then, at night, after donning some overalls on Block 3, that I twice scrambled into the stinking sewers.

In the manhole, the hinged grate which had once been

locked with padlocks, now broken and covered in silt, appeared from above to be locked.

The route now branched in three directions using wider pipes. One ran between Blocks 12 and 13, 22 and 23, then broke left and ran by the kitchen and then, beyond the final watchtower, near Block 28 it turned slightly right and came up beyond the railroad tracks.

This pipe was very long, about 800 meters. It had one great advantage, a safe exit, but it also had a great disadvantage: it was dreadfully silted up. I followed it for barely 60 m to see how easily one could move inside and I climbed out, completely exhausted.

It was an ideally dark night.

I was filthy; I washed and changed on Block 3. I must admit that I lost interest for some time.

Going the other direction, the sewer was dryer and it was easier to move along it; it was also much shorter.

It ran between Blocks 4 and 15, 5 and 16 and then continued straight as far as Blocks 10 and 21 and straight on.

It rose upwards—it had less water and waste matter from the blocks. But it came up two meters beyond a watchtower.

The slab covering the exit beyond the fence, even if prepared by colleagues during the day outside by the gravel pit, was difficult to raise at night without making a noise, and it was right by the soldiers in the watchtower.

The third branch remained, the shortest at about 40 meters, and an extension of the previous one.

It contained the most water. It ran between Blocks 1 and 12 and went under the wire between the administrative offices and a newly erected building. It came up on the road and was pretty visible, especially from the hauptwache [main gate guardhouse] in the light.

They had once put up a Christmas tree for us there. But now there would be no tree.

There was also the so-called underground "submarine" with a permanent crew, but I could not include it in my plans.[59]

I could now take the risk of escaping, but I continued to feel that this was not the right time for me to get out.

One evening, we came to the conclusion that a full-scale war was being waged against us.

We usually got our information from the political department, the Commandant's office and the hospital through SS men who were working for both sides, and would send it on to us through the Volksdeutschen and Reichsdeutschen working alongside us.

Some of the SS had formerly been NCOs in the Polish Army,[60] who clearly wanted us to know that, in the event of something happening, they would be with us and would even give us a key to the armory.

In fact we would not need to wait for their keys, since our lads in the locksmiths' shop had already made copies of all of them—and though the NCOs were two-faced and unpleasant people, even they had their uses, often warning us of the authorities' planned moves and always doing so accurately.

---

[59] Some sources claim that a few inmates had discovered a disused underground fuel tank, which they equipped with electricity and a well-concealed periscope! However, it is unclear to what use they put it and indeed whether or not the story is actually true. Otherwise, Pilecki's reference is obscure and, given Auschwitz's location, odd to say the least. Furthermore, there is supposedly no record or trace of such an installation at the camp today. Translator's note.

[60] These are likely to have been Volksdeutscher. Translator's note.

# 1943...

Apparently, Grabner no longer trusted his own people and tried to keep things hush-hush up to the last minute, with the list of those to be shipped out held a secret. He shared his decisions with Palitzsch.

A blocksperre [block lock-down] was held on the 7th of March.

The lists were sent over to the blocks and the blocks were suddenly locked. Inmates' numbers, exclusively Polish ones, were now called out and they were ordered to prepare for a transport.

Only the numbers of those whose cases had been wrapped up, or in whom the political department no longer had any interest, were read out.

The transports were to leave for other camps, which supposedly were very much better than Auschwitz.

We learned secretly that the first ones would go to the better camps; the later ones to the worse ones.

There was a mixed reaction on the blocks. Some were glad to be going to better camps and that they were not to be shot here. Others worried that they were not going, that their cases were still open and that they might be shot. Meanwhile, others were very unhappy to be leaving, for here they had got a good job after years' of hard work, and there they would again have to be a zugang, with only the fittest surviving, and they might not make it to the top again.

However, the general feeling was that going was a good thing, for nowhere else could there be a hellhole like this one.

In any case, no one asked us.

Had it been daytime and the blocks open, we could have done something about it.

Someone wanting to remain could "fall sick," but nothing could be done at night.

My number was read out early on the first night (7th–8th).

We were ordered to get our things and move to Block 12, now deliberately quite empty, and so off we went with our stuff.

Block 19 was similarly filled and numbers were read out there three evenings in a row (the 7th, 8th and 9th of March); altogether about 6,000.

We were also locked up in Blocks 12 and 19, and could communicate only through the windows.

Dr. 2 [Władysław Dering] came to the stairwell and through the glass in the door indicated that if I wanted to stay, I would have to be sick.

Given my underground work and my status in the inmates' work world, this was worth consideration.

On the 10th of March (of '43) they had us out by 6:00 a.m. in fives, in columns, on the "Red Alley."

Here German military doctors conducted a medical examination of those inmates who had been selected by the political department to be shipped out.

I was standing near Colonel 11 [Tadeusz Reklewski] and Kazio 39 [Pilecki's nephew, Kazimierz Radwański].

My brain was turning over feverishly, working out who was going and who was staying behind.

A tightly knit group of lads with whom I had been working was to leave. My instinct was to go with them.

The medical commission was amazed at the health and excellent physical condition of the Polish inmates, for the most part well fed (with the exception of the newly arrived zugangs), shaking their heads and saying: "Where have these people been?"

In addition to "Canada" and parcels, to a certain extent our organization deserved credit for this—now the results were there for all to see...

But my responsibility was the continuity of our work here... Who would I be with?... I began to discuss the issue with some of the other fellows...

Colonel 11 [Tadeusz Reklewski] and Kazio 39 [Pilecki's nephew, Kazimierz Radwański] were glad to be going. They had been assigned to Buchenwald, supposedly one of the better camps.

My friend Colonel 11 [Tadeusz Reklewski] felt that, despite everything, my duty was to stay on in this hellhole.

I had plenty of time to think it over. The examinations were going very slowly.

We stood the whole day and part of the night.

With Colonel 11 [Tadeusz Reklewski] and Second Lieutenant 61 [Konstanty Piekarski] we reached the head of the line about 2:00 a.m.

Long before, I had decided to try to stay in Auschwitz.

From 169 [Stanisław Barański], who was able to move about freely, I had got a truss from the krankenbau, even though I did not have a hernia.

By 2:00 a.m. the commission was tired.

Colonel 11 [Tadeusz Reklewski], over a dozen years older than me and a weakling in comparison, was passed as fit for work by the commission and put on the transport.

But when I stood naked before the commission with my truss over my nonexistent hernia, the doctors waved me on saying: "Weg! [Move along!] We don't need chaps like him!" I was not accepted for the transport.

I marched off to Block 12 and after reporting in with my card excusing me from the transport, I was immediately sent off to Block 6 back to my own bunk, and the following day I went back to my normal job in the parcel office.

On the 11th of March, after rejecting those unfit for work, or those who tried to pretend that they were, they shipped out five thousand healthy Poles (with a few others to increase the numbers).

The main schreibstube [office] sent over to the parcel office a detailed list with the numbers of those inmates who had been shipped out, so as to be able to forward any food parcels coming for them; we were therefore able accurately to confirm that these five thousand Poles had been sent in five different directions, more or less a thousand to each of the following camps: Buchenwald, Neuengamme, Flossenbürg, Gross-Rosen and Sachsenhausen.

Our organization's basic leadership had managed to wriggle out of this transport—and so our work went on.

A week later, on the first Sunday, we again received a surprise.

In order to avoid a last-minute rush of work just before a transport, it was decided to do it calmly ahead of time.

That day, all the remaining Poles on every block had to present themselves to a medical commission, which put next to each inmate's number the letters A or U,[61] indicating his category as "fit" or "unfit" for work.

This was sprung on us, preventing any of the dodges hitherto used.

I wondered what to do about it. To get an "A" meant leaving on the next transport and to worse camps, since I had not gone to the better ones.

Although we were told that those unfit for work would be sent to Dachau where they would be in the hospital and so on,

---

[61] Probably abbreviations for *arbeitsfähig* (fit for work) and *arbeitsunfähig* (unfit for work). Translator's note.

knowing the authorities at the time, I felt getting a "U" would probably lead to "the gas and the chimney."

I had to find a way out.

In any event I decided against the truss. The medical commission to which I presented myself, without a closer examination, sent me on my way putting the letter "A" by my number on the list.

I looked in good shape.

The German military doctors, looking at the Poles' fine physiques, once again expressed surprise saying loudly: "We could field a fine regiment with men like these!"

Now that I was goods to be shipped out, I had to come up with something, for I didn't want to go to a "worse" camp, given that I had not gone to a "better" one.

SS men heading kommandos with specific duties very willingly requested Polish craftsmen. They always preferred to work with the Poles, who were the best workers. However, owing to the authorities' directives at this time, they could not be seen to be doing this too obviously.

It was also hard to pretend to be a craftsman in the parcel office. Yet somehow, with the help of Dr. 2 [Władysław Dering] and 149 [name unknown], I was requested by the head of the parcel office among an overall number of five who were considered essential workers.

Nor was I included in a new transport which left in two waves (on the 11th and 12th of April). Both to Mauthausen.

They shipped out 2,500 Poles.

Altogether then, in March and April (of '43) they shipped out 7,500 fit Poles.

It was then that I decided that to stay on was becoming too difficult.

After more than two and a half years I would have to start all over again, with "new boys."

On the morning of the 13th of April I went to the cellar in Block 17, where Captain 159 [Stanisław Machowski] (from HQ in Warsaw) was working in a separate little room. I knew him by sight; he had been pointed out to me several times by Second Lieutenant Stasiek 156 [Stanisław Wierzbicki] (who had been shot) and Major 85 [Zygmunt Bohdanowski], but I had not yet spoken to him, for he had been put in the care of our member 138 [name unknown], and we spoke for the first time.

I told him: "I have been inside for two years and seven months. I have had a job to do here. Lately I have had no instructions. Now the Germans have shipped out our best people with whom I've been working. I would have to start from scratch. I can see no further point in staying here. Therefore, I'm going to leave."

Captain 159 [Stanisław Machowski] looked at me in some surprise and said: "Yes. I can see that, but can one pick and choose when one wants to come to Auschwitz and when one wants to leave?" I replied: "One can."

From that moment on all my energies were directed at finding the best way to escape.

I then spoke to Major 85 [Zygmunt Bohdanowski], who at the time was in the hospital with Dr. 2 [Władysław Dering]; supposedly ill, he was resting there and had thus been able to avoid the transports, for they had not been taking the sick for the time being. He was an "A," but before getting out I managed to fix him up with a job in the parcel office.

I went to see him as someone who knew the Auschwitz/Oświęcim area well, asking which way he would go and which direction he recommended. Zygmunt looked at me in disbelief saying: "If anyone else had said that, I would have thought he was kidding, but since it's you, I'm sure you'll get out. I'd head for Trzebinia and Chrzanów."

I pulled out from under my jacket a 1:100,000 map of the Oświęcim [Auschwitz] area, which I had got from 76 [Bernard Świerczyna], and showed it to him.

I intended to head for Kęty.[62]

We said goodbye warmly. I turned over to him, "Bohdan"— Major 85 [Zygmunt Bohdanowski], responsibility for everything, should it come to a fight.

I went to see my friend 59 [Henryk Bartosiewicz] and turned over to him the organizational side of things, relying too on the naturally brave Colonel 121 [Juliusz Gilewicz], who was the organization's official head and a friend of 59 [Henryk Bartosiewicz].

Now it was time to go... really go...

There is always a difference between saying you will do something and actually doing it. A long time before, many years before, I had worked on myself to be able to fuse the two.

But above all I was a believer, and I believed that if God wanted to help me, I would definitely make it...

There was also another reason hastening my decision. I learnt through Dr. 2 [Władysław Dering] from zugangs who had come from the Pawiak that 161 [Bolesław Kuczbara], who had escaped from Auschwitz with the "arbeitsdiensts," had been picked up in Warsaw and was now being held in the Pawiak.

Having little confidence in the man—and because of rumors about his past and because of his unscrupulous work here collecting gold from dead people's crowns and because of the business with the "decorations" which he had painted in honor of Colonel 121's [Juliusz Gilewicz's] and 59's [Henryk Bartosiewicz's] work for us—I felt that to save his own life,

---

[62] That would have been due south, and 180 degrees away from the northerly route which Bohdanowski recommended. Translator's note.

he might agree to cooperate with the Germans and start spilling the beans.

I spoke to Dr. 2 [Władysław Dering], 59 [Henryk Bartosiewicz] and 106 [name unknown] about this, and felt that those whom he knew to be the organization's leadership needed to get out.

In mid-March my colleague and friend 164 [Edmund Zabawski] had informed me that one of our colleagues, whom I knew by sight, Jasiek 170 [Jan Redzej], was planning to get out of the camp and that if I wanted to send out a report, he could take it.

I got to know Jasiek and took an immediate liking to him.

I liked the constant smile on his mug, his broad shoulders and his direct manner. In a word, a first-rate fellow.

I told him about the possibility of using the sewers as a last-ditch approach and asked him how he was planning to get out.

He replied that going into town on a dray to get bread from the bakery, he had often seen the civilian bakers' bicycles standing by the bakery. If there was no other way, he'd grab a bike and just "go for it."

I was against this. After a while he came to see me with the news that if we could get into the bakery, there was a huge, heavy, studded door with two leaves which could be opened.

In order to have a good look at this door, with the permission of the kapo of his own *brotabladungskommando* [bread-unloading kommando], Jasiek transferred for a few days to the bakery, supposedly to fill up on bread.

At the time Jasiek weighed 96 kg.[63] The kapo liked him as an experienced and cheerful worker.

It was the end of March.

After five days in the bakery, Jasiek returned downhearted. The work at the bakery was very hard.

Over the course of five days Jasiek had sweated off 6 kg. He now weighed only 90 kg. But worse than that, he had come to the conclusion that the door could not be opened... A mighty lock in one of the leaves which, when locked with a key, slid a large pin into the other leaf, might not be a problem if the bolts (four in all) on both leaves were slid back, but there was also an outside hook which held the leaves together when the door was closed.

The hard work and that hook had discouraged Jaś.

So for a time we did not talk about the bakery, focusing instead on the sewers.

Meanwhile two innovations were introduced into the camp.

During the first years we had had roll call three times a day. In addition to the other brutal, though primitive, ways of finishing us off, the roll calls with the extended punishment parades were also a quiet way of finishing us off.

Then there was a change in the murder methods... to more civilized ones...by which thousands were killed daily by gas and phenol; the daily number brought in for gassing reached 8,000.

As part of this "cultural" improvement, having abandoned finishing off people with clubs, it was decided that this quiet way of finishing off people by keeping them on punishment parades showed modest results compared to the equally quiet way of finishing off people with gas, and was ludicrous; so in 1942 the midday roll call was abolished.

---

[63] Approximately 211 lbs. Translator's note.

After that there were two roll calls. On Sundays, as before, there was a single roll call at 10:30 a.m.

Now (in the spring of '43) the innovation was the abolition of another roll call, the morning one, and the introduction for the häftlings of civilian clothes, of which there were thousands left behind by people who had been gassed.

An inmate working inside the camp within the wire was allowed to wear civilian clothing with a red stripe painted in oil paint across the shoulders and around the waist on the jacket, and up the trouser legs.

No one who worked outside and left the camp enclosure was allowed to wear civilian clothing, except kapos and unterkapos.

In any event, there was a huge difference between now and then.

The lads now slept on beds (bunks). They slept under fluffy blankets, taken from "Canada" and which had belonged to people from Holland who had been gassed. Those who remained in camp, in the morning donned fine woollen civilian clothing, spoilt rather by the bright stripes, and went off to work like office workers, without having to stand for roll call.

The lunch break was not disturbed by any roll call or standing at attention.

There was just the evening roll call, which by now was not stressful. We were not out there long. Even on the day when it was discovered that three of the lads had got away from the hospital there was no punishment parade. They simply conducted a thorough search for the escapees, not wanting these witnesses roaming free.

A great effort was made to improve radically Auschwitz's dreadful reputation, which had already spread.

An announcement was made that the camp would be

changed from a "concentration" camp to an *arbeitslager* [labor camp]—in any event there were no more beatings.

At least that is how it was for us in the stammlager [main camp].

I compared camp impressions from '40 and '41—and found it hard to believe that things had been like that, within the same walls and with some of the same people.

I remembered the winter of '40–'41 when an SS man, in the presence of more than a dozen of us, had suddenly flown into a rage and killed two inmates and then, seeing our eyes fixed on him, had turned to us and suddenly, as if needing to justify himself, spat out quickly: "Das ist ein Vernichtungslager! [This is a death camp!]"

Now every effort was made to erase any suggestion, even in people's minds, that things could have been like that . . .

It would be interesting to see how they could erase memories of the gas chambers and the by-now six crematoria . . .

There was no change in the attitude towards escapees who had been caught . . .

Two more were hanged on the parade ground as a deterrent to any would-be imitators.

Then Jaś and I gave each other a look saying: "Alright. Both sides can play at this. We'll try to get out and let them try to catch us."

When Jasiek had recovered somewhat from his trial period in the bakery, I asked him whether the "damned hook" on the door could not be opened. Jasiek explained that it probably could be done, since it was held by a screw and nut, with the nut on the inside of the door.

Over the next few days Jasiek, bringing in bread from the bakery on the dray, made imprints in fresh bread of the nut and the key to the padlock on the window in the bakery room where the freshly baked bread was stacked.

Using this imprint, a friend of Jasiek's, a locksmith at Industriehof I, made a wrench for the nut. My former colleague from the TAP, Warrant Officer 28 [Szczepan Rzeczkowski], made a key to the padlock in the same shop. Both were ready within the day.

Jasiek was discreetly able to check if they fitted.

The key to the padlock had been made just in case, for, as Jasiek said, it was next to impossible to open the window even a little.

But from making these implements, it was still a long way to getting out.

It was barely a small step on the road towards an escape.

First of all, both of us needed to be in the bakery, and as far as I was concerned, I could really only turn up there for a very short time, for it would be immediately apparent that I was not a baker, and the physical job of carrying the flour sacks had already been grabbed and was zealously guarded by fellows pretending to be bakers.

Furthermore, even if I could get into the bakery, I could spend only a short period of time there, for the authorities in the parcel office could not become aware of it, since I had only recently been considered indispensable there and specifically requested.

A unilateral change of kommando made the authorities suspect an escape attempt, especially if it involved a move from such a good kommando as the parcel office, and one could quickly end up in the Penal Company, as had Olek 167 [Aleksander Bugajski].

As I weighed the obstacles to be overcome on the bakery route, I kept thinking of the sewers which, however, also had their complications... and I kept coming back to the bakery.

Finally, Jasiek and I reached a firm conclusion to go out

through the bakery. To overcome all the obstacles, get in on the night shift and, as far as I was concerned, for just a single night.

All that remained was... to carry it out!

Saying nothing for the time being even to Jasiek, I went to see 92 [Wacław Weszke], whose friend had taken over as arbeitsdienst [work assignment leader] from Mietek. Through him, saying nothing of the reason for this move, I got Jaś transferred to the bakery by telling him that Jaś was really a baker by trade and that he was doing the rounds of the kommandos for no real reason, which was really beneath an "old number's" dignity...

The following day Jasiek ran up to me with the news that out of the blue he had received a card for the bakery, that his kapo was upset to lose him and was unhappy, but had reconciled himself to it. I told Jasiek where the card had come from and he went off to the bakery. Within a couple of days he was an "old hand" at baking.

The bakery kapo, a Czech whom Jasiek had impressed with his sense of humor and strength, made him his deputy, an unterkapo, and willingly agreed to take the day shift, while Jasiek with a kommando of inmates did nights.

There were only a few days left until Easter.

We decided to take advantage of Easter when, under the influence of vodka, things were a little more relaxed and the SS, the kapos and all the camp authorities were less vigilant.

There had been a time when Fritzsch [Karl Fritzsch] or Aumeier [Hans Aumeier] would have sent a kapo to the bunker if they had smelled of vodka, but times had changed.

Drinking vodka was still officially forbidden, on pain of the bunker. Yet sex with women was forbidden on pain not only of the bunker but of the Penal Company, but here too things were more relaxed.

Not only the SS men, but häftlings had sex with German women in SS uniforms, who were the "authorities" in the women's camp and were often recruited from streetwalkers; and inmates returning from work in their columns often exchanged knowing glances with these SS women.

A certain percentage of these liaisons were discovered and a great many inmates, usually kapos or block chiefs, were in the bunker, and only avoided the Penal Company owing to their status with the authorities.

Block chief 171 [name unknown] was also among those in the bunker for similar offenses.

Now that the camp régime was less strict, inmates began relationships with women.

Couples formed, bringing romantic baggage.

Nor were the SS men innocent in this area. For some months now we had seen a formerly unknown sight: SS men being led out of our bunker on Block 11, without their belts, for a half-hour exercise period twice a day. The SS men had been locked up for having had sex with a woman.

Strictly speaking, for an offense like that, such as sex with a woman who was an "untermensch" ["subhuman"], the SS men faced a much stiffer penalty—a special penal prison for the SS, to which much later Palitzsch himself would be sentenced for many years for a relationship with a Jewish girl, Katti.

But that was later. For the time being, the milder form of punishment in the bunker was applied, or they even walked away scot-free. For here too there was a code of silence, and SS men picking up girls in Rajsko was kept an inside secret. If only because the Commandant himself too had sins on his conscience. "Gold lust" had consumed him. Working very discreetly with Erik in the tannery, he collected gold, precious stones and valuables; had he imposed stiffer penalties on his men, he could have expected revenge on the part of a punished SS man in the form of a denunciation. Therefore, he made an effort to turn a blind eye to his subordinates' infractions.

However, if a häftling had "gold lust," it always ended in his death, for after an interrogation in the bunker and a search of the places he had indicated, the SS usually finished off the häftling in order to get rid of a witness to how much gold they had taken from him.

Everyone died, irrespective of their nationality.

In this way two German bastards also died: Block 22 chief [Reinhard Weinhold] and Kapo Walter [Walterscheid].

Second Lieutenant 164 [Edmund Zabawski] wanted to join us "going home," but he decided against, fearing for his family. He gave us his family's address in the town of Z [Bochnia]. He wrote discreetly saying that they could expect a visit from a friend of his and he gave us the password agreed with his family, as well as an underground contact in Z [Bochnia].

In the parcel office I transferred from the night to the day shift.

Easter fell on the 25th of April (in '43).

The weather was sunny and fine. Spring, with the grass shooting up and the buds on the trees turning into leaves and flowers, was when one always wanted the most to be free again.

In the morning of Holy Saturday, the 24th of April, I started complaining of a headache in the parcel office. Who knew that my head never hurt?

In the afternoon, I did not return to work. On the block I also complained of pains in my joints and calves.

The block chief, a rather placid German and always polite

towards workers in the parcel office, hearing what I was on purpose loudly telling the orderly about these symptomatic pains, said worriedly: "Du hast Fleckfieber. Gehe schnell nach Krankenbau! [You have typhus. Get off at once to the hospital!]."[64] Pretending to be unwilling to go to the hospital, I went off reluctantly.

Near the hospital I sought out Edek 57 [Edward Ciesielski]. I told him that I needed to be in the hospital that same day, preferably in the typhus block, where he worked in the storeroom, but on the condition that he would arrange for me to enter (be admitted) informally and to be discharged a few days later.

Edek did not think long. He never did things by halves.

By the afternoon of Holy Saturday the dispensary had stopped working. Edek, using his own methods, completed all the formalities to admit me by way of the dispensary (on Block 28) to the typhus block and, still taking advantage of the lack of staff on Holy Saturday, took me to the hospital himself.

There, avoiding the usual route (a bath and turning in one's personal belongings), he led me to a small private room on the ground floor, where I undressed, handing my things over to a friend of Edek's. He then ushered me into a ground-floor ward run by 172 [Janusz Młynarski].

A bed was found for me and Edek entrusted me to 172 [Janusz Młynarski], who remembered me from my earlier brush with typhus.

He now reckoned that this was a second bout, although I did not look ill at all; he just shook his head and asked neither me nor Edek any indiscreet questions.

---

[64] More correctly: "Du hast Fleckfieber. Gehe schnell zum Krankenbau!" Translator's note.

I gratefully squeezed Edek's hand and told him, as he was leaving, that I had to get out in two days' time.

The bakery did not work on Easter Sunday, but would start up on the following day, Monday.

I calculated that I needed to get out and try to get to work on a start-up day like that, when my arrival (a psychological touch this) would be less obvious and easier to accept by people thinking that some change in the bakery's staffing had been made over the holiday.

I spent Saturday night in a ward on Block 20 and had a beautiful dream: I dash into some kind of shed where a magnificent horse is standing, and had I not been a cavalryman and not known the correct terms for horses' coat colors, I would have said it was as white as milk. I quickly throw a saddle on the horse which is prancing on its tether. Someone hurries in with a saddle blanket. I tell him not to interrupt me; I don't have time. I tighten the girth with my teeth (a habit of mine from 1919–1920),[65] leap into the saddle and ride out of the shed on the magnificent horse. Oh how I longed for that horse...

Easter Sunday. I am still lying on my bed in Block 20.

Edek pops in from time to time see if I need anything.

By the afternoon I had decided to have a chat with Edek.

Edek had been brought here as a boy and after two years in Auschwitz, he was turning twenty.

He had been picked up with a pistol in his pocket. He thought that they might not release him from Auschwitz and often said to me: "Mr. Tomek, Sir, I'm counting on you..."

So, on Sunday afternoon, I said to him: "Edek, let's not beat about the bush, I'm getting out. Since you got me into the

---

[65] The Polish–Bolshevik War. Translator's note.

hospital avoiding the usual formalities and you're going to throw me out tomorrow—once again fixing it informally so that I won't have to go through quarantine and, contrary to the rules, not back to my "home" Block 6 from which I came, but to Block 15—whom are they going to nab after I escape? You. Therefore, I suggest you join me."

Edek considered for barely a minute or two. He didn't even ask how. He decided that we would go together.

When, shortly afterwards, Jasiek came to the window and told me that I had to get out the next day and be on Block 15, I told him that everything was fine, but that Edek was coming too.

Janek clutched his head, but when he learned that Edek, whom he did not know, was a first-rate chap, his usual cheerful expression returned and he said: "Well, that's that, then."

That evening Edek stormed at the block chief that Poles were no longer welcome there, that he was fed up and would go "back to the camp" the next day. The block chief, a German, liked Edek and tried to calm him down saying that he saw no reason why he should abandon a good job as a storeman and that he wouldn't let him go, for what would be the point of Edek kicking around in some other job when here he did not have a great deal to do and as much food as he wanted? However, Edek would not be persuaded. He continued to maintain that he would not remain, for he was treated badly as a Pole and so on and so on.

The block chief finally lost his temper and told him: "Then go where you want, you idiot!"

Echoes of this reached the ward where I was lying. For several hours orderlies and pflegers from the whole block kept running up to 172 [Janusz Młynarski] asking each other what had come over Edek. He's giving up such a great job.

Since they saw that Edek had been coming to me, they asked me whether he had told me why he was leaving the block. I replied that he was obviously an impetuous young man.

I spent Sunday night in the same bed and again dreamt of horses.

I dreamt that a cart on which a number of us were sitting was harnessed to a pair of horses, but there were three other horses ahead of them harnessed abreast. The horses were moving briskly. The cart suddenly ran into heavy mud. The horses had trouble making any headway with the cart, but they succeeded in pulling it onto a dry road and then it went quickly on its way.

On the morning of Easter Monday, Edek brought me a *zettel* (card) transferring me to Block 15. He also had one for himself for Block 15. Our colleague 173 [Władysław Fejkiel] had helped Edek to get these cards filled out.

I got up, put on my clothes which were lying in the small room nearby, and went off with Edek to Block 15.

Here we went to the block schreibstube [office] to report to the block chief, a German. The atmosphere here was festive. The block chief, clearly having had a few vodkas, was energetically playing cards with the kapos.

We stood at attention and reported efficiently and by the book our transfer to this block. The supervisor said in German: "Clearly 'old numbers.' What a pleasure to hear them report in," and beamed. But then he suddenly frowned: "Why have you come to my block?"

"We're bakers."

"Bakers, eh? Okay," said the chief glancing simultaneously at his papers, "does the bakery kapo know about this?"

"Jawohl! We've already spoken to the kapo; he's taking us on."

We had not seen the bakery kapo at all, but since we had chosen to deceive everyone in authority, we needed to press on.

"Alright, hand over your zettels and go to the room."

We handed over the cards transferring us from Block 20 to Block 15 and went off the bakers' room.

Jasiek was already waiting for us in the room, but he intentionally did not come up to us at once.

We stood before the kapo and told him that we were bakers, that we knew how to operate an automated bakery (which they were about to set up) and that, as bakers, we had been transferred to Block 15 where the block chief knew us (in truth, he had met us only a moment before), that we were "old numbers" and that we would not let his kommando down.

The kapo, sitting at the table, was clearly surprised and uncertain, but before he could come to a decision, Jasiek began whispering to him and smiling. The kapo smiled too, but continued to say nothing. (Later Jasiek told us that he had spoken more or less as follows to the kapo: "Kapo, here's a couple of chumps who've been taken in; they think that they'll fill up on bread in the bakery and that we have an easy job. Let me have them on the night shift and I'll show them what's what," he showed a huge fist, "so that one night in the bakery will be enough for them.")

Meanwhile, to mark our new friendship, we handed over to the kapo an apple, sugar and some jam, which I had from a parcel received from home.

The kapo smiled at Jasiek, then looked at the apple and the sugar. Maybe he was sizing us up as a function of the parcels we might be able to give him in the future. Then he looked at us and finally said:

"Alright then, let's see what sort of bakers you are."

The bell for roll call which, given that this was a holiday, was held before 11:00 a.m., cut short any further conversation with the kapo and put off an intimate conversation with Jasiek.

The roll call passed off without incident or confusion. For the time being the numbers tallied.

Standing there in my rank I thought that if everything went as planned, then this would be my last roll call in Auschwitz. I reckoned that I had had about 2,500 of them.

And what a wide range of them; different years, different blocks.

Yes, the camp régime was continually becoming milder...

After roll call, the three of us gathered on top bunks in the bakers' room and talked loudly about food parcels, and this and that, since unknown häftlings were sitting all around us. However, from time to time we did discuss the matter which for us was critical.

Jasiek, who immediately got on famously with Edek, pretended that he was interested in us because of our Easter parcels.

The idea was to go to the bakery that very night, as our plan to deceive the authorities wouldn't stand up for long. Moreover, I had to be invisible to my friends in Block 6 and the workers at the parcel office, since news from them that I had been seen in camp in full health would certainly have attracted the attention of the kapo and the head of the parcel department, which could have led to me sharing Olek's fate.

It was still to be expected that the bakery kapo would mention us to the block chief and that it would emerge that neither of them knew us. Therefore, we had to move fast and take care of every problem.

Eight bakers went to the bakery for the night shift.

It had been established that eight was the number needed in the bakery at night. That was what had been entered in the blockführerstube [SS guardroom] at the gate and it could not be changed. In any case, we could not change it.

The night shift consisted of inmates who had no intention of giving up their spot for anyone.

On the plus side was the fact that Jasiek was already on that shift, but two other slots had to be found. The trickiest bit would be to convince two bakers, without arousing suspicion, not to go work that night and let us take their places.

They were suspicious and afraid that we wanted to take their jobs. Who knows, maybe we were good bakers (we had not wanted to pretend that we weren't), and the kapo would kick them out of the bakery and bring us on full-time in their place. We argued that the automated bakery was about to be set up and that everyone would be needed.

That we were "old numbers" who knew how to find ourselves another spot, especially if they were telling us that this was not so great and that the work was hard, we'd go just the once, we'd see what the work was like and if we didn't want to go again, we'd find ourselves another spot.

It's difficult to be specific here about all the arguments and methods we used, at the same time we had to pretend that we didn't care all that much while pushing forward the sugar, the gingerbread, the apples. We gave out all the parcels we had, with the exception of a small jar of honey, which I had got from home.

It was hard work.

We had long before decided that we could not return from the bakery, since first of all I would be sent to the Penal Company (for changing kommando without permission), then it would be apparent in the bakery that we were not bakers, we would never again be taken on to work there, and the kapo would kick us off the kommando.

But in order not to be able to come back, one first had to get out.

And now there was no space on the night shift.

About three in the afternoon, one of the bakers finally agreed to give up his place just for the one night, but we still needed another place.

Meanwhile I had been running around to friends for various items. I went around very carefully to Block 6 for some essential things, supposedly for Platoon Sergeant 40 [Tadeusz Szydlik] (Block 18a) who was sick and who knew of my plan. There I changed my boots twice.

I went over to First Lieutenant 76 [Bernard Świerczyna] (Block 27), who gave me some warm underwear for the journey, and for me and Edek navy-blue ski pants which we put on under our clothes.

My friend 101 [Witold Kosztowny] (Block 28) gave me a navy-blue windbreaker for the journey.

We were running out of time and there was still room for only one of us in the bakery.

Running with a pair of high boots which, after trying them on, were unsuitable because they were uncomfortable, I almost bumped into the Lagerältester [Head Inmate]. I left them in the corridor of Block 25 by the block chief 80's [Alfred Włodarczyk's] door, and, for lack of time, did not go in to explain. Rushing out of Block 25 I bumped into Captain 11—,[66] whom I bid a warm farewell without any explanation.

---

[66] It is unclear to whom Pilecki is referring, since the number is cut off at the edge of the page after the first two digits (11). Indeed, it could not have been 11, who was a Colonel, Tadeusz Reklewski, and who, in any event, had been transported to another camp in Germany a month earlier. It could have been Captain 114 [Tadeusz Paolone]. Translator's note.

I partially changed on Block 22 in the presence of Colonel 122 [Teofil Dziama], Captain 60 [Stanisław Kazuba] and 92 [Wacław Weszke]. Watching from a top bunk as I hastily put on the windbreaker and ski pants under my camp "stripes," they worriedly shook their heads and Captain 60 [Stanisław Kazuba] amusingly said his favorite phrase: "Errrr, I dunno about this!!"

I then said goodbye to my friend 59 [Henryk Bartosiewicz], who gave me a few dollars and German marks for the journey.

I made the rest of my preparations for the journey on the top bunk of my friend First Lieutenant 98 [name unknown]; Officer Cadet 99 [name unknown] was right there, but sleeping soundly and I did not want to wake him.

On Block 15 it was some minutes past 17:00 when we finally found a baker who agreed to give up his spot—whether because he wanted to have a couple of "old numbers," rich inmates, as future friends, or because he just wanted to rest that night—and who took us at our word that we were not pulling the wool over his eyes and would not take his job.

By 18:00 we were ready.

Jasiek put on some civvies that I had managed to wangle for him some time before from First Lieutenant 76 [Bernard Świerczyna] who, as an unterkapo, was allowed to go to work outside the camp in civilian clothes.

He had wide bright stripes painted on his shoulders and around his waist with red paint (to prevent a häftling escaping, he was visible at a distance).

Obviously, no one knew that 118 [name unknown] had painted those stripes not with varnish but with water-soluble paint.

At 18:20, the SS man on the gate called out in a carrying voice: "Bäckerei! [Bakery!]"

On this signal all of us on the bakery night shift ran out of Block 15 and rushed over to the gate.

It was a sunny day. The camp had the day off. Inmates were taking a walk. Running from the block to the gate I came across a few fellows who stared at me in surprise, wondering where I was off to with the bakers, since I had such a good job in the parcel office.

I recognized First Lieutenant 20 [Jan Kupiec] and Second Lieutenant 174 [Jan Olszowski], but I wasn't bothered—they were my friends.

In front of the gate we lined up in two ranks, ready to march out. Right until the last minute we weren't sure that one of the bakers who had given up his spot for us wouldn't change his mind and run over to the gate.

Then one of us newcomers would have had to stay behind.

The remaining two would have had to go without him, for even if they had wanted to back out, they could not do so at the gate.

But eight of us, the right number, were there.

As many as five SS men surrounded us.

As we were being counted the *Scharführer* [SS equivalent to a Staff Sergeant] called out from the window of the blockführerstube [SS guardroom] to our escort: "Paßt auf! [Be careful!]" Did they know something? There was in fact another reason. It was a Monday, when a new bakers' escort took over for the whole week.

We set off.

I thought then about how many times I had gone through the gate, but never like this. I knew now that I could not return under any circumstances. I felt joy and as if I had wings. But it would still be some time before I could use them.

We marched along the road by the tannery. I had not been

there for a long time. Walking by, I kept looking at the tannery's buildings and yard, running through in my mind all the jobs I had held there and the faces of the lads, some of whom were no longer alive.

Where the road we were following from the camp arrived at the road on which stood the little town's houses, we split into two small detachments. Two bakers and as many as three SS men went to the right towards the bridge and the "small bakery."

The disproportionately heavy escort for those two and the light one for us, since only two SS men continued with six inmates, was due to the fact that those three SS men were planning some holiday booze-up.

We marched off to the left. I eventually saw the "large bakery," the day shift of bakers coming out to greet us and the great menacing studded door, which would be the scene of our life-and-death struggle that night.

Inside the bakery on the left was a separate room holding coal. There we stacked our clothes, undressing completely owing to the high temperature.

It was pretty dark in there.

We each stacked our clothes, separating them into those we needed to take and those we would leave behind: our "stripes."

One of our two SS men, the smaller one, as if scenting something, immediately began inspecting the door, shaking his head and saying it was not secure enough.

The eloquent Jasio smilingly began to convince him that it was in fact the opposite.

The heavy, studded door was closed with a great lock, the key to which the SS man was carrying on his belt, a spare key hung in a recess in the wall, behind glass which had to be broken to retrieve the key.

The SS man's suspiciousness was fuelled perhaps by instinct, but also by the sense of duty, which the new guard (like a new broom) wanted to demonstrate on the first day.

In this respect, Monday was not an ideal day.

By the end of the week the SS men had become more used to the workers and were less likely to be vigilant.

A new guard did have the benefit though of coming, like Edek and me, for the first time and, not knowing that we had just arrived and that we were new, made no distinction in supervision between us and the other inmates.

What did we do in the bakery?

Civilian bakers, who came in from town and who also worked in two shifts, were in charge of the actual baking.

Over the course of a night we were meant to bake a specific number of loaves of bread. A baking team which did not complete the designated number of loaves at work went to the bunker—civilian bakers and inmates alike.

Therefore, everything was done at the double.

Over the course of a night we were meant to finish five batches. We were to put the bread in the ovens five times and then take it out five times.

We were going to try to escape from the bakery after the second batch, for after the first one it would be too soon.

Meanwhile the first, second, third and fourth batches came and went, and we still could not leave the bakery.

Just as when one plays solitaire, the cards have to fall a certain way and you have to sort and shuffle them for the game to work out, so here too, with bakers rushing around getting flour, sawdust, coal and water, and carrying off the baked loaves, our paths kept crossing in different directions, complicated by the SS men on duty walking about; the cards would have to fall so that at one given moment we would be near the door and out of the line of vision of both the SS men and the other bakers.

And the stake for this game of solitaire was—our lives...

We were locked up in the bakery in order to complete the task which had to be done quickly, and we could not get in the way of the other bakers. We were drenched in sweat owing to the great heat. We drank water by the bucket.

We were able to lull the SS men and the bakers by giving the impression that we were doing nothing but work.

In our eyes we were like wild animals locked up in a cage, using all their cunning to create the conditions to get out of the cage that very night.

The hours were passing... the "solitaire" was—not working out... for the time being it was impossible to set up an escape...

Opportunities came and then went.

The nervous tension lessened, then increased.

The door was in full view. The SS men walked back and forth right by it.

It was impossible to open the padlocked window, since there was always someone nearby.

When after midnight we passed from Monday to Tuesday, things became a little more relaxed.

One of the SS men stretched out and went to sleep, or at least pretended to. In any case, he was not walking about.

The bakers were also exhausted.

When around two o'clock the fourth batch was done and only one remained, the bakers took a longish break and had something to eat.

The three of us were on edge.

Janek had discreetly started to dress. Edek and I covered

his movements by, out of apparent zeal, carrying coal and then water to get ready for the final batch.

In reality we were preparing ourselves for the final effort—to escape.

Then, seizing a moment when the SS man was walking away from the door towards the main baking hall, Janek, counting on the fact that he would not turn around for two or three minutes, slid out fully dressed and quickly undid the nut, which easily gave way under Janek's iron grip; he pushed the screw together with the hook, which fell on the other side of the door.

When the SS man returned, Jasio disappeared into the coal bunker.

We were using wheelbarrows to carry the coal.

During the SS man's next round and when he had his back to the door, Jasio quickly and silently slipped back the two upper and the two lower bolts. We with our wheelbarrows took turns to screen him from view.

The exhausted bakers were all sitting or lying in the baking hall.

The bolts took more time than had the nut.

Jasiek went fully dressed to the lavatory by the door in full view of the SS man who did not react to the fact that he was dressed, perhaps, as a newcomer, thinking that this was normal in the morning.

For the time being things seemed to be going well.

Suddenly, the unexpected happened. Driven by some sixth sense or simply on an impulse, the SS man walked over to the door and stood in front of it, about half a meter away, and began to inspect it.

I had put down my wheelbarrow about 4 meters behind him. Edek also froze by the coal.

We were both waiting for the SS man to shout out loudly, whereupon, as if on a command, we would rush him, immobilize him and tie him up.

Why did he not notice anything? Did he have his eyes open, or was his mind on other things? I have never been able to understand.

I daresay that the following day in the bunker he must have racked his brains about that one.

He turned away from the door and calmly walked off towards the ovens and when he was about 6 meters from the door, Jasiek slipped out of the lavatory, I quickly made a dash for my things and with Jaś I pushed hard on the door.

At that moment Edek, right behind the SS man's back, dashed quickly and quietly with a knife to the bed with the sleeping SS man and cut the telephone wire in two places, taking the piece of wire as a souvenir.

Meanwhile the door, which Jaś and I were pushing, bent outwards, but would not yield.

The SS man was walking away from us and was now eight, and a moment later nine, meters away from us.

We redoubled our pressure on the door, which kept bending, but still would not yield, for after all we had never opened it and we had no certainty that it would open. Had we thought of it, we would surely have broken out in a cold sweat, but there was no time for fear.

Meanwhile Edek dashed from the SS man's bed to the coal bunker for his things stashed there.

Jasiek was strong, and my strength was doubled by all the nervous tension, but the door seemed stronger than us...

We put everything we had into that door when... suddenly and noiselessly—it flew open before us...

**Jan Redzej (Pilecki's comrade—code no. 170) —Inmate No. 5430.**

**Edward Ciesielski (Pilecki's comrade—code no. 57) —Inmate No. 12969.**

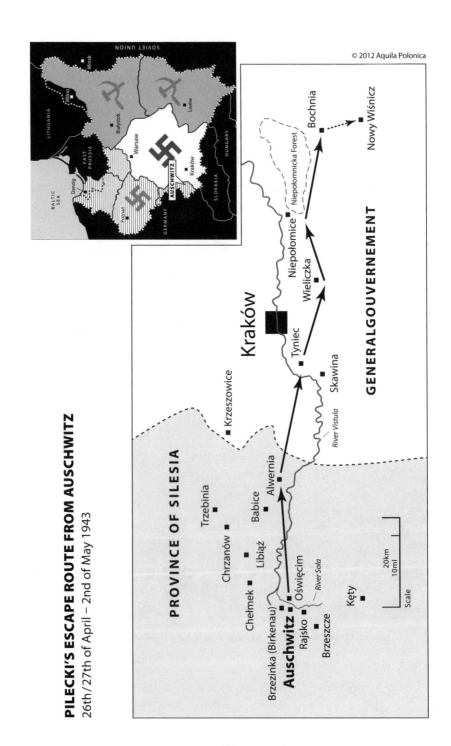

**PILECKI'S ESCAPE ROUTE FROM AUSCHWITZ**
26th/27th of April – 2nd of May 1943

© 2012 Aquila Polonica

Cold blew on our heated heads, the stars twinkled in the sky as if winking to us...

This all happened in the blink of an eye...

A leap into the dark unknown, followed by a dash, Jasiek, me and Edek in that order.

At the same time shots followed us.

It's hard to judge how fast we were running. The bullets missed. Our legs, arms and bodies tore at the air.

When we were more or less 100 meters from the bakery, I began to call out "Jasiek! Jasiek!..." But Jasiek continued to charge ahead like a racehorse. If I could only catch him... grab him by the shoulder... and stop him... but the distance between the three of us did not vary and we all charged ahead at more or less the same speed.

Nine shots rang out behind us. Then there was silence. The SS man must have dashed to the telephone. The one who had been asleep was probably for the first minute quite disoriented.

I wanted to stop Jasiek because I had planned to take a route at right angles to the one we were now dashing along. After about 200 to 300 meters I managed to do this. Jasiek slowed down, I caught up with him and Edek too.

"Well?" asked Jasio panting.

"I think that's it, for the time being," I replied.

"You said you had a route planned."

Correct, I did have a route. I was to cross the River Soła and double back along the opposite bank towards the camp and continue south towards Kęty. But Jasiek haring off like that to the north had changed everything. It was too late to double back. It was after two in the morning. We needed to hurry.

"Well, what now?" the others inquired.

"Nothing, let's get dressed," I said to Edek, "I'm going

another way." The two of us were naked, wearing swimming trunks with our clothes in a bundle under our arms.

We had been running some distance from the Soła, but parallel to it and going north.

Now, after dressing and leaving our striped pants, which we had mistakenly taken with us, well hidden in the bushes, I led them to the river bank (the left one) and then followed it north in the bushes.

When we asked Edek if he had the powdered tobacco, he said that he did, but that all of it had spilt while we had been running. If the dogs picked up our scent, they would have their fill of tobacco.

I had dried and rubbed this tobacco quite a long time before, while working in the spoon shop (in the tannery), from which we had once been planning for some of the lads to escape.

To be sure, it had now fallen out rather too quickly, but it still might cover some of our scent.

Not changing our chosen northerly heading, we were confronted by a fork in the river. The Soła flowed into the Vistula, but before that on the right was a railroad bridge which, if the information we had gathered was correct, had a sentry on it all the time.

"Tomek, where are you going?" asked Jasio.

"Stow it! There's no other way and we don't have much time. We must take the shortest route."

We approached the bridge. I was in front. I had rubber soles, Jasio was about 10–15 paces behind me and Edek brought up the rear.

Carefully, keeping my eyes on the hut to the left of one of the bridge's abutments, I climbed up the railroad embankment and onto the bridge.

The other fellows followed.

Treading softly, we began to cross the bridge quite quickly. We covered a third... then half... we were already approaching the opposite bank... and the end of the bridge... for the time being nothing stood in our way...

Finally we reached the end of the bridge and jumped quickly down from the embankment to the left onto grass and a field.

Quite unexpectedly we had managed to cross the bridge without a problem.

The sentries must have been enjoying the holiday in pleasant company.

I then picked an easterly heading, along the Vistula and on the left-hand side of the railroad tracks.

It was easy to navigate, as the sky was full of twinkling stars.

We already felt to some extent free. But a certain sense of danger still lay between us and a full feeling of freedom.

We began to run cross-country.

The little town of Oświęcim [Auschwitz] lay to our right.

We jumped over ditches, crossed roads and ran across ploughed fields, getting closer to or drawing away from the Vistula as it meandered.

Only later did we marvel at how much effort a man can expend when he is running on nervous energy.

We got onto ploughed fields that ran uphill. We slid down cement banks, or scrambled up like cats on other ones—part of some canal system. As we followed the tracks, a train roared by.

Finally, after several kilometers, at the time it seemed like ten to us (it was a little less), from a rise we saw ahead of us fences, barracks, watchtowers, wire... Before us was a camp with the familiar searchlights creeping over the ground...

For a moment we almost froze. Then we came to the conclusion that it was so-called "Buna," a subcamp of ours.

We had no time to change our heading.

Dawn was beginning to light up the sky...

We began rapidly to skirt the camp to the left. We came across some wire. We again began to slide down and clamber up banks... We crossed canals on footbridges. At one spot we carefully crossed a footbridge over which foaming water was pouring... We skirted the wire, wading through the water. Finally, we also left this camp behind us.

We ran up against (for we were still able to run) the bank of the Vistula and we began to follow it, looking for somewhere to hide during the day, just in case.

Day was dawning. There was no real cover for us. The dark line of woods could be seen far away on the horizon. It was now quite light.

There was a village here on the bank of the Vistula. Boats belonging to its inhabitants rocked on the water.

I decided to take a boat over the Vistula. The boats were secured with chains to stakes. The chains were locked with padlocks. We examined these chains. One of them consisted of two halves, linked with a screw.

Jasiek took out the wrench (a piece of metal with a hole for the nut) with which he had undone the nut in the bakery.

We were astonished at the coincidence. The wrench was an exact fit for the nut. We undid it. The chain's two halves fell apart.

The sun was coming up.

We got into the boat and pushed off.

At any moment someone could come out of one of the houses in the village, barely a few dozen meters away.

A dozen or so meters before the opposite bank, the boat hit some shallows. We had no time to shove it off. We jumped into the water and pushed on, wading to the bank in water up to our waists.

Our bodies and joints, warmed by a night of running, reacted accordingly to the cold water. For the time being we felt nothing, leaping onto the bank of the Vistula.

About two kilometers away was a dark line of woods.

The woods, so dear to me and which I had missed for many years, were now our salvation and the first real cover we had encountered.

It would not be true to say that we ran over to this salvation. We had no strength left for running. We walked at a brisk pace, and sometimes slowed down for lack of strength.

The sun was now shining brightly.

We could hear the roar of motorcycles on the roads in the distance, perhaps even in pursuit of us...

We walked slowly...

Edek's and my clothes looked a little suspicious at close quarters, but at a distance made an unobtrusively dark impression. Jasio's fine civilian suit, however, was clearly visible at a distance with its bright red stripes.

Some people could be seen working in the fields in the distance. They must have spotted us.

The woods slowly grew closer.

Odd—for the first time in my life I could smell the woods from over a hundred yards away.

A powerful smell assailed all our senses, together with the merry chirping of the birds, a breath of damp, the smell of resin... our eyes bored into the depths of the mysterious wood, now almost upon us.

We went in to a depth of over a dozen trees and lay down on the soft moss.

Lying on my back, my thoughts rose above the treetops and happily formed a great question mark. A metamorphosis. What a contrast with the camp in which I felt that I had spent a thousand years...

The pines whispered, gently waving their huge tops...

Scraps of blue sky could be seen between the tree trunks. The dew shone like little jewels on the bushes and grass... In places the sun's rays broke through, lighting up the lives of thousands of small creatures... the world of little beetles, bugs and butterflies... the world of birds, unchanging for a thousand years, followed its usual routine and, flocking and scattering, hummed with its own life...

And yet, despite so many sounds of woodland life, all around us was silence... a deep silence... a silence far from the roar of humanity... far from man's scheming... a silence in which there was not a living soul...

We did not count.

We were just returning to the land of the living and we were yet to be counted as members of the human race.

How glad we were not to have seen any people so far.

We had decided to keep as far away from them as possible for as long as we could.

However, it was difficult to survive very long without people... We had no food at all. For the time being we were not that hungry. We ate some lettuce and drank from a stream...

We were enchanted by everything.

We were in love with the world... just not with its people...
I had a small container of honey which had been sent from
home and a teaspoon. I treated Jasio and Edek to a spoonful
each, myself too.

As we lay, we talked over the night's events.

Jasio was balding, so he didn't need a cap. Edek and I
had shaved heads. In order to conceal our lack of hair
from other people we had taken two civilian caps from the
bakers' belongings in the bakery, but Edek had lost his
while running through the bushes during the night. He now
tied a woman's kerchief on his head. So we called him
Ewunia.

Jasio, just to be different, called himself Adam and, looking
at a green branch, chose Gałązka [Twig] for a surname.
It really matched his 90 kg physique!

After Jasio washed out the red stripes on his suit in a
stream and I had dried out four banknotes which had got wet
in my shoe, we marched on eastwards through the woods,
dashing across small areas of open ground, and skirting the
larger ones along the woods' edge.

Our rule was to give people as wide a berth as possible...

Just before evening, we had a minor run-in with a
gamekeeper, who had spotted us in the distance as we were
eating up the last of the honey... and, wanting to stop us, had
blocked our path, so I scrambled into some young-growth
trees, which were conveniently near... They were so dense,
that we could only crawl through. Amongst these trees
I changed heading and emerged by a road.

We dashed across and again got into some young-growth
trees.

The gamekeeper lost our trail, we kept to the road because,

according to the road signs, it led to the small town of Z [Babice],[67] which lay on our route.

We approached the town after sundown.

A ruined castle stood on a hill before the town.

We skirted to the left of the open ground in front of the town. We slipped over a road between the houses and headed for the wooded hill, straight towards the castle ruins.

Near the ruins, on the side of the hill, terribly tired, we lay down to sleep buried in the previous year's leaves. Thus passed Tuesday (the 27th of April).

Edek fell asleep immediately.

After our cold bath, Jasiek and I had inflammation of the joints and I also had an inflammation of the sciatic nerve.

The last hour I had pushed on by willpower alone. In addition to the pain in my right hip, the pain in my knee joints, especially when going down slopes, was so severe that I could only walk "gritting my teeth."

Now, when I was lying down, the pain was less intense, but it still bothered me.

Jasiek felt no pain lying down and also fell asleep.

I was unable to fall asleep. Taking advantage of this, I began to consider what to do next.

Eight kilometers away lay the border between Silesia, annexed by the Third Reich, and the Generalgouvernement,[68] which we had to cross.

---

[67] Pilecki confuses the letters, using Z for their ultimate destination Bochnia, as well as for this intermediate location which Adam Cyra says is Babice; see Cyra, *Ochotnik do Auschwitz. Witold Pilecki (1901–1948)* (Oświęcim: Chrześcijańskie Stowarzyszenie Rodzin Oświęcimskich, 2000), p. 398. Cyra also says that IX is Bochnia, op. cit., p. 404. Translator's note.

[68] The part of occupied Poland that the Nazis ran as a separate administrative entity, using the ancient Polish city of Kraków as its capital. Warsaw, Poland's capital, was within the Generalgouvernement. Translator's note.

For long hours, half dozing, I worked on a plan how to get to and then across this frontier and where we would go after that. When suddenly, a kind of epiphany hit me and I sat up in the leaves... sucking in my breath from the pain...

I remembered the year of '42. I was working in the spoon shop (the tannery) where 19 [Tadeusz Słowiaczek] was working as schreiber [clerk] and with whom I had often had very frank conversations.

He told me to whom he wrote letters, that his uncle was a priest right by the border, that his parish straddled the border and that, as parish priest, he was allowed to cross it with a cart driver, whom he could, if he had to, leave on the other side...

It was only about 7 or 8 kilometers to the little town where my friend's relative was the parish priest.

In his sleep Edek began to say something, at first not very clearly, but then he began asking some Bronek or other whether he had brought him some bread (he was hungry and so he was dreaming of food). He suddenly leapt to his feet and asked so loudly that Jasiek woke up:

"Well? Has he brought the bread?"

"Who's supposed to have brought the bread?"

"Bronek, of course!"

"Don't worry, my friend. Can't you see the wood, the castle and us sleeping in the leaves? You've been dreaming... "

Edek lay down.

But now I stood up. It was four o'clock. I had decided to reach the priest in the morning. We did not have too many kilometers, but painful joints. The pain in my knees meant that I could barely move my legs. Jasiek got up stretching, but staggered and began to slip down the hillside. He almost fainted from the pain in his knee joints. However, he controlled himself.

The initial steps were hard and painful, especially when going downhill.

It took us quite some time to cover these seven or eight kilometers, meandering a bit. At first it went slowly, then a little faster.

Jasiek, in order to obtain some information, and as the best dressed amongst us and not needing to hide his lack of hair, went up to a local on his way to work and walked along chatting with him.

We were approaching the town of II [Alwernia].

A small church could be seen on a wooded hill.

Jasiek left the local and joined us, bringing the information that the place we were seeking matched the one we could see, which was near the hill with the church.

Picking our way between fields we reached a road on which stood a customs post. The border itself was further along, on a hill.

It was seven o'clock. There were a couple of people already in the post who were studying us carefully at a distance.

However, we crossed the road, then went over a stream by a bridge and carried on in full view of these people, trying to walk briskly and jauntily.

We finally reached the wooded hill and once we had covered several dozen meters up the slope, we fell to the ground exhausted.

And, as if on cue, the bell in the church tower, which was at the top of the hill, rang out . . .

"It can't be helped, my dear Jasiek, you've got to go to the church. You're the most presentable of us and you're the only one of us who can go in, for you can be bareheaded."

So I sent Jasiek off to see the priest, whom he was to tell

that we had been together, there in hell, with his brother Franciszek and his brother's two sons, Tadek and Lolek.

Jasio went off and was gone a long time.

He eventually returned looking doubtful, and said that he had waited in the church for the priest who came to say mass and that he had spoken to him. But the priest had been unwilling to believe that we had managed to escape from Auschwitz and had stated openly that he was afraid that this could be some kind of trap.

I thought to myself, when he saw Jasiek smiling from ear to ear it must have been hard for him, on hearing the name Auschwitz, to believe immediately that Jasiek had been imprisoned there for over two and a half years. And that he had managed to escape.

I sent Jasio back, for the mass might end, and I coached him carefully on which of his relations had been on which block, where his nephews had gone, on what block their father now was. I even told him what they had put in their last Christmas letters.

Jasio went off. The mass ended. Jasio went up to the priest. He told him everything, adding that two of his mates were in the bushes and that they could not come out on account of their lack of hair and odd combination of clothes.

The priest believed him and accompanied Jasio back to us.

On seeing us, he wrung his hands. He finally believed the whole story. He started coming to see us in the bushes every half hour, bringing milk, coffee, rolls, bread, sugar, butter and other delicacies.

It turned out that this was not the priest we had been thinking of, who was about two kilometers away.

He knew the other priest and the story of his family in Auschwitz.

He could not bring us into his house, for there were too many people about in the square.

We were actually very comfortable there among the young spruces and bushes.

The priest gave us some ointment to rub into our joints. We now wrote our first letters home, which the priest then posted for us.

In the evening, when it was quite dark, the priest gave us a good guide.

There are still good people on this earth, we said to one another.

Thus ended Wednesday (the 28th of April).

We said goodbye to the priest. Our knee joints now hurt less. At ten o'clock in the evening we followed our guide with a view to crossing the border.

The guide led us for a long time, taking a roundabout way, then pointed to a spot and said that that was the best place. He then went back.

Perhaps it was the safest spot for the very reason that it was filled with felled trees, wire and crisscrossed with ditches, and so the border patrol must have felt that no one would want to take this route and was watching elsewhere.

It took us a good hour to cross a 150-meter belt.

We now proceeded quickly over varying terrain, but for the most part keeping to the road.

The night was dark. There was no danger of being spotted at a distance. However, we could bump into a patrol, but some kind of animal alertness, or was it instinct, continued to guide us safely.

Sometimes, when the road went in the wrong direction, we left it and walked cross-country, using the stars to navigate, pushing through woods, tumbling into holes, scrambling up slopes.

We walked the whole night covering, so it seemed to us, a great deal of ground.

The first gleam of dawn found us in a rather large village, which dragged on for kilometers. In the village the road veered left. Our route lay at an angle to the right. Since we had spotted in the distance on the road to the left the first group of people of the day, we turned right at an angle and continued across pastures and a meadow.

The sun rose. It was Thursday.

We were on completely open ground. It was risky crossing it in daylight. We found a large bush where we spent the whole day, unable to fall asleep, since the ground was wet and it was hard to sleep sitting on a stone or the branches of a bush.

In the evening, when the sun had gone down but it was still light enough to see, Jasiek went off on a reconnaissance along our line of march. He appeared shortly with the news that the Vistula lay nearby to the right and, if we did not want to abandon our heading, we would have to get across here. There were boats and a ferryman who could take us to the other side.

We decided to cross on the ferryman's boat. We left our bush and approached the river. The ferryman eyed us. We got on the ferry. The boat cast off. We safely disembarked on the far bank. When we paid him in marks, the ferryman looked at us even more oddly.

Before us lay III [the spires of the Benedictine Monastery at Tyniec] and the town of IV [Tyniec] itself.

We followed the main road through the town. People were returning home after work. Some tardy cows were hurrying back to their pens. Local people, standing by their front doors, looked at us curiously.

We were very hungry and equally thirsty for something hot. The nights were cold. I had last slept on Sunday night in the Auschwitz hospital, but we were not yet ready to go up to people's homes.

At the end of the town an older man was standing on the left by his front door looking at us. He appeared so friendly, that I told Edek to ask him for some milk.

Edek went up to him and asked if he could buy some milk. The man began to beckon us and invite us in saying: "Come in, come in… I'll get you some milk… "

There was something about his words which had nothing to do with milk, but he looked so honest that we decided to venture into his house.

When we went in and he had introduced his family to us, his wife and children, he then stopped in front of us and said: "I'm not going to ask you a thing… but you can't walk around looking like that!"

He then explained that he had seen much in the Great War and that he wanted to know nothing. He fed us hot milk, noodles, eggs, bread, and suggested that we spend the night in the barn where he would lock us in. "I realize," he said, "that you don't know me and that you might have reservations, so I won't insist, but if you trust me, stay and don't worry."

His face and eyes and all of him were so transparently honest that I decided to stay.

We spent the night locked in the barn, once again under lock and key, and yet we slept peacefully on a real pillow— something we had not seen in years.

Thus ended Thursday, the 29th of April.

In the morning our host unlocked us alone, without the police. He fed us and watered us. We had a good talk. We changed some money. He was an honest, decent, patriotic Pole.

There are such people... He was called 175 [Piotr Mazurkiewicz]. His whole family had welcomed us warmly. We told them where we were coming from. We wrote some more letters to our families. It goes without saying that they were not to addresses known to the authorities in Auschwitz.

After breakfast, we continued over the fields and through the woods passing V [unidentified location] and VI [unidentified location] to our left. We were heading for VII [Wieliczka].

We spent Friday night in a hut standing on its own in a field, where a young married couple and their children were living. We arrived late and we left before they rose. We paid and went on our way.

We skirted VII [Wieliczka] and headed for the forest VIII [the Niepołomnicka Forest].

It was Saturday the 1st of May as we entered the forest smelling of resin. The weather was beautiful and the sun cast its golden rays through the tree trunks onto the cone-strewn ground. Squirrels were clambering up, deer ran by.

Jasio and I took turns leading the way; Edek brought up the rear.

The day had so far passed without incident. We were hungry. At 14:00 in the afternoon Jasio was leading. We came out onto a wide road which led in the right direction. Jasio led us along the road. About 16:00 we reached a somewhat wider stream with a bridge over it. Beyond the bridge were some buildings: on the left a forester's house and a few sheds, and on the right some other buildings.

Jasio advanced quite boldly towards the bridge and the forester's house. Things had been going our way for so long that we had stopped being cautious. We were lulled by the fact that we saw no movement, no people, and the green shutters of the forester's house were all closed.

Walking past the house, we looked into the yard behind it leading to the sheds. A German soldier, quite possibly from the field police and carrying a rifle, was in the yard heading towards the road and towards us. We made no outward reaction at all in order to keep walking as far as possible and we were about ten paces beyond the house. Our reactions were all internal. However, the policeman reacted outwardly.

"Halt!"

We walk on, pretending not to hear.

"Halt," rings out again behind us and we hear the sound of a rifle being cocked. We all calmly stop, a smile on our faces. The soldier is on the other side of the yard wall about 30–35 meters away. Another soldier quickly comes out of a hut about 60 meters away. So we say:

"Ja, ja. Alles gut . . . , " and calmly turn towards them.

Seeing how calm we are the first soldier, who had been prepared to fire, lowered his weapon. Seeing that, I say calmly:

"Lads, run for it!" and we all take off in different directions. Jasiek to the right at right angles to our heading, Edek along the road we were following, and I head between them to the right at a slant.

Once again I have to emphasize that it is difficult to describe how we ran. Each one of us ran as best he could. I leapt over tree trunks, a nursery fence, bushes.

A great many shots rang out. Some of them whistled past my ear.

I suddenly felt, perhaps in my spinal cord, that someone was aiming at me.

Something hit my right shoulder. "Bastard!" I thought, "he's got me." But I felt no pain. I ran on, drawing rapidly away.

I could see Edek far off to my left. I shouted out to him. He spotted me and we began to converge running in the same direction. We were a good 400 meters from the forester's house and they were still firing at us. Since they could no longer see us, I assumed that they were firing at Jasiek, perhaps they had killed him.

Meanwhile, Edek and I sat down on a fallen tree.

I had to tend to my bleeding wound. My right shoulder had been shot through, but the bone was untouched. My clothes too had been harmlessly shot through several times. My pants and windbreaker had altogether four holes. After wrapping a handkerchief around my wound, Edek and I set off heading east.

Edek suggested we stay in a hollow by the tree, but I felt that we needed to get out of the area as quickly as possible, since the Germans might get on the telephone and organize a larger sweep.

I felt that Jasiek might be in trouble, for the firing continued, but not in our direction.

An hour later, we arrived at some village where, without beating about the bush, we said: "We're the lads from the forest," that there had been three of us, but now we were two. They had heard shots and maybe our colleague had been killed...

These honest folk gave us milk and bread and a guide who led us to a ferry. We crossed a small river on the ferry and found ourselves in some larger village with a church. Here we encountered German soldiers, but they were searching the village for food and paid us no attention, taking us for locals.

Finally, after leaving this village we saw in the distance the town of IX [Bochnia]—our initial destination. However, since 164's [Edmund Zabawski's] family's house was on the other side of town, and it was already 7:30 in the evening (curfew was at 8:00), I did not want to go through town given our appearance, so Edek and I spent the night in some fellow's attic whose house we had reached by skirting the town to the east and north.

On the morning of Sunday the 2nd of May, we set off on the short journey to Mr. and Mrs. 176 [the Oboras].

We approached their house and on the porch we saw an elderly couple who were 164's [Edmund Zabawski's] parents-in-law, a young lady who was his wife, and their little daughter Marysia.

The couple smiled, greeted us politely and, asking no questions, invited us in. Inside we introduced ourselves as friends of 164 [Edmund Zabawski]. We were invited further inside and on opening the door to the last room, we saw Jasio sleeping soundly on a bed.

We woke him up and embraced warmly.

Jasio, well dressed, had walked through the town the previous evening and had turned up at the house. That was the reason why our hosts, warned by him of our impending arrival, had smilingly invited us in, saying nothing.

Jasio's clothes and the bundle he had been carrying under his arm had been shot through in several places. He himself was unhurt.

My wound was not serious. We had all managed to get away.

The 176s [the Oboras] and Mrs. 177 [Helena Zabawska] showed us the kind of goodwill and hospitality that one finds only in one's own family and in one's own home after a long absence.

At this juncture we should have repeated several times a day that . . . there are still good people on this earth.

They listened with great interest and with obvious kindly sincerity as we described our experiences in Auschwitz with our friend and their loved one 164 [Edmund Zabawski].

After we had got to know each other, had developed a degree of trust and exchanged the agreed passwords, I asked them to put me in touch with someone from the military underground. A few hours later I was talking to Leon 178 [Leon Wandasiewicz]; after exchanging passwords, I asked him to put me in touch with the local commander.

Leon presented me with the option of speaking to one of two gentlemen: the first from northern district IX [Bochnia], the other from southern district, who lived about 7 kilometers away in the little town of X [Nowy Wiśnicz]. I said that it was all the same to me. Leon suggested that we go to see the commander in the town of X [Nowy Wiśnicz], since they were friends.

I stayed with Mr. and Mrs. 176 [Obora] on Sunday and Monday (the 2nd and 3rd of May). On Tuesday morning, dressed in some decent clothes belonging to Leon, I set off alongside him to X [Nowy Wiśnicz]. Jasio and Edek stayed behind as guests of Mr. and Mrs. 176 [Obora].

It was a beautiful sunny day. We walked along, cheerfully chatting. Leon was pushing a bicycle which he would use to get home, since he expected that the local commander would put me up.

As I walked, I reflected on how many experiences I had had over the course of the last few years and that now they had come to an end. Yet fate had again prepared an extraordinary surprise for me.

More or less halfway there, in a little wood, we sat down on some tree stumps to rest.

I asked Leon out of curiosity the name of the commander we were going to see, since I was shortly to meet him.

Leon replied in two words: a Christian name and surname... two words which would have meant nothing to anyone else, but which for me were exceptional... and represented an extraordinary and strange coincidence.

The local commander had the same name that I had had in Auschwitz...

So I had spent all those days in hell under his name... and he had been completely unaware of it.

And now my steps were leading me to... the owner of that name.

Was it fate? Blind fate? If indeed it was fate, it was surely not blind!

I gulped and fell silent and Leon asked:

"Why so quiet?"

"It's nothing, I'm just a bit tired."

I was calculating how many days I had spent in Auschwitz.

In that hell behind the wire there had been 947 of them. Almost 1,000...

"Let's go a little faster," I said "I have an unusual surprise for you and the commander. Come on, let's go."

We drew near to the lovely town of X [Nowy Wiśnicz], spreading over valleys and hills and with a fine castle on a hill.

Walking along I thought, well, yes, I was supposed to have been born in IX [Bochnia]. It was here that 158 [Zygmunt Ważyński] had come to take care of business for me with Father 160 [Kuc].

A man was sitting with his wife and daughters on the veranda of a small house surrounded by a garden. We went up to them. Leon whispered to me that I could talk openly.

I introduced myself with the name I had used in Auschwitz. He replied:

"I'm also Tomasz."

"But I'm Tomasz."

"I'm also Tomasz," he said in surprise.

Leon listened to this exchange in astonishment, as did the man's wife.

"But I was born here." I now proceeded to name the day, year and month, which I had repeated so many times in Auschwitz at every change of block or kommando, and for the lists drawn up by the kapos.

The man almost leapt from his chair:

"What's going on here? Those are my personal details."

"Yes, they are, but they have gone through far more with me than with you." And I told him that I had been in Auschwitz for two years and seven months and that now I had escaped.

There was no knowing how anyone might react to this. My namesake and the owner of the name which had seemed to be my own for a thousand years opened his arms. We embraced warmly and became instant friends.

"But how did this happen?" he asked.

I asked whether he knew Dr. 83 [Helena Pawłowska] in Warsaw. Yes, he did and had stayed there. Yes, false identity papers had been made for him there; he had left before they were ready. I had then used them as one of several fake sets I had had at the time.

I stayed three and half months with the 179s [the Serafińskis].

We sent word through friends to Father 160 [Kuc] that he should erase in the parish register the information written in pencil next to my name, which had once been so vital for me.

From here I formed a detachment, helped by 84 [Tomasz Serafiński] and 180 [Andrzej Możdżeń], with a view, if Warsaw accepted my plan, to attacking Auschwitz after coordinating with the lads inside.

I and 180 [Andrzej Możdżeń] had some German weapons and uniforms. I wrote a letter to my family and to my friend 25 [Stefan Bielecki], who had escaped from Auschwitz with a report and who was now in Warsaw and working in one of the [Home Army] High Command's sections.

I wrote a letter to 44 [Wincenty Gawron] in XI [Warsaw], who had also escaped from Auschwitz with a report, wanting to make contact and continue our work.

On the 1st of June, my friend 25 [Stefan Bielecki] flew in from Warsaw as if on wings, bringing me the valuable information that Mrs. E.O. [Eleonora Ostrowska], to whom I had been writing letters from Auschwitz, was still living peacefully. The Gestapo threatened only families with collective responsibility. They had no need or interest in getting involved with someone who in their eyes was only a friend. They had no trace of my family and did not know its name.

My friend 25 [Stefan Bielecki] also brought me some papers and money.

I discussed the matter with him, telling him that for the time being I was not about to go to Warsaw while I still had some hope that they would let me attack Auschwitz from the outside. Only if I received a direct order to desist, then I would go to Warsaw.

My friend, saddened that he would have to return alone despite having promised my family to bring me back with him, left for Warsaw.

On the 5th of June, the local Gestapo man and an SS man from Auschwitz appeared, first of all at Tomek's (my name-sake's) mother's house asking about her son's whereabouts. She replied that he had been living nearby for years.

They went round to Tomek's.

At that moment I was not far away.

The SS man must have been already briefed by the local Gestapo man that 84 [Tomasz Serafiński] had been living there a long time. He took one look at his face and at the piece of paper in his hand (he was probably comparing him to my picture with the puffed-out cheeks).

He asked whether there would be a good fruit crop in the autumn and left.

Working in X [Nowy Wiśnicz] I met some first-rate people and fine Poles; in addition to Mr. and Mrs. 179 [the Serafińskis], there was also Mr. 181 [Józef Roman].

Then 25 [Stefan Bielecki] sent from Warsaw a parcel containing some of the latest methods for dealing with the occupying forces and a letter, in which he wrote that Warsaw was very favorably disposed to...(reading this a frisson of pleasure ran through me, assuming it to be the attack on Auschwitz)... but then followed the words... awarding me a decoration for my work in Auschwitz. However, he still held out hope that the operation would be equally successful.

However, in July I received a letter with the tragic news that General Grot [Stefan Rowecki][69] had been arrested.

Given the current somewhat tense situation in Warsaw, I realized that I could not expect an answer to the Auschwitz question, so I decided to go to Warsaw.

By the 23rd of August I was in Warsaw. Jasio arrived in September and Edek in December.

In Warsaw, I worked in one of High Command's cells.

I kept presenting in the appropriate quarters the issue of the lads still in Auschwitz and the need to set up a proper organization there.

---

[69] Lieutenant General Stefan "Grot" Rowecki was commander of the Polish Home Army (Armia Krajowa, or AK); see footnote 42, p. 146. Translator's note.

I learned that 161 [Bolesław Kuczbara], while in the Pawiak, had "shopped" the leadership of the Auschwitz organization and that he had agreed to work for the Germans.

He was released from the Pawiak and walked around Warsaw with a pistol in his pocket; he was shortly thereafter liquidated on Napoleon Square.

I exchanged letters with the lads in Auschwitz through their families on the outside. I kept up their spirits, but I felt that this was not enough.

Then came the news that several of the lads in Auschwitz from the leadership of our organization had been shot (perhaps as a result of 161's [Bolesław Kuczbara's] testimony).

I saw in the Kedyw [70] on a list of people to be liquidated the name of Wilhelm Westrych, who had once saved me in Auschwitz. I knew that he was a bastard, but even if I had wanted to do something about it, it was now too late, since there was a note next to his name: "carried out" and a date...

On the street I bumped into Sławek [Sławek Szpakowski], with whom I had once wielded a pickaxe in Auschwitz, dreaming of the dinner he would one day stand me in Warsaw. We were both optimists and, as one had said in those days, we had unrealistic dreams, yet now here we both were in Warsaw and still alive.

He was carrying a parcel and on seeing me almost dropped it.

I had dinner at his place several times and the menu was the one we had devised there in hell...

I was staying in the same house from which I had gone to

---

[70] Kedyw (Kierownictwo Dywersji—Guerrilla Warfare and Sabotage Command) was an elite section of the Polish Home Army, whose mission was sabotage, propaganda and armed action against the enemy. Translator's note.

Auschwitz in 1940 and where I had been writing letters from camp to Mrs. E.O. [Eleonora Ostrowska], but one floor up.

It afforded me the satisfaction of a certain challenge to the authorities.

For the duration of the Occupation no one turned up at Mrs. E.O.'s [Eleonora Ostrowska's] about my disappearance from Auschwitz. Neither did anyone go to Jasio's sister, nor to Edek's family.

In the autumn of 1943, I presented my plan for an operation at Auschwitz to Kedyw's Head of Plans ("Wilk," "Zygmunt" [Major Karol Jabłoński]) who said to me:

"When the war's over I'll show you a file full of reports on Auschwitz, all yours are there too..."

I wrote my final report on Auschwitz on 20 typewritten pages, and on the last page those chaps who had brought out reports wrote in their own hand whom they had told what and when.

I collected eight such statements, for the rest of them were either no longer alive or not in Warsaw.

In addition to my work in a certain department of High Command, I was busy taking care of families of Auschwitz inmates, both those who were still alive and those who had perished.

No. 86 [Aleksander Paliński] helped me with this. We received money for this work from a well-organized cell, consisting of three ladies 182 [names unknown], who devoted a great deal of effort to inmates and their families.

Through these ladies I was one day informed that there was someone in whose operational area Auschwitz lay. That this fellow was a real "pistol," that he was running a first-rate operation and that we might be able to get in touch with the inmates in Auschwitz through him, since communications in the field had recently broken down.

This gentleman was leaving and I couldn't see him; however, since he was so effective and claimed that he could get in touch with the inmates... I wanted to help him and provided the name of a friend, an Auschwitz inmate, Murzyn [Leon Murzyn], and that he could use Tomasz's name saying, for clarification, that Tomasz had gone away for Easter.

Among the sound fellows, I met several fellows from Auschwitz who were not at all sound (they had been released earlier) and who claimed that I too had been released.

On the 10th of June 1944, on Marszałkowska Street someone suddenly opened his arms saying:

"I don't believe that they could've released you from Auschwitz!"

I replied that I didn't think that they could have released him either. It was Olek 167 [Aleksander Bugajski]. Like a cat, this lucky devil always landed on all fours. He had wangled his way out of the Penal Company as a doctor and had been shipped off to Ravensbrück,[71] from which he had escaped.

The ladies 182 [names unknown] informed me that the gentleman who worked in the Auschwitz area was going there again and would like to see me.

I hurried off to meet him. I arrived a few minutes before the gentleman. The ladies remained discreetly in another room, awaiting the outcome of this meeting of aces.

I waited for a while, assuming that some kind of eagle would appear. The door opened and... in rolled a chubby ball, small, bald and with a turned-up nose. But, outward appearances are misleading. We sit down and this gentleman briskly gets things moving by saying:

"Now what if I take... a board... and paint a black man

---

[71] Ravensbrück is better known as a women's concentration camp, but there was a small men's camp adjacent. Translator's note.

on it...and I take this board...with the painted black man...and creep up to the Auschwitz wall...?"

I stood up, excused myself and went through to the ladies:

"Who's this you've put me in touch with? Can one have a serious conversation with him?"

"But of course, he's a wonderful organizer and he...," they reeled off his rank.

I returned thinking that this must be his way of breaking the ice and vowed to be patient. The gentleman, when I had resumed my seat at the table, seeing that the black man had not really worked, said:

"Well...what if instead of a black man I painted St. Thomas...or...an Easter cake?!"

I have to admit that I was cracking up inside from laughter and thought that I might break the chair into the wood of whose arms I was pressing my fingers...to stop myself from bursting out with laughter.

I got up and said that unfortunately I could not continue our conversation that day, since I had an urgent appointment elsewhere.

I am not making this up; this really happened.

At the end of July 1944, a week before the outbreak of the [Warsaw] Uprising, someone stopped me as I was riding a bicycle along Filtrowa Street, calling out "Hello!" I stopped unwillingly, as one did in those days of underground work. A man came over. At first I did not recognize him, but this lasted only a moment. It was my Auschwitz friend, Captain 116 [Zygmunt Pawłowicz].

Jasiek and I took part in the [1944 Warsaw] Uprising, serving in the same sector. There is a description of our actions and of my friend's death in the history of 1 Battalion "Group–Chrobry II"

Edek took five bullets during an operation, but made it.

My friend 25 [Stefan Bielecki] was seriously wounded during the Uprising.

During it I also ran into 44 [Wincenty Gawron].

Later, somewhere else, I met some fellows who had been in Auschwitz until almost the end (January 1945): 183 [name unknown] and 184 [name unknown]. It was music to my ears to hear them talk about the fallout from the bakery escape. About how the camp had had a good laugh that the authorities had been bamboozled, and about the fact that no reprisals had been taken against any of the lads! With the exception of the SS men who had been on duty, who had done time in the bunker.

I now mention the number of people who died in Auschwitz.

When I left Auschwitz the then-current number was a bit over 121,000. About 23,000 had been shipped out and released. About 97,000 inmates with prison numbers had been killed.

This has nothing to do with the people who were sent en masse to the gas chambers and burnt, without being formally processed into the camp.

On the basis of calculations made by the kommandos working in the vicinity, there were over 2 million such victims up to the time of my departure from Auschwitz.

I offer these numbers cautiously so as not to exaggerae and so that these daily numbers can be carefully examined.

Fellows who were there longer than I was and who witnessed the daily gassing of 8,000 people give a number of somewhere around 5 million.[72]

---

[72] It is now widely accepted that about 1.1 million died in Auschwitz throughout the war, of whom about 90 percent were Jews. Translator's note.

# SUMMER 1945

I would now like to say what I felt when I was back amongst the living, coming from a place about which one can honestly say: he who entered died; he who got out was reborn. What was my impression not of the very finest or the worst amongst us, but of the general mass of humanity, when I had been reborn on earth?

At times I felt that I was wandering through a great house and would suddenly open the door to a room in which there were only children: "...Ah, the children are playing..."

Yes, the leap was too great from what for us was important and what people, fussing, enjoying themselves and worrying, think is important.

But that is not all...A kind of widespread dishonesty had now become all too evident. There was some destructive agent at work trying to blur the boundary between false-hood and truth, and it was there for all to see.

The truth had become so elastic that it was stretched to cover everything that had become convenient to hide.

The boundary between honesty and common dishonesty had been meticulously blurred.

What I have written so far in these few dozen pages is unimportant, especially for those who will read them just for thrills, but here I would like to write in letters larger unfortunately than any on the typewriter for all those heads, which beneath their perfectly parted hair contain nothing but the proverbial sawdust and who can surely thank their mothers for only their well-formed skulls stopping the sawdust seeping out: let them take a moment to consider their own lives, let them look around and begin on their own to fight the falsehood, the lies and the self-interest, which are artfully presented as meaningful, the truth and even a great cause.

**APPENDICES**

# APPENDIX 1

## Glossary of English, German and Polish Terms and Acronyms

| | |
|---|---|
| AK | – Armia Krajowa: the military arm of the Polish Underground State during World War II; also known as the Home Army |
| Aleja Szucha | – shorthand reference to Gestapo headquarters in occupied Warsaw, which were located on Aleja Szucha |
| Arbeitsdienst | – work assignment office or leader |
| arbeitsfähig | – fit for work |
| Arbeitskommando | – a camp work detail |
| Arbeitslager | – a labor camp |
| arbeitsunfähig | – unfit for work |
| Armia Krajowa | – the military arm of the Polish Underground State during World War II; also known as the AK or the Home Army |
| Aufräumungskommando | – salvage Kommando |
| Awo | – camp slang for a kind of broth |
| Bademeister | – a washroom supervisor |
| Baderaum | – refers to communal washing facilities in the camp |

| | |
|---|---|
| Baubüro | – a construction site office |
| Bekleidungskammer | – the clothing storeroom |
| Bekleidungswerkstätte | – the clothing workshop |
| Binden | – armbands |
| Blockältester | – a block chief or leader (this position was held by an inmate) |
| Blockführer | – an SS block supervisor |
| Blockführerstube | – an SS guardroom |
| Blocksperre | – confinement to blocks, or block lock-down |
| Brotabladungskommando | – bread-unloading Kommando |
| Bunker | – confinement cell used for punishment; different types of bunkers provided for varying levels of punishment |
| "Canada" | – the Auschwitz name for stores of goods looted from people (mainly Jews) who were sent straight to the gas chambers[1] |
| Durchfall | – "the runs," or dysentery |
| Effektenkammer | – the storeroom for inmates' personal belongings |
| Erkennungsdienst | – the records office |
| Fahrbereitschaft | – the motor pool |
| Funkstelle | – the SS garrison's radio room |
| Gemeiner | – as used by Pilecki, refers to a low-level SS man |
| Gemeinschaftslager | – a camp for civilian workers; at Auschwitz, virtually all such workers would have been forced laborers conscripted from the German-occupied territories |

---

[1] The country Canada was seen as a symbol of wealth. At Auschwitz, "Canada" was enormous, and its overspill extension in Birkenau alone ("Canada II") consisted of thirty large barrack huts.

| | |
|---|---|
| Generalgouvernement | – the part of occupied Poland that the Nazi Germans ran as a separate administrative entity using the ancient Polish city of Kraków as its capital. Warsaw, Poland's capital, was within the Generalgouvernement. |
| Gestapo | – Geheime Staatspolizei (Secret State Police): the Nazi German secret police |
| Große Postenkette | – the outer security perimeter |
| Häftling | – a camp inmate or prisoner |
| Häftlingsküche | – the camp inmates' kitchen |
| Harmense | – a small subcamp of Auschwitz |
| Hauptscharführer | – the equivalent in the German SS of Master Sergeant |
| Hauptwache | – the main gate guard or guardhouse |
| Home Army | – the military arm of the Polish Underground State during World War II; also known as the Armia Krajowa or AK |
| Kapo | – a supervisor or "trusty" (this position was held by an inmate) |
| Kedyw | – Kierownictwo Dywersji (Guerrilla Warfare and Sabotage Command): an elite branch of the Polish Home Army, whose mission was sabotage, propaganda and armed action against the Nazi Germans |

| | |
|---|---|
| Kiesgrube | – a gravel pit |
| KL Auschwitz | – Konzentrationslager Auschwitz (Auschwitz Concentration Camp) |
| Kleine Postenkette | – the inner security perimeter |
| kommandiert | – ordered to stay at work |
| Kommando | – a camp work detail |
| Krankenbau | – the camp hospital |
| Kriegsgefangenenlager | – a prisoner of war camp |
| KZN | – Pilecki conflates the Konfederacja Zbrojna (The Armed Confederation—KZ) with the Konfederacja Narodu (The Confederation of the Nation—KN). The KZ was the autonomous military arm of the KN, a Polish underground resistance organization that was formed early in World War II and subsequently integrated into the ZWZ (precursor of the Home Army) |
| Lagerältester | – the Head Inmate at the camp |
| Lagerführer | – Camp Head; as Auschwitz grew beyond the main camp, each subordinate camp was supervised by an SS Lagerführer, all under the ultimate authority of the Lagerkommandant |
| Lagerkapo | – the discipline Kapo (this position was held by an inmate) |
| Lagerkommandant | – the Camp Commandant |
| Landwirtschaftskommando | – farming Kommando |

| | |
|---|---|
| Laufschritt | – doing things at the double |
| Lederfabrik | – literally, "leather factory"; Pilecki also refers to it as the tannery |
| Meldung | – a report |
| Muselmann | – camp jargon for an inmate on his last legs; pl. Musselmänner |
| NCO | – a non-commissioned officer |
| NIE | – Niepodległość (Independence): a Polish deep-cover anti-communist resistance movement, to be activated when the Soviet Army arrived in Poland in the final stages of World War II |
| Oberkapo | – a senior Kapo (this position was held by an inmate) |
| Obersturmführer | – the equivalent in the German SS of First Lieutenant |
| Ofensetzer | – a stove fitter |
| Pawiak | – the Pawiak Prison in Warsaw |
| PE | – physical exercise |
| Pfleger | – a nurse |
| Postenkette | – the security perimeter |
| Postzensurstelle | – the mail censorship office |
| POW | – a prisoner of war |
| PZP | – Polski Związek Powstańczy (Polish Insurrectionary Organization): a name under which the Home Army often hid its identity. |
| Rapportführer | – an SS officer responsible for discipline and roll calls in the camp |
| Reichsdeutsche | – a German person from the German Reich; pl. Reichsdeutschen |

| | |
|---|---|
| Scharführer | – the equivalent in the German SS of Staff Sergeant |
| Schonungsblock | – the convalescence block |
| Schreiber | – a clerk (this position was held by an inmate) |
| Schreibstube | – camp term for an office |
| Schutzhäftling | – a camp inmate or prisoner held under indefinite detention pursuant to the Nazi German law of Schutzhaft (protective custody) |
| Senior Uhlan | – the rank in a Polish uhlan cavalry regiment equivalent to Private First Class |
| SK | – Strafkompanie (Penal Company); assignment to the SK, where treatment of inmates was even more brutal than in the rest of the camp, was one of many forms of punishment meted out to camp inmates |
| SOE | – Special Operations Executive, a clandestine British organization whose mission was to encourage and facilitate espionage, sabotage and reconnaissance behind enemy lines |
| SS | – Schutzstaffel (Protective Guard): an elite paramilitary unit of the German Nazi party which operated under its own command structure separate from the regular German Armed Forces (the Wehrmacht) |

| | | |
|---|---|---|
| Stammlager | – | the main or core camp at Auschwitz |
| Stehbunker | – | the "standing bunker," one of the most severe of the punishment confinements |
| Strafkompanie | – | Penal Company, also known as the SK; assignment to the SK, where treatment of inmates was even more brutal than in the rest of the camp, was one of many forms of punishment meted out to camp inmates |
| Strassenbaukommando | – | road-construction Kommando |
| Stubendienst | – | a room supervisor (this position was held by an inmate) |
| TAP | – | Tajna Armia Polska (the Polish Secret Army): a Polish underground resistance organization formed early in World War II that was subsequently integrated into the ZWZ (precursor of the Home Army) |
| Tierpfleger | – | an animal or veterinary nurse |
| Übermenschen | – | "supermen" |
| Unterkapo | – | a deputy Kapo (this position was held by an inmate) |
| Untermensch | – | a "subhuman"; pl. Untermenschen |
| Verkehrsabkürzungen | – | literally, "traffic short-cuts"; apparently jargon used in the SS garrison's radio room referring to the German cipher keys |
| Vernichtungslager | – | an extermination camp |
| Virtuti Militari | – | Poland's highest award for gallantry |
| volksdeutsch | – | ethnically German |

| | |
|---|---|
| Volksdeutsche | – an ethnic German, from outside the German Reich; pl. Volksdeutschen, Volksdeutscher |
| Volksliste | – the German People's Register |
| Vorarbeiter | – a foreman; pl. Vorarbeiteren |
| Waschraum | – a washroom |
| Winkel | – an identification triangle worn by a camp inmate |
| Zettel | – a camp assignment card |
| Zugang | – a new camp inmate, or a new transport of inmates to the camp |
| ZWZ | – Związek Walki Zbrojnej (The Union for Armed Combat): the Polish underground resistance organization into which smaller resistance organizations were integrated, eventually renamed the Armia Krajowa (AK, or Home Army) |

# APPENDIX 2

## German-Language Positions and Ranks at Auschwitz Mentioned by Pilecki[1]

---

### SS PERSONNEL

#### Positions:

Lagerkommandant – the Camp Commandant

Lagerführer – Camp Head; as Auschwitz grew beyond the main camp, each subordinate camp was supervised by an SS Lagerführer, all under the ultimate authority of the Lagerkommandant

Rapportführer – an SS officer responsible for discipline and roll calls in the camp

Blockführer – an SS block supervisor

Gemeiner – as used by Pilecki, refers to a low-level SS man

#### Ranks:

Obersturmführer – the equivalent in the German SS of First Lieutenant

---

[1] In approximately descending order of authority, where appropriate.

343

Hauptscharführer – the equivalent in the German SS of Master Sergeant

Scharführer – the equivalent in the German SS of Staff Sergeant

## INMATES

Lagerältester – the Head Inmate at the camp

Lagerkapo – the discipline Kapo

Oberkapo – a senior Kapo

Kapo – a work supervisor or "trusty"

Unterkapo – a deputy Kapo

Häftling – a camp inmate or prisoner

Schutzhäftling – a camp inmate or prisoner held under indefinite detention pursuant to the Nazi German law of Schutzhaft (protective custody)

Zugang – a new camp inmate, or a new transport of inmates to the camp

**At Work:**

Arbeitsdienst – work assignment office or leader

Vorarbeiter – a foreman; pl. Vorarbeiteren

Pfleger – a nurse

Schreiber – a clerk

Tierpfleger – an animal or veterinary nurse

**In the Blocks:**

Blockältester – a block chief or leader

Stubendienst – a room supervisor

Bademeister – a washroom supervisor

# APPENDIX 3

Index of People and Places Referred to by Pilecki with Either a Code
Number or Letter

(Military ranks and titles are included, where known.)

## PEOPLE

1    Colonel Władysław Surmacki; also called Władek

2    Captain Dr. Władysław Dering; also called Władek
or Dziunko

3    Cavalry Captain Jerzy de Virion

4    Second Lieutenant Alfred Stössel; also called Fredek

5    Roman Zagner

6    Second Lieutenant Tadeusz Burski; also called Tadek

7    Captain Michał Romanowicz; also called Michał
or Captain Michał

8    Captain Ferdynand Trojnicki; also called Fred

9    Corporal Czesław Wąsowski; also called Czesiek

10    Name unknown; called Jurek

11    Colonel Tadeusz Reklewski; also called Colonel R

12    Dr. Edward Nowak

13    Zofia Szczerbowska

14    Sergeant Antoni Woźniak; also called Antek

15    Officer Cadet Witold Szymkowiak; also called Witold

16    Jan Pilecki; also called Pilecki (no relation to author Witold Pilecki)

17    Władysław Kupiec; also called Władek

18    Bolesław Kupiec; also called Bolek

19    Tadeusz Słowiaczek; also called Tadek

20    First Lieutenant Jan Kupiec; also called Janek

21    Tadeusz Pietrzykowski; also called Tadek

22    Antoni Rosa; also called Antek

23    Colonel Aleksander Stawarz

24    Lieutenant Colonel Karol Kumuniecki

25    Stefan Bielecki; also called Czesław III

26    Officer Cadet Platoon Sergeant Stanisław Maringe; also called Stasiek

27    First Lieutenant Jerzy Poraziński; also called Jurek

28    Warrant Officer Szczepan Rzeczkowski; also called Szczepan

29    First Lieutenant Włodzimierz Makaliński; also called Włodek

30    Captain Eugeniusz Triebling; also called Geniek

31    Karol Świętorzecki

32    Leszek Cenzartowicz

33    Stanisław Kocjan

34    Name unknown

35    Officer Cadet Remigiusz Niewiarowski

36    Stanisław Arct

37    Name unknown

38    Major Chmielewski [first name unknown]; also called Sęp II

39    Kazimierz Radwański; also called Kazio (author Witold Pilecki's nephew)

40    Platoon Sergeant Tadeusz Szydlik

41  Stanisław Stawiszyński

42  Tadeusz Lech

43  Antoni Koszczyński

44  Wincenty Gawron; also called Wicek

45  Stanisław Gutkiewicz

46  Wiktor Śniegucki

47  Name unknown

48  Stanisław Ozimek; also called Stach

49  Jan Dangel; also called Janek

50  Jan Mielcarek; also called "Wernyhora"

51  Does not appear

52  Tadeusz Myszkowski; also called Tadek

53  Józef Chramiec

54  Stefan Gaik

55  Mieczysław Wagner

56  Zbigniew Różak

57  Edward Ciesielski; also called Edek

58  Andrzej Marduła

59  Henryk Bartosiewicz

60  Captain Stanisław Kazuba

61  Second Lieutenant Konstanty Piekarski

62  Colonel Jan Karcz

63  Lieutenant Colonel Jerzy Zalewski

64  Lieutenant Colonel Kazimierz Rawicz; in the camp under the name Jan Hilkner

65  Name unknown

66  Name unknown

67  Second Lieutenant Czesław Darkowski

68  Mieczysław Januszewski

69  Professor Roman Rybarski, former member of Parliament

| 70 | Stanisław Dubois, former member of Parliament |
| 71 | Jan Mosdorf, former member of Parliament (per Pilecki) |
| 72 | Konstanty Jagiełło, former member of Parliament (per Pilecki) |
| 73 | Piotr Kownacki, former member of Parliament |
| 74 | Kiliański [first name unknown], former member of Parliament |
| 75 | Stefan Niebudek, former member of Parliament |
| 76 | First Lieutenant Bernard Świerczyna |
| 77 | Zbigniew Ruszczyński |
| 78 | Name unknown |
| 79 | Name unknown |
| 80 | Alfred Włodarczyk |
| 81 | Alojz Pohl |
| 82 | Major Jan Włodarkiewicz; also called Janek W. (promoted to Lieutenant Colonel in 1941, per Pilecki) |
| 83 | Dr. Helena Pawłowska |
| 84 | Lieutenant Tomasz Serafiński; also called Tomek (he and his wife together are no. 179) |
| 85 | Major Zygmunt Bohdanowski; also called Bohdan (promoted to Lieutenant Colonel in 1941, per Pilecki) |
| 86 | Aleksander Paliński |
| 87 | Father Zygmunt Ruszczak |
| 88 | Captain Tadeusz Dziedzic |
| 89 | Karel Stransky |
| 90 | Officer Cadet [name unknown] |
| 91 | Corporal Stanisław Polkowski |
| 92 | Wacław Weszke |
| 93 | Name unknown |
| 94 | Officer Cadet [name unknown] |

| | |
|---|---|
| 95 | Name unknown |
| 96 | Tadeusz Stulgiński |
| 97 | Jan Machnowski; also called Janek |
| 98 | First Lieutenant [name unknown] |
| 99 | Officer Cadet [name unknown] |
| 100 | Name unknown |
| 101 | Witold Kosztowny |
| 102 | Dr. Rudolf Diem |
| 103 | Name unknown |
| 104 | Józef Putek, former member of Parliament |
| 105 | Edward Berlin |
| 106 | Name unknown |
| 107 | Name unknown |
| 108 | Stanisław Dobrowolski |
| 109 | Second Lieutenant [name unknown] |
| 110 | Andrzej Makowski-Gąsienica |
| 111 | Name unknown |
| 112 | Officer Cadet Stanisław Jaster |
| 113 | Sokołowski [first name unknown] |
| 114 | Captain Tadeusz Paolone |
| 115 | First Lieutenant [name unknown] |
| 116 | Captain Zygmunt Pawłowicz; in the camp as Julian Trzęsimiech |
| 117 | First Lieutenant Eugeniusz Zaturski |
| 118 | Name unknown |
| 119 | Cavalry Sergeant Jan Miksa |
| 120 | Dr. Zygmunt Zakrzewski |
| 121 | Colonel Juliusz Gilewicz |
| 122 | Lieutenant Colonel Teofil Dziama |
| 123 | Senior Uhlan Stefan Stępień |
| 124 | Captain Tadeusz Chróścicki (father) |

| | |
|---|---|
| 125 | Tadeusz Lucjan Chrościcki (son) |
| 126 | Tadeusz Czechowski |
| 127 | Name unknown |
| 128 | Name unknown |
| 129 | Leon Kukiełka |
| 130 | Name unknown |
| 131 | Name unknown |
| 132 | Name unknown |
| 133 | Name unknown |
| 134 | Name unknown |
| 135 | Name unknown |
| 136 | Name unknown |
| 137 | Name unknown |
| 138 | Name unknown |
| 139 | Name unknown |
| 140 | Name unknown |
| 141 | Name unknown |
| 142 | Name unknown; lawyer |
| 143 | Name unknown |
| 144 | Name unknown |
| 145 | Dr. [name unknown] |
| 146 | Captain Dr. Henryk Suchnicki |
| 147 | Name unknown |
| 148 | Name unknown |
| 149 | Name unknown |
| 150 | Major Edward Gött-Getyński |
| 151 | Name unknown |
| 152 | Name unknown |
| 153 | Name unknown |
| 154 | Name unknown |

155     Name unknown

156     Second Lieutenant Stanisław Wierzbicki; also called Stasiek

157     Czesław Sikora

158     Zygmunt Ważyński

159     Captain Stanisław Machowski

160     Father Kuc [first name unknown]

161     Bolesław Kuczbara

162     Cavalry Captain Włodzimierz Koliński

163     Second Lieutenant Mieczysław Koliński

164     Second Lieutenant Edmund Zabawski

165     Second Lieutenant Henryk Szklarz

166     Platoon Sergeant [name unknown]

167     Second Lieutenant Aleksander Bugajski; also called Olek

168     First Lieutenant Witold Wierusz

169     Stanisław Barański

170     Jan Redzej; also called Jasiek, Jasio, Jaś, Janek; in the camp as Jan Retko

171     Name unknown

172     Janusz Młynarski

173     Dr. Władysław Fejkiel

174     Second Lieutenant Jan Olszowski

175     Piotr Mazurkiewicz

176     Mr. and Mrs. Obora

177     Helena Zabawska

178     Leon Wandasiewicz

179     Mr. and Mrs. Tomasz Serafiński (Tomasz Serafiński alone is referred to as no. 84)

180     Andrzej Możdżeń

181     Józef Roman

182    Three ladies [names unknown]

183    Name unknown

184    Name unknown

E.O.    Eleonora Ostrowska (author Witold Pilecki's sister-in-law)


## PLACES

I        Does not appear

II       Alwernia

III      The spires of the Benedictine Monastery at Tyniec

IV      Tyniec

V       Unidentified location

VI      Unidentified location

VII     Wieliczka

VIII    The Niepołomnicka Forest

IX      Bochnia[1]

X       Nowy Wiśnicz

XI      Warsaw

Z       Babice and/or Bochnia[1]


## THE FIRST AUSCHWITZ INMATES

The first Auschwitz inmates were brought in from the Oranien-burg concentration camp in May 1940. Pilecki describes them

---

[1] Pilecki confuses the letter Z and the number IX, using Z both for the town of Bochnia and an intermediate location which Adam Cyra says is Babice; see Cyra, *Ochotnik do Auschwitz: Witold Pilecki (1901–1948)* (Oświęcim: Chrześcijańskie Stowarzyszenie Rodzin Oświęcimskich, 2000), p. 398. Cyra also says that IX is Bochnia, op. cit., p. 404. Translator's note.

as "30 Germans, or aspiring Germans...chosen to be our tormentors." They bore the first Auschwitz inmate numbers: 1 to 30. Of these, in his text Pilecki identifies names with numbers for only eight, as follows:

| | |
|---|---|
| 1 | Bronisław Brodniewicz (also written Brodniewitsch); also called Bruno[2] |
| 2 | Otto Küsel; also called Otto |
| 3 | Artur Balke |
| 4 | Fritz Biessgen; also called "Mateczka" ("Mom") |
| 5 | Hans Bock; also called "Tata" ("Daddy") |
| 6–17 | Not named |
| 18 | Konrad Lang |
| 19 | Jonny (*sic*) Lechenich |
| 20–29 | Not named |
| 30 | Leon Wieczorek (also written Wietschorek); also called Leo[2] |

---

[2] Pilecki refers to Bruno and Leo, inmate numbers 1 and 30, as "ex-Poles working for the Germans."

# APPENDIX 4

## Chronology of Witold Pilecki's 1945 Auschwitz Report[1]

### 1940

**19th of September**

Deliberately walks into a German SS street round-up, Warsaw. *p. 11*

**22nd of September**

First day in camp: inmate no. 4859. *p. 14*

**September–December**

Daily camp routine. *p. 25*

Punished: on the wheelbarrows. *p. 33*

Begins setting up a military organization: the first "five." *p. 36*

Doing "physical exercise." Jews and priests harnessed to rollers. *p. 39*

Becomes a stove fitter. *p. 42*

Serious killing starts up again. Weakening, but could not admit to others. *p. 56*

Gets into the small carpenters sho*p. p. 60*

A few "camp pictures." *p. 65*

Silesians. *p. 69*

---

[1] This is an approximate chronology of some key experiences in Pilecki's Report. The chronology is only approximate because in many cases, Pilecki does not give specific months or days, nor does his Report proceed in strictly chronological order.

# 1940

### September–December (continued)

Hunger—"the hardest battle in my life." *p. 72*

Punishments in Auschwitz. *p. 73*

### Christmas 1940

The first parcels from home—no food allowed. *p. 79*

# 1941

### Early 1941

First transport of priests from Auschwitz to Dachau. *p. 156*

### January

Sick: in the hospital, overrun by lice. Saved by Dr. Władysław Dering. *p. 82*

### February

A month of rest: more time to set up "fives." *p. 91*

SS men Grabner and Palitzsch—paid "by the head" for killing inmates. *p. 92*

New meaning for "organize." *p. 93*

Taking advantage of "friendly" Kapos. *p. 94*

### 6th of March

Summoned to the records office over photo. *p. 97*

### 7th of March

Summoned to the main office for not writing to family. *p. 99*

### March

Sets up second "five." *p. 105*

### Spring

Camp orchestra formed. *p. 106*

New camp word: "Muselmann." *p. 120*

# 1941

### Spring (continued)

Collective responsibility for escapes. An heroic priest (Father Maksimilian Kolbe).  *p. 125*

### April–May

Great transports of Polish prisoners from Pawiak Prison—many friends arrive.  *p. 106*

Difference between indoor and outdoor jobs.  *p. 110*

Saving friends.  *p. 116*

### June

Outbreak of the German–Bolshevik War.  *p. 131*

### July

Nephew Kazimierz Radwański brought into camp.  *p. 120*

Camp grows. New subcamps include Buna and Birkenau. Most of those who build them die.  *p. 121*

### August

First Bolshevik prisoners of war brought in and gassed.  *p. 131*

### Autumn

Two hundred inmates released.  *p. 123*

Worries family might buy him out. Clandestinely sends two letters to them.  *p. 125*

### November

The organization grows, based on mutual trust. Choosing leaders.  *p. 129*

More than a thousand naked Bolshevik POWs herded into crematorium.  *p. 132*

Church bells.  *p. 136*

Sets up a fourth "five." Begins bringing senior officers into the organization; suggests Kazimierz Rawicz as leader.  *p. 138*

# 1941

### November (continued)

The political cell.  *p. 139*

Carpentry and woodcarving "elite." A warm bath in the tannery tank.  *p. 140*

### December

Beaten for a "smile" that enrages an SS man.  *p. 143*

Promoted in Warsaw.  *p. 145*

Barbers.  *p. 146*

Lining up to receive money sent by families, one could see who was still alive—only six out of his "hundred."  *p. 150*

"Seidler week."  *p. 154*

### Christmas 1941

Second Christmas in Auschwitz. Another parcel from home— no food allowed.  *p. 150*

# 1942[2]

### Early 1942

Change in attitude toward Jews.  *p. 155*

### February

Remaining Bolshevik POWs finished off; Bolshevik POW revolt quashed.  *p. 157*

Orders from Berlin prohibit use of collective responsibility for escapes and the beating of inmates.  *p. 159*

Typhus-infected lice cultivated and released onto coats of SS men.  *p. 159*

---

2 At this point in the Report, Pilecki says: "owing to a lack of time . . . I must write almost in shorthand."

# 1942

### February (continued)

Gas chambers hastily built in Rajsko-Berkenau. *p. 160*

Inspectors see only "good" view of Auschwitz. Camp tyrants hung by inmates. *p.164*

Begins building radio transmitter; broadcasts until autumn 1942. Clandestinely sends out German cipher keys and receives medicine. *p. 168*

### 16th of March

One hundred and twenty Polish women brought in for interrogation. That evening: bloody corpses in pieces with severed heads, hands, breasts. *p. 173*

### March

Another Warsaw transport brings friends and information. *p. 165*

First daily gassings of people. Two new crematoria with electric ovens. *p. 173*

Buried bodies dug up and burnt. *p. 174*

First large female transports begin. *p. 176*

### Spring

SS man Klehr kills with phenol injections. *p. 179*

Plans are developed for eventual action by the organization. *p. 183*

### Easter

Typhus taking a terrible toll. *p. 186*

### June

Superior officer Kazimierz Rawicz sent to Mauthausen, replaced by Juliusz Gilewicz. *p. 186*

### July

Second transport of priests from Auschwitz to Dachau. *p. 156*

# 1942

## Summer

Transports keep coming—the numbers processed in camp now higher than 40,000. But vast majority go straight to Rajsko-Birkenau without processing, where they are gassed. Mostly Jews from France, Czechoslovakia, Holland and other European countries. *p. 187*

"Canada." *p. 196*

Four inmates escape in the Camp Commandant's car, dressed in SS uniforms. *p. 204*

"Sick tourists": inmates in the hospital taken to gas chambers. *p. 207*

The Jewish "Strangler." *p. 211*

Women all moved to Rajsko-Birkenau, where they die in terrible conditions. Great flea infestation in the women's blocks. *p. 213*

## August–September

Tyhpus patients taken from hospital to gas chambers. *p. 219*

A new expression: "de-lifing." *p. 221*

Ill with typhus: recovering, thanks to comrades' care. *p. 221*

Rajsko-Birkenau bombed by air. *p. 223*

Prepares new plans for the organization in the event of military action. *p. 226*

## October–Autumn

Back to work in the tanners' Kommando. Items left by people who had been gassed are burned, but first searched for valuables by inmates. *p. 228*

"Able to take over the camp on more or less a daily basis"—awaiting orders from Home Army High Command. *p. 230*

The different Lublin pacifications. *p. 231*

The Volksliste. *p. 233*

New transport from Pawiak Prison: surprised by inmates' good physical condition and morale. No one in Warsaw had seriously considered that Auschwitz could represent an active asset. *p. 239*

The gold "organization." *p. 244*

# 1942

### Late Autumn

Germans begin sexual experiments on inmates. *p. 252*

### Christmas 1942

Third Christmas in Auschwitz. Parcels from home—food now allowed. *p. 245*

Daring daylight escape by inmate Bolesław Kuczbara and two Arbeitsdiensts (work assignment leaders). *p. 245*

# 1943

### January

Poles on Block 27, suspected of being organized, are punished. The "educated" group is tortured, interrogated, and finally shot in March 1943. The less educated are sent to the gravel pit to be worked to death. *p. 249*

Seven inmates escape through the SS kitchen. *p. 260*

New German policy: escapees' families will be put in cam*p. p. 260*

### February

Moves to the parcel Kommando, dealing with avalanche of food parcels arriving from inmates' families. *p. 255*

Nearly twenty thousand Gypsies brought to Birkenau; the men are finished off "Auschwitz style." *p. 262*

Audacious inmate escape via "Diogenes's Barrel." *p. 262*

Investigates the sewers as possible escape route. *p. 266*

### 7th–11th of March

Fakes a hernia to escape transport with five thousand Poles to other camps—his responsibility is continuity of his work in Auschwitz. *p. 270*

### March–Spring

Gets to know Jan Redzej, who is planning an escape through the bakery. *p. 276*

# 1943

### March–Spring (continued)

Abolition of morning roll call. Civilian clothing for some inmates.  *p. 278*

Relationships between men (both SS and inmates) and women in the camp.  *p. 281*

### 11th–12th of April

Avoids another transport of twenty-five hundred Poles.  *p. 273*

### 13th of April

Decides to escape.  *p. 274*

### 24th of April, Holy Saturday

Fakes the symptoms of typhus; gets into hospital with help of Edward Ciesielski. Only one night's opportunity for escape through bakery. Jan Redzej and Edward Ciesielski will go too. *p. 283*

### 27th of April

Around 2 a.m., before the last batch of bread for the night is put in the oven, they make their move...  *p. 298*

### 27th April–2nd May

Fleeing to freedom.  *p. 301*

### 4th of May

Meets a commander of the local military underground: Tomasz Serafiński, the man under whose identity Pilecki has been in Auschwitz for nearly three years. *p. 319*

### July

General Grot (Stefan Rowecki, head of the Home Army) is arrested by the Germans.  *p. 323*

### 23rd of August

Back in Warsaw. *p. 323*

# 1943

## Autumn

Works in one of the High Command's cells. Keeps pressing for liberation of Auschwitz. Writes twenty-page report on Auschwitz. *p. 323*

# 1944

A few post-Auschwitz experiences, including the Warsaw Uprising. *p. 326*

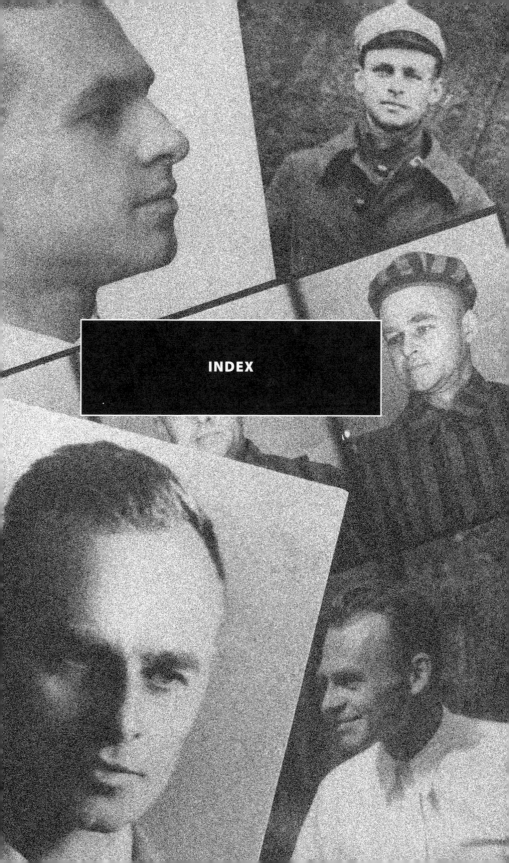

# INDEX

*Preceding page:*
Portraits of Witold Pilecki.

Pilecki Family

# INDEX

Page numbers in *italics* indicate illustrative material

## Code Numbers of People

1 (Colonel Władysław Surmacki; Władek), xx, xxvii, 36–37, 59, 106, 149, 153–154, 165, 240
2 (Captain Dr. Władysław Dering; Władek or Dziunko). *See* Dering, Captain Dr. Władysław
3 (Cavalry Captain Jerzy de Virion), 37, 59, 102, 240
4 (Second Lieutenant Alfred Stössel; Fredek), 37, 91, 116, 168, 226, 241–242
5 (Roman Zagner), 37, 241
6 (Second Lieutenant Tadeusz Burski; Tadek), 37, 87, 91
7 (Captain Michał Romanowicz; Michał or Captain Michał), 47, 53–54, 56, 58
8 (Captain Ferdynand Trojnicki; Fred), 60, 61, 64, 168
9 (Corporal Czesław Wąsowski; Czesiek), 62–64, 104, 153
10 (name unknown; Jurek), 64
11 (Colonel Tadeusz Reklewski; Colonel R), 51, 81, 270–271, 291n66
12 (Dr. Edward Nowak), 87–88
13 (Zofia Szczerbowska), 97
14 (Sergeant Antoni Woźniak; Antek), 104–105, 153, 240
15 (Officer Cadet Witold Szymkowiak; Witold), 105, 186
16 (Jan Pilecki; no relation to Witold Pilecki), 105
17 (Władysław Kupiec; Władek), 105, 115
18 (Bolesław Kupiec; Bolek), 105
19 (Tadeusz Słowiaczek; Tadek), 105, 131–132, 215, 309, 311
20 (First Lieutenant Jan Kupiec; Janek), 105
21 (Tadeusz Pietrzykowski; Tadek), 105, 114, 206
22 (Antoni Rosa; Antek), 105
23 (Colonel Aleksander Stawarz), 105, 165, 184, 187
24 (Lieutenant Colonel Karol Kumuniecki), 105, 165, 184, 232, 249
25 (Stefan Bielecki; Czesław III), 106, 116–117, 166–167, 239–240, 322–323, 328
26 (Officer Cadet Platoon Sergeant Stanisław Maringe; Stasiek), 106, 116, 212, 240
27 (First Lieutenant Jerzy Poraziński; Jurek), 106, 116, 212
28 (Warrant Officer Szczepan Rzeczkowski; Szczepan), 106, 280
29 (First Lieutenant Włodzimierz Makaliński; Włodek), 106, 117, 163, 204, 240
30 (Captain Eugeniusz Triebling; Geniek), 106, 217–218
31 (Karol Świętorzecki), 24, 113
32 (Leszek Cenzartowicz), 114
33 (Stanisław Kocjan), 116
34 (name unknown), 116, 240
35 (Officer Cadet Remigiusz Niewiarowski), 116, 240
36 (Stanisław Arct), 116, 241

37 (name unknown), 116, 241
38 (Major Chmielewski, first name unknown; Sęp II), 117, 241
39 (Kazimierz Radwański; Kazio; nephew of Pilecki), 120, 184, 225, 250, 270, 271
40 (Platoon Sergeant Tadeusz Szydlik), 120–121, 291
41 (Stanisław Stawiszyński), 106n29, 121, 207, 233, 239, 241
42 (Tadeusz Lech), 121, 128–129
43 (Antoni Koszczyński), 121
44 (Wincenty Gawron; Wicek), 21, 106n29, 121, 128, 141, 150, 165–167, 322, 328
45 (Stanisław Gutkiewicz), 106n29, 121, 128, 150, 163
46 (Wiktor Śniegucki), 121
47 (name unknown), 125
48 (Stanisław Ozimek; Stach), 125, 241
49 (Jan Dangel; Janek), 125, 241, 247
50 (Jan Mielcarek; Wernyhora), 129, 216, 217
52 (Tadeusz Myszkowski; Tadek), 128, 167, 168, 215
53 (Józef Chramiec), 129, 217
54 (Stefan Gaik), 129, 217
55 (Mieczysław Wagner), 129
56 (Zbigniew Różak), 129
57 (Edward Ciesielski; Edek), xlix, 129, 224–225, 254, 299, 319, 323, 325, 328. See also escape of
    Pilecki from Auschwitz
58 (Andrzej Marduła), 129, 217
59 (Henryk Bartosiewicz). See Bartosiewicz, Henryk
60 (Captain Stanisław Kazuba), 138, 183, 227, 292
61 (Second Lieutenant Konstanty Piekarski), 138, 145, 168, 183, 226, 228, 244, 266, 271
62 (Colonel Jan Karcz), 138, 160–163, 167–168, 207–208
63 (Lieutenant Colonel Jerzy Zalewski), 138
64 (Lieutenant Colonel Kazimierz Rawicz; in camp as Jan Hilkner), lii, 139, 140, 162, 163,
    183–184, 186
65 (name unknown), 139
66 (name unknown), 139
67 (Second Lieutenant Czesław Darkowski), 139, 186
68 (Mieczysław Januszewski), 139, 166, 168
69 (Professor Roman Rybarski; former member of Parliament), 139, 150, 166
70 (Stanisław Dubois; former member of Parliament), 139, 150, 187
71 (Jan Mosdorf; former member of Parliament, per Pilecki), 139, 216, 217
72 (Konstanty Jagiełło; former member of Parliament, per Pilecki), 139
73 (Piotr Kownacki; former member of Parliament), 139, 216, 217
74 (Kiliański, first name unknown; former member of Parliament), 139
75 (Stefan Niebudek; former member of Parliament), 139
76 (First Lieutenant Bernard Świerczyna), 140, 184, 225–226, 240, 243, 249, 275, 291, 292
77 (Zbigniew Ruszczyński), 140, 168, 243
78 (name unknown), 140
79 (name unknown), 140
80 (Alfred Włodarczyk), 70, 150, 218, 221, 291
81 (Alojz Pohl), 150
82 (Major Jan Włodarkiewicz; Janek W.), xlvi, 17, 125, 146
83 (Dr. Helena Pawłowska), 152–153, 321
84 (Lieutenant Tomasz Serafiński; Tomek). See Serafiński, Lieutenant Tomasz
85 (Major Zygmunt Bohdanowski; Bohdan), 146, 165, 183, 184, 227, 241, 250, 274, 275
86 (Aleksander Paliński), 154, 325
87 (Father Zygmunt Ruszczak), 157
88 (Captain Tadeusz Dziedzic), 160, 239
89 (Karel Stransky), 163
90 (Officer Cadet, name unknown), 165, 243, 252
91 (Corporal Stanisław Polkowski), 165, 216, 217

92 (Wacław Weszke), 165, 216, 281, 292
93 (name unknown), 165
94 (Officer Cadet, name unknown), 165, 216, 217, 243
95 (name unknown), 165, 216
96 (Tadeusz Stulgiński), 165
97 (Jan Machnowski; Janek), 140–141, 165
98 (First Lieutenant, name unknown), 166, 292
99 (Officer Cadet, name unknown), 166, 292
100 (name unknown), 166, 223, 224
101 (Witold Kosztowny), 166, 224, 252–254, 291
102 (Dr. Rudolf Diem), 166, 244
103 (name unknown), 166
104 (Józef Putek; former member of Parliament), 167
105 (Edward Berlin), 167, 239
106 (name unknown), 167, 216, 276
107 (name unknown), 167
108 (Stanisław Dobrowolski), 167, 239, 241
109 (Second Lieutenant, name unknown), 167
110 (Andrzej Makowski-Gąsienica), 167, 266
111 (name unknown), 167, 215–217, 222
112 (Officer Cadet Stanisław Jaster), 168, 204
113 (Sokołowski, first name unknown), 168
114 (Captain Tadeusz Paolone), 183, 227, 291n66
115 (First Lieutenant, name unknown), 183
116 (Captain Zygmunt Pawłowicz; in camp as Julian Trzęsimiech), 183–184, 227, 327
117 (First Lieutenant Eugeniusz Zaturski), 184, 240, 241, 243, 250
118 (name unknown), 184, 226, 266, 292
119 (Cavalry Sergeant Jan Miksa), 184, 186
120 (Dr. Zygmunt Zakrzewski), 184, 241
121 (Colonel Juliusz Gilewicz), xx, 186–187, 226–228, 244, 275
122 (Lieutenant Colonel Teofil Dziama), 187, 232, 292
123 (Senior Uhlan Stefan Stępień), 204
124 (Captain Tadeusz Chróścicki; father), 212, 241
125 (Tadeusz Lucjan Chróścicki; son), 212–213, 241
126 (Tadeusz Czechowski), 217
127 (name unknown), 215
128 (name unknown), 218
129 (Leon Kukiełka), 218, 226, 239, 241
130 (name unknown), 218, 226, 241
131 (name unknown), 218, 241
132 (name unknown), 218
133 (name unknown), 218
134 (name unknown), 218
135 (name unknown), 218
136 (name unknown), 218
137 (name unknown), 218
138 (name unknown), 218, 240, 274
139 (name unknown), 218
140 (name unknown), 218
141 (name unknown), 218
142 (lawyer, name unknown), 218, 249
143 (name unknown), 218
144 (name unknown), 218
145 (Dr., name unknown), 224, 226
146 (Captain Dr. Henryk Suchnicki), 224, 226, 239
147 (name unknown), 226

148 (name unknown), 226
149 (name unknown), 226, 273
150 (Major Edward Gött-Getyński), 227, 249
151 (name unknown), 232
152 (name unknown), 232
153 (name unknown), 232
154 (name unknown), 232
155 (name unknown), 232
156 (Second Lieutenant Stanisław Wierzbicki; Stasiek), 232, 239–242, 250–251, 274
157 (Czesław Sikora), 239, 241, 242
158 (Zygmunt Ważyński), 239–242, 320
159 (Captain Stanisław Machowski), 240, 274
160 (Father Kuc), 240, 320, 321
161 (Bolesław Kuczbara), 244–245, 275, 324
162 (Cavalry Captain Włodzimierz Koliński), 249
163 (Second Lieutenant Mieczysław Koliński), 249
164 (Second Lieutenant Edmund Zabawski), 259, 276, 283, 317–318
165 (Second Lieutenant Henryk Szklarz), 259
166 (Platoon Sergeant, name unknown), 259
167 (Second Lieutenant Aleksander Bugajski; Olek), 259–262, 265–266, 280, 289, 326
168 (First Lieutenant Witold Wierusz), 260–262, 265
169 (Stanisław Barański), 271
170 (Jan Redzej; Jasiek, Jasio, Jaś, Janek; in camp as Jan Retko), *xlix*, 276–277, *299*, 319, 323,
         325, 328. *See also* escape of Pilecki from Auschwitz
171 (name unknown), 282
172 (Janusz Młynarski), 284, 286
173 (Dr. Władysław Fejkiel), 287
174 (Second Lieutenant Jan Olszowski), 293
175 (Piotr Mazurkiewicz), 314–315
176 (Mr. and Mrs. Obora), 318–319
177 (Helena Zabawska), 318
178 (Leon Wandasiewicz), 319–321
179 (Mr. and Mrs. Serafiński), 321–323. *See also* Serafiński, Lieutenant Tomasz
180 (Andrzej Możdżeń), 321–322
181 (Józef Roman), 323
182 (three ladies, names unknown), 325–327
183 (name unknown), 328
184 (name unknown), 328

## A

AK. *See* Polish Home Army
Aleja Szucha (Gestapo headquarters in Warsaw), 117, 123, 152, 165
Aloiz ("Bloody Aloiz," Kapo), 23–25, 33, 35, 38, 39, 70, 164
Alsatian (dog belonging to SS man "Pearly"/"Perełka"), 65, 75
Alwernia (location II), map *300*, 310
Anders, General Władysław, liv
animals, cared for by inmate kommandos or work details, 110, 113–114, 140, 146
Antek (Antoni Rosa; 22), 105
Antek (Sergeant Antoni Woźniak; 14), 104–105, 153, 240
"Arbeit macht frei" gate, Auschwitz, 14, *15*, 59, 115
Arbeitsdienst (work assignment office), ZOW members in, 166
Arbeitsdiensts (work assignment leaders), 42, 139, 166, 245, 265–266, 275, 281
arbeitsfähig (fit for work), 272
Arbeitskommando (camp work detail), 33, 35, 39, 99, 138, 234
Arbeitslager (labor camp), 279
arbeitsunfähig (unfit for work), 272

Arct, Stanisław (36), 116, 241
armbands (Binden), 94
Armia Krajowa. *See* Polish Home Army
arms store, reserve under baubüro or construction site office, 235
arrest of Pilecki, xlviii, 11–12
Aufräumungskommando (salvage Kommando), *197, 200–202*
Aumeier, Hans, 205, 281
Auschwitz. *See also* escapes from Auschwitz; Jews at Auschwitz-Birkenau; military
        attacks on Auschwitz; Polish inmates in Auschwitz; releases of
        inmates from Auschwitz; SS garrison at Auschwitz; *specific buildings
        and sites*
    "Arbeit macht frei" gate, 14, *15,* 59, 115
    arrival and admission to, 13–25
    assignment card (Zettel), 287–288
    bell at, 136–137
    Bolshevik POWs at, xvi, xxxix, li, 16, 132–136, *134,* 157
    construction of buildings and roads at, *44,* 56–58, *111–112,* 122–123
    daily routine at, 25–36
    as death camp, 135, 279
    as work camp, 278–279
    different nationalities at, 209
    fencing, perimeter and interior (the "wire"), 14, *15,* 28, *29,* 31, 41, 47, 51, 55–56,
        66–67, *111,* 125, 132, 135–137, 140, 157, *192,* 215, 223, 242, 245, 262, 267, 278,
        304, 320
    first thirty German inmates at, role of, 93–97, 352–353
    identity and reputation of, 18, 164, 278–279
    importance of telling world about, 254
    inmate identity photographs, *xxxviii, 21, 30, 43, 89, 95–96, 162, 299, 333*
    inspection of, 107, 164, 170
    maps of environs, camp layout and location, *9–10, 300*
    mission of Pilecki in, xlii–xliv, 36
    number of inmates at, 121–122, 187, 209
    Pilecki in, xlviii–liii
    Polish political prisoners, used for, xxxix, xlii–xliii, 23
    political versus criminal prisoners in, xlii–xliii
    self-sufficiency of, 110
    subcamps of, 122–123
    survival expectations/death rates, 19, 49, 150–151, 186, 328–329
awo (camp slang for a broth), 27

**B**

Babice (possible identification of Z), map *300,* 308
Bademeister (washroom supervisor), 20
Baderaum (communal washing facility), 20
bakery, escape through, 276–277, 279–281, 287–298
Balke, Artur (inmate no. 3), 94, *95,* 104–105, 115, 121, 123, 140
Baltosiński (Baltaziński), 64–65
Barański, Stanisław (169), 271
barbers, 146–149, 176
barracks/blocks. *See* blocks/barracks
Bartosiewicz, Henryk (59)
        beating of Pilecki by Kapo Walter, present at, 145
        Christmas tree with Polish eagle erected by, 150
        Karcz's interrogation by political department and, 160
        Kuczbara's certificate for, 244, 275–276
        leadership of ZOW turned over to, 275, 276
        Pilecki's farewell to, 292
        recruitment activities, 139, 165

recruitment by Pilecki, 138
sense of humor and good-heartedness of, 169–173
tannery, Pilecki's movement to, 228
ZOW plan of eventual action, development of, 184, 226
basket-weaving Kommando, 255
bathing facilities, 20, 26, 84, 141–142, 149, 214
Baubüro (construction site office), 37, 59, 118, 166, 174, 235, 260, 266
Baworowski, Władysław, 19
beatings and punishments of inmates. *See also* torture and interrogation
    beatings, 13, 17, 19, 23, 26, 34–35, 39–41, 52–53, 56–57, 66, 69–71, 106–107, 117, 132,
        136, 165, 238, 243
    bench beatings, 73, 82, 97, 219
    "black hole," 74, 158
    bunker punishment, 28, 67, 69, 73–74, 106, 126n34, 142, 158, 160, 167–168, 184, 196,
        206, 241–243, 246, 250, 251, 281–283, 295, 298, 328
    cessation of beatings, 159, 179, 279
    collective responsibility. *See* collective responsibility for escapes
    "death selection," 126-127, 137
    hanging, 67, 80, 137, 206, 260, 279,
    order forbidding, 159
    pole, inmates hung by arms from, 75
    punishment parade, 66–69, 137, 154, 205, 250, 277, 278
    shooting, xl, 14, 28, 29, 66n18, 75–79, 77, 92,126–127, 149, 157, 159, 166, 187, 204,
        207, 234–236, 238, 241, 251, 258, 269, 274
    Stehbunker (standing bunker), 74, 158
    testicles, crushing of, 65
beatings experienced by Pilecki
    bunk, for improper making up of, 132
    convalescence, end of, 104
    front teeth, loss of, 20
    preemptive beating of Stubendiensts (room supervisors), 24
    smile or smirk, beaten for, 144–145
Bednarek, Emil, 70
Bekleidungskammer (clothing storeroom), 196, 248–250, 251
Bekleidungswerkstätte (clothing workshop), 255
Belgian inmates at Auschwitz, 209
bell at Auschwitz, 136–137, 138, 234, 289. *See also* gong; siren at Auschwitz
bench beatings. *See* beatings and punishments of inmates
Benedictine Abbey, Tyniec (location III), 313
Berlin, Edward (105), 167, 239
Bielecki, Stefan (Czesław III; 25), 106, 116–117, 166–167, 239–240, 322–323, 328
Biessgen, Fritz (inmate no. 4; "Mateczka" or "Mom"), 94, 95, 228
Binden (armbands), 94
Birkenau (Brzezinka, also called Rajsko). *See also* gas chambers; Jews at Auschwitz-
        Birkenau
    Bolshevik POWs, 136, 157
    Bruno moved to, 246
    construction of, 122–123
    crematoria constructed at, 174–175, *178*, 187
    female inmates moved to, 213, 215
    Gypsies in, 262, *263, 264*
    Karcz moved to, 163
    sexual experiments on inmates from, 253
    Silesians moved to, 163
    SS men picking up women at, 282
    ZOW members saved and admitted as zugangs to, 182

Black August, 53

"black hole," 74, 158

black man, proposal to creep up on Auschwitz with board painted with, 326–327

Blockältesters (block chiefs), 28, 32, 69, 94

Blockführers (SS block supervisors), 69

Blockführerstube (SS guardroom), 100, 205, 290, 293

blocks/barracks

"a" added to block number designated first floor (above ground floor), 23

at Auschwitz main camp, construction of new, 20n3, 122

at Birkenau, construction of, carpenters dying in, 122–123

bunks in, 132, 143, *147*, 164, 216–217, 271, 278, 289, 292

deployment of by ZOW, in the event of military action, 226–227

designation of blocks by ground and first floors, 23

flea infestation in, 214–215

"freedom" block, 124, 153

map of main Auschwitz camp, *10*

new numbering system, 20n3

numbers of, mentioned in Report:

Blocks 1–10 (new nos.; female inmates' blocks), 176

Block 1, 176, 227, 267

Block 2, 176, 227

Block 3/3a, 71, 84, 103, 104, 132, 176, 227, 234, 236, 250, 256, 266–267

Block 4 (new no.), 176, 227, 267

Block 5 (new no.), 154, 176, 227, 267

Block 5 (old no.; the "youngsters' block"), 64–65, 72, 80–81

Block 6 (new no.), 176, 227, 259, 271, 286, 289, 291

Block 6 (old no.), 170

Block 7 (new no.), 176, 227

Block 8 (new no.), 176, 227

Block 8 (old no.), 61

Block 9 (new no.), 176, 227

Block 9 (old no.; small carpentry shop, main Schreibstube or office), 42, 60, 81, 99, 104, 107

Block 10 (new no.; location of German medical experiments), 176, 227, 252–254, 267

Block 10 (old no.), 23

Block 11 (old no.; Zugang block), 116

Block 11 (new no., old no. Block 13; location of the SK [Strafkompanie or Penal Company], the bunkers and interrogation cells; adjacent to "Wall of Tears"), 32, 73–75, 77, 92, 103, 131, *134*, 158, 227, 238, 241, 247, 282

Block 12 (new no.), 132, 143, 227, 266–267, 270–271

Block 12 (old no.; Zugang block), 75–77, 116

Block 13 (new no.), 227, 267

Block 13 (old no.). *See* Block 11 (new no.)

Block 14 (new no.), 227, 236

Block 14 (old no.). *See* Block 19 (new no.)

Block 15 (new no.), 227, 236, 267, 286–288, 292–293

Block 15 (old no.). *See* Block 20 (new no.)

Block 16 (new no.), 227, 234, 236, 267

Block 17 (new no.), 227, 236, 274

Block 17/17a (old no.). *See* Block 25 (new no.)

Block 18/18a (new no.), 227, 236, 291

Block 18 (old no.). *See* Block 26 (new no.)

Block 19 (new no., old Block 14; the Schonungsblock or convalescence block), 120, 227, 270

Block 20 (new no., old no. Block 15; hospital, location of information box), 82, 84, 88, 91, 97, 101–103, 159, 179, 180, 218–220, 223–224, 227, 232, 285, 288
Block 21 (new no.), 149, 227, 238, 267
Block 22 (new no.), 227, 234, 244–245, 248, 267, 283, 292
Block 23 (new no.), 227, 267
Block 24 (new no.), 227
Block 25 (new no., old no. Block 17/17a), 23, 49, 70–71, 84, 100, 132, 138, 143, 150, 163, 186, 216, 222, 227, 291
Block 26 (new no., old no. Block 18; communal washing facilities, Erkennungsdienst or records office), 20, 70, 84, 97, 149, 227, 234
Block 27 (new no.; Bekleidungskammer or clothing storeroom), 220, 227, 238, 248–249, 291
Block 28 (new no.; hospital), 179, 218, 220, 222–223, 226–227, 241, 267, 284, 291
Blocksperre (confinement to blocks), 121, 158, 269
Bloody Aloiz (Kapo), 23–25, 33, 35, 38, 39, 70, 164
Bochnia (location Z/IX), 153, 240, 283, map 300, 308n67, 317, 319, 320, 352n1
Bock, Hans (inmate no. 5; "Tata" or "Daddy"), 94
Bohdan (Major Zygmunt Bohdanowski; 85), 146, 165, 183, 184, 227, 241, 250, 274, 275
Bohdanowski, Major Zygmunt (Bohdan; 85), 146, 165, 183, 184, 227, 241, 250, 274, 275
Bolek (Bolesław Kupiec; 18), 105
Bolsheviks. See Soviet Union
bombing of Auschwitz, 223
Bonitz, Bernard, 53
boxing matches between inmates and Kapos, 204–205, 246
bread-unloading Kommando (Brotabladungskommando), 276
Brodniewitsch, Bruno (Lagerältester Bronisław Brodniewicz; inmate no. 1), 30, 31, 63, 73, 94, 236, 246, 249, 353n2
Brotabladungskommando (bread-unloading Kommando), 276
Bruno (Lagerältester Bruno Brodniewitsch/Bronisław Brodniewicz ; inmate no. 1). See Brodniewitsch, Bruno.
Brzezinka. See Birkenau
Buchenwald, 16, 271, 272
Bugajski, Second Lieutenant Aleksander (Olek; 167), 259–262, 265–266, 280, 289, 326
Bulgarian inmates at Auschwitz, 209
Buna, 122, 169, 205, 304
bunker punishment. See beatings and punishments of inmates; torture and interrogation
bunks. See blocks/barracks
burial of inmates alive by SS men, 71–72
Burski, Second Lieutenant Tadeusz (Tadek; 6), 37, 87, 91

**C**

camp heads (Lagerführers), 41, 42, 154, 205, 338, 343
"Canada," 196–204, 197–202, 218, 220, 225, 245, 257, 270, 278
Captain Michał (Captain Michał Romanowicz; Michał; 7), 47, 53–54, 56, 58
carpenter, Pilecki's work as, 60–65, 72, 80–82, 104–105, 114–116, 120–121, 123, 127–129, 132, 140–141, 167, 215–216
cell organization of ZOW. See "fives," ZOW organized in
censorship office, mail (Postzensurstelle), 100–104, 124
Cenzartowicz, Leszek (32), 114
character, camp as proving ground of, 50
Chełmno, 264
children at Auschwitz
    family, Palitzsch's execution of, 76–79

of German camp authorities, 142
Jewish children, 188, *190–191, 192,* 195
Lublin boys killed by phenol, 232
patriotic songs, schoolboys imprisoned for, 120
sexual abuse of boy inmates by Leo (Leon Wietschorek), 80–81
in small group killed in crematorium, 247–248
shoes of, 228
typhus patients, gassing of, 220
Chmielewski, Major (first name unknown; Sęp II; 38), 117, 241
Chramiec, Józef (53), 129, 217
Christmas at Auschwitz
    1940, 72–73, 79–80
    1941, 150
    1942, 245–252, 266, 268
Chrobry II, 1 Battalion of Group–, 328
Chrościcki, Captain Tadeusz (124; father), 212, 241
Chrościcki, Tadeusz Lucjan (125; son), 212–213, 241
church. *See also* priests; religion; Christmas at Auschwitz; Easter at Auschwitz
    assistance to Pilecki during escape, 309–312
    bells, 47, 136–137, 310
    parish records, changed to protect Pilecki's assumed identity, 152–153, 240, 321
    services, including mass, communion, confession, 157
Ciesielski, Edward (Edek; 57), *xlix,* 129, 224–225, 254, *299,* 319, 323, 325, 328. *See also* escape of
    Pilecki from Auschwitz
cigarettes, 27, 145, 302
cipher keys, German (Verkehrsabkürzungen), 169
civilian forced laborers, camp for (Gemeinschaftslager), 169
clothing
    Bekleidungskammer (clothing storeroom), 196, 248–250, 251
    Bekleidungswerkstätte (clothing workshop), 255
    for escape from Auschwitz, 291–292, 301–302, 305, 307
    of gassed Jews and other inmates, 195–203, *197–202,* 221, 278
    knitting wool, use of, 228
    of Pflegers (nurses), 219–220
    of inmates, 14–17, *16,* 20, 23, 62, 79, 278, 292
collective responsibility for escapes
    on arrival and admission to Auschwitz, 14
    families of escapees, threats to, 261, 322
    food, access to, 67
    order forbidding, 159, 251
    punishment parade, 66–69, 154, 205
    ten men shot for every escapee, 125–127
Colonel R (Colonel Tadeusz Reklewski; 11), 51, 81, 270–271, 291n66
communism
    anti-communist Polish resistance movement, Pilecki's involvement with, xvi,
        xxiii, lii, liii–liv
    Auschwitz, communist political prisoners in, xliin4
    Soviet Union in WWII and after, xi–xiii
confinement to blocks (Blocksperre), 121, 158, 269
conscientious objectors, 23n6
convalescence block (Schonungsblock), 120, 138, 220
corpses
    of boys murdered with phenol, 232
    brought back to roll call by inmates, 57, 107
    dug up and burned, 174–175
    naked, taken to crematoria as, 224

numbers on, 182
piling up of, 224
of Polish female inmates, 174
crematoria, 27, 34, 113, 132–136, 174–175, *178*, 187, 223, 224, 247–248, 279
croton oil, 184–185
Cyra, Adam, xx, xxi, 308n67, 352n1
Czech inmates at Auschwitz, 163, 187, 209, 257, 281
Czechowski, Tadeusz (126), 217
Czesiek (Corporal Czesław Wąsowski; 9), 62–64, 104, 153
Czesław III (Stefan Bielecki; 25), 106, 116–117, 166–167, 239–240, 322–323, 328
Czetwertyński family, 116

**D**

Dachau, xii, 125, 156–157, 272
"Daddy" or "Tata" (Hans Bock; inmate no. 5), 94
daily routine at Auschwitz, 25–36
Dangel, Jan (Janek; 49), 125, 241, 247
Darkowski, Second Lieutenant Czesław (67), 139, 186
Davies, Norman, xi–xiii
"de-lifing," 221
death camp, Auschwitz as, 135, 279
death notices for inmates, 155
death rates/survival expectations at Auschwitz, 19, 49, 150–151, 186, 328–329
"death selection," 126–127, 137
"delousing," gassing referred to as, 219, 221
delousings, 84, 91, 132, 215, 221, 226, 265
Dering, Captain Dr. Władysław (Władek or Dziunko; 2)
anti-typhus shots obtained by, 169, 217
diagnosis of Pilecki's pneumonia by, 87–88
in first "five" of ZOW, 36–37
freezing of naked inmates, as witness to, 149
hospital, position in, 98–99, 116, 143, 166
inmate photo, *89*
inquiries after Pilecki's health by, 59
Kuczbara and, 244, 275
Pflegers, typhus patients saved by dressing as, 220
Pilecki's plans to escape from Auschwitz and, 275, 276
Pilecki's second fever, treatment of, 222, 223, 226
in TAP, 240
transport of Polish inmates and, 270, 273, 274
Triebling's blood infection cured by, 218
Uris sued by, 36n9
warning to Pilecki about office summons, 98
diamonds and gold, 203–204, 229–230, 243–244, 246, 257, 275, 282–283
Diem, Dr. Rudolf (102), 166, 244
"Diogenes' barrel" escape, 262–265
discipline Kapos (Lagerkapos), 63, 138, 158
Dobrowolski, Stanisław (108), 167, 239, 241
dogs at Auschwitz, 13–14, 65, 67, 75, 114, 179, 209, 302
double, doing things at the (Laufschritt), 25–26, 34, 42, 63, 295
dreams of Pilecki prior to escape, 285, 287
Drozd, Franciszek, 71, 83
Dubois, Stanisław (former member of Parliament; 70), 139, 150, 187
dunce's cap, 67
Dunikowski, Professor, 140–141
Durchfall (dysentery), 55–56

Dutch inmates at Auschwitz, 209, 278
dysentery (Durchfall), 55–56
Dziama, Lieutenant Colonel Teofil (122), 187, 232, 292
Dziedzic, Captain Tadeusz (88), 160, 239
Dziunko (Captain Dr. Władysław Dering or Władek; 2). *See* Dering, Captain Dr. Władysław

**E**

Easter at Auschwitz, 186, 281, 283, 285, 287, 289, 326
eating. *See* food and drink
Edek (Edward Ciesielski; 57), *xlix*, 129, 224–225, 254, *299*, 319, 323, 325, 328. *See also* escape of
    Pilecki from Auschwitz
Effektenkammer (storeroom for inmates' possessions), 70–71, 79
E.O. (Eleonora Ostrowska, sister-in-law of Pilecki), 100, 103, 153, 322, 325
Erik (Erik Grönke), 141–142, 145, 167, 203, 216, 229, 282
Erkennungsdienst (records office), 97, 99, 234
escape of Pilecki from Auschwitz (with Edward Ciesielski and Jan Redzej), lii, 279–323
    bakery, via, 276–277, 279–281, 287–298
    to border between Silesia (German Third Reich) and the Generalgouverne-
        ment, 301–308
    from border to Bochnia, 314–319
    clothing used in, 291–292, 301–302, 305, 307
    crossing the border, 308–313
    decision to escape, 279–281
    dreams prior to escape, 285, 287
    farewells and gathering of supplies for, 291–292
    food and drink during, 306–307, 309, 311, 314
    map of escape route, *300*
    medical issues during, 308, 309–310, 312, 316–318
    plans for, 230, 251, 261, 266–268, 273–277
    Serafińskis, Pilecki's stay with, xix, *xlix*, 319–323
    shot at by German soldiers, 301, 316–317
    SS men and, 293–298, 301, 328
    tobacco used to cover scent trail, 302
escapes from Auschwitz. *See also* collective responsibility for escapes
    Bugajski and Wierusz's plans for, 259–262, 265–266
    Camp Commandant's car, using, 204–205
    captured escapees, punishment/execution of, 67–68, 206, 279
    "Diogenes' barrel," 262–265
    families of escapees, threats to, 261, 322
    first case of, 65–65
    Kommando change associated by camp authorities with, 266, 280
    perimeter fencing, reinforcement and electrification of, 66–67
    senior officers, planned camp revolt and escape by, 105–106
    sewers, via, 259–260, 266–268
    by SK inmates, 212–213
    SS men drugged for purposes of, 261
    SS uniforms used for, 204–205, 245–246
    "wet job," Pilecki's protest against, 262
    ZOW's opposition to, 126, 262
    ZOW's organization of, 166–167, 226, 241
    ZOW's sending of reports via, 159, 167, 260
ethnic Germans (Volksdeutschen), 53, 60, 150, 184, 249, 268, 342
European territorial boundaries (1939), map *vi*
*Exodus* (Uris), 36n9

# F

Fahrbereitschaft (motor pool), 116
"Falcon" ("Sokół") organization of Czechs, 163
families, of Auschwitz inmates
 death notices to, 155
 escaped inmates, threats against families of, 261, 322
 freedom of inmates bought by, 11, 91, 114, 123, 125
 Jewish inmates' letters home, 156, 188, 210
 money sent by, 151
 parcels sent by, 79, 150, 245, 246, 255–259, 270, 288–290
 Pilecki's post-escape contacts with, 324, 325
 threat of accountability for inmate actions, 237–238
 Volksliste, inmates urged by families to sign, 233
 Zabawski's family and Pilecki's escape from Auschwitz, 276, 283, 317–318
family, Palitzsch's execution of, 77–79
family, of Pilecki
 background of, xliv, *xlv*
 escape from Auschwitz, after, 322
 failure of Pilecki to write letters to, questioning about, 98–104
 letters of Pilecki to, 125
 nephew of Pilecki sent to Auschwitz, family news from, 120
 photographs of, *xxviii, xlvi*
 Report, seldom mentioned in, liii
farming Kommando (Landwirtschaftskommando), 97
Fejkiel, Dr. Władysław (173), 287
female inmates at Auschwitz
 arrival of, 176–179
 Birkenau, moved to, 213, 215
 Blocks 1–10 (new nos.), first housed in, 176
 building construction, work on, *44*
 deterioration of, 176–179, 208–209, 213
 escaped inmates, threats against families of, 261
 fence built to block off area for, 157, 215
 flea infestation, 213–215
 gassing of, 213
 German prostitutes and female criminals as authorities over, 173, 176, 282
 Jewish women, 188, 209–210
 Palitzsch's sexual relationship with Jewish inmate Katti, 282
 Polish political prisoners, arrival and execution of, 173–174
 sexual experiments on, 252–254
 shaving of heads and body hair of, 176
 shot by Palitzsch, 76
 in small group killed in crematorium, 247, 248
 SS men and other inmates having sex with, 281–282
fencing, perimeter and interior. *See* Auschwitz—fencing, perimeter and interior
fish ponds, 167
"fives," as Pilecki's term for groups generally, 11, 13, 33, 39, 42, 46, 47
"fives," ZOW organized in, xlviii–li, 36–38, 93
 first five, 36–38, 47
 second five, 105
 third five, 106
 fourth five, 138
 in Baubüro (construction site office), 59, 166

Makaliński introduced to all 42 cells, 163
political cell, 139–140, 150
recruitment of, 47, 91, 97, 105, 121, 129, 138–140, 165–168, 183–184, 186–187, 218,
    226, 232, 240
Silesians in, 70, 150
flea infestation in female barracks, 213–215
Florczyk, Heniek, 91
Flossenbürg, 272
food and drink
    on admission and arrival, 18, 19
    awo (camp slang for a broth), 27
    barbers' access to, 149
    from "Canada," 245
    at Christmas, 72, 80, 245
    cigarettes, trading food for, 27
    collective responsibility for escapes and loss of access to, 67
    dead inmates, parcels sent to, 257–259, 270
    dog meat, consumption of, 114
    dysentery and, 55–56
    energy requirements versus, 57
    escape from Auschwitz, during, 306–307, 309, 311, 314
    experience of hunger, difficulty of describing, 72
    family parcels to inmates and, 79, 150, 245, 246, 256–259, 270, 288, 290
    Jewish arrivals, taken from, 188, 196
    liquids, excessive reliance on, 26–27
    livestock, as work detail, 113–114
    local population, additional food provided by, 97
    mangelwurzels, 55
    salad dressing/vinegar, fed to inmates hung from poles, 75
    second illness of Pilecki, extras provided by comrades during, 226
    sickness, ability of Pilecki to eat while suffering from, 86
    small carpenter shop, Pilecki's receipt of extra food while working in, 64–65, 72
    storerooms, smell of food from, 58
    from Stubendiensts (room supervisors), 130
    transport to Auschwitz, during, 12
    turnips carried into camp, 143–144
    use as test in recruiting inmates for ZOW, 130
    vodka, 205, 262, 281, 287
football matches, 204–205
forced laborers, civilian, camp for (Gemeinschaftslager), 169
foremen (Vorarbeiteren), 34, 45, 47, 53, 60, 61, 69
Fred (Captain Ferdynand Trojnicki; 8), 60, 61, 64, 168
Fredek (Second Lieutenant Alfred Stössel; 4), 37, 91, 116, 168, 226, 241–242
"freedom" block, 124, 153
freezing of inmates by exposure after hot shower, 149
French inmates at Auschwitz, 209, 257
Fritzsch, Karl, 42, 281
Funkstelle (radio room), 168, 169
Fusek (friend of Janek Machnowski), 141

**G**

Gaik, Stefan (54), 129, 217
Gajowniczek, Franciszek, 127n35
garden of Camp Commandant, Pilecki's work on, 45, 47–48, 51–53
Garliński, Jarek, xxii, xxiii, xxv, liv
Garliński, Józef, xx, xxi, 223n50

gas chambers
    construction of, 160, *177*
    crematorium, Bolshevik POWs gassed in, 132–136
    daily gassings, 173, 277
    female inmates, gassing of, 213
    hospital patients taken to, 207
    ill or weak-looking inmates picked for, 220–221
    interior photo, *161*
    Jews, gassing of, 195
    pacification campaign in Lublin region and, 231–232
    Prussic acid, 131–132
    reputation of Auschwitz and, 279
    sealed room, Bolshevik POWs gassed in, 131–132, *134*
    "sick tourists," 207
    typhus block patients taken to, 219–220
    Zyklon B, 134, *194*, 195
Gąska, Izak ("the Strangler"), 211
Gawron, Wincenty (Wicek; 44), *21*, 106n29, 121, 128, 141, 150, 165–167, 322, 328
Gemeiner (refers to low-level SS man), 235
Gemeinschaftslager (camp for civilian forced laborers), 169
Generalgouvernement, maps *x* and *300*, 308
Geniek (Captain Eugeniusz Triebling; 30), 106, 217–218
German cipher keys (verkehrsabkürzungen), 169
German citizens (Reichsdeutschen), 249, 268
German inmates, xlii–xliii, 23, 28, 42, 52, 65, 82, 93, 136, 159, 165, 173, 176, 205–206, 209, 212,
    227, 249, 253, 258, 282–283, 286–287
German songs, inmates required to sing, 160
German words in Pilecki's Report, xxi, xxiv
German–Bolshevik war, Russian POWs from, xvi, xxxix, li, 132–136, *134*, 157
Germans, ethnic (Volksdeutschen), 53, 60, 150, 184, 249, 268, 342
Gestapo, map *10*, 73n21, 90, 117, 146n42, 322–323. *See also* Aleja Szucha; political department
    at Auschwitz (Gestapo)
Gierych, Bolesław, 80
Gilewicz, Colonel Juliusz (121), xx, 186–187, 226–228, 244, 275
"go for the wires," 28, *29*
gold and diamonds, 203–204, 229–230, 243–244, 246, 257, 275, 282–283
gong, 136. *See also* bell at Auschwitz; siren at Auschwitz
    morning, 25, 28, 33, 99
    lunch/afternoon, 35
    escapes, 68
    evening, 35, 67, 154, 160
Gött-Getyński, Major Edward (150), 227, 249
Grabner, Maximilian, *90*, 92, 166, 184–186, 233, 235, 239, 269
gravel in wheelbarrows, moving, 33–35, 63–64
gravel pit (Kiesgrube), 250
Greek inmates at Auschwitz, 209, 253
Grönke, Erik, 141–142, 145, 167, 203, 216, 229, 282
Gross-Rosen, 272
Grot (Lieutenant General Stefan Rowecki), 146, 323
GULag, xii
Gutkiewicz, Stanisław (45), 106n29, 121, 128, 150, 163
Gypsies in Auschwitz-Birkenau, 253, 262, *263*, *264*

**H**

Häftling, as term for inmate, 20n4, 23
Häftlingsküche (inmates' kitchen), 257

hangings
    of camp authorities by inmates, 53, 164–165
    of inmates. *See* beatings and punishments of inmates; suicides by inmates
Harmense Kommando, 166–167
Hauptscharführer (the equivalent in the German SS of Master Sergeant), 69n19, 78
Hauptwache (main gate guard or guardhouse), 205, 235, 267
head inmates (Lagerältesters), *30*, 31, 94, 158, 291
health issues. *See* Krankenbau; medical issues
hernia faked by Pilecki to avoid transport to another camp, 271, 273
Hilkner, Jan (assumed name of Lieutenant Colonel Kazimierz Rawicz; 64), lii, 139, 140, *162*,
    163, 183–184, 186
Himmler, Heinrich, 170, *171*
Hitler, Adolph, xi
Hofman, Krzysztof (Krzyś), 91
Home Army. *See* Polish Home Army
homosexuals, 23
honorifics and titles, inmate abandonment of, 51
hospital. *See* Krankenbau
Hrebenda, Janek, 87, 91
"Hulajnoga" ("Scooter"; Kapo), 167, 215
humor, inmates' sense of, 58, 169–173, 246
"hundreds," 53, 54, 56, 108, 144, 151, 228, 235, 247
hunger. *See* food and drink

I

I. G. Farben works near Auschwitz, bombing of, 223n51
illnesses. *See* Krankenbau; medical issues
Industriehof I, Auschwitz, 60, 104, 122, 140, 169, 280
Industriehof II, Auschwitz, 53, 58, 65, 68
information box, sabotage of, 159–160
inmates' resistance organization. *See* ZOW
insanity of camp life, 17–18, 32–33, 59
inspection of Auschwitz, 107, 164, 170
intellectuals/intelligentsia, 17–18, 34–35, 40, 118–120, 163, 250–251
interrogation. *See* torture and interrogation
"Isjago," 218
Italy, Pilecki's military service in, in 1945, xix, xxxv, *xlix*, lii
Iwo II, 240

J

Jabłoński, Major Karol (Wilk; Zygmunt), 325
Jagiełło, Konstanty (former member of Parliament, per Pilecki; 72), 139
Janek (Jan Dangel; 49), 125, 241, 247
Janek (First Lieutenant Jan Kupiec; 20), 105
Janek (Jan Machnowski; 97), 140–141, 165
Janek, Jasiek, Jasio, Jaś (Jan Redzej, in camp as Jan Retko; 170), *xlix*, 276–277, *299*, 319, 323,
    325, 328. *See also* escape of Pilecki from Auschwitz
Janek W. (Major Jan Włodarkiewicz; 82), *xlvi*, 17, 125, 146
Januszewski, Mieczysław (68), 139, 166, 168
Jaś, Janek, Jasiek, Jasio (Jan Redzej, in camp as Jan Retko; 170), *xlix*, 276–277, *299*, 319, 323,
    325, 328. *See also* escape of Pilecki from Auschwitz
Jasiek, Jasio, Jaś, Janek (Jan Redzej, in camp as Jan Retko; 170), *xlix*, 276–277, *299*, 319, 323,
    325, 328. *See also* escape of Pilecki from Auschwitz
Jasieński, Second Lieutenant Stefan, xliv

Jasio, Jaś, Janek, Jasiek (Jan Redzej, in camp as Jan Retko; 170), *xlix*, 276–277, *299*, 319, 323, 325, 328. *See also* escape of Pilecki from Auschwitz
Jaster, Officer Cadet Stanisław (112), 168, 204
Jehovah's Witnesses, 23
Jews at Auschwitz-Birkenau, 187–204
    arrival and division of, 187–188, *189–193*
    change in attitude towards, 155–156
    corpses dug up and burnt by, 175
    deaths, number of, 329n72
    gassing of, 195
    letters sent home from, 156, 188, 210
    new Jewish arrivals sent directly to Birkenau, 156
    Palitzsch's sexual relationship with Jewish inmate Katti, 282
    parcels sent to dead inmates, 257
    possessions of, 188, 195–204, *197–202*
    rollers, inmates attached to, 41
    sexual experiments on, 253
    SK, removal from, 155
    SK, sent to, 32, 211
    "the Strangler" (Izak Gąska), 211
    stripping of, 188–195
    testicles, crushing of, 65
    ZOW's reports on, xli, li
Jonny (Jonny Lechenich; inmate no. 19), 94–97, 158
Jurek (First Lieutenant Jerzy Poraziński; 27), 106, 116, 212
Jurek (name unknown; 10), 64

**K**

Kapos (inmates who were supervisors or "trusties")
    clothing of gassed Jews worn by, 196–203
    experimentally drugged with barbiturates for escape purposes, 262
    first thirty German inmates at Auschwitz, 93–97, 352–353
    helpful, 94–97, 140–142, 158
    killed by camp inmates, xl. *See also* killing of camp authorities by camp inmates
    Lagerkapos (discipline Kapos), 63, 138, 158
    mass shooting of Polish inmates (28th of October 1942), collection of names for, 233–234, 235
    role of, 28–31
    yellow armbands worn by, 20
Karcz, Colonel Jan (62), 138, 160–163, 167–168, 207–208
Katti (Jewish inmate having sexual relationship with Palitzsch), 282
Kazik (Kapo), 24, 36, 49
Kazio (Kazimierz Radwański, nephew of Pilecki; 39), 120, 184, 225, 250, 270, 271
Kazuba, Captain Stanisław (60), 138, 183, 227, 292
Kedyw, 324, 325
Kiesgrube (gravel pit), 250
Kiliański (first name unknown; former member of Parliament; 74), 139
killing of camp authorities by camp inmates, xl
    by hanging, 53, 164–165
    by typhus-infected lice, 159, 186, 216
KL Auschwitz (Konzentrationslager Auschwitz—Auschwitz Concentration Camp), map *10*, 18. *See also* Auschwitz
Klehr (SS man), 179–182, 185–186, 207, 224, 226
knitting wool, use of, 228
Kocjan, Stanisław (33), 116

Kolbe, Father Maksymilian, 127n35
Koliński, Cavalry Captain Włodzimierz (162), 249
Koliński, Second Lieutenant Mieczysław (163), 249
Kommandos (work details), 25, 31, *111–112*
    Arbeitsdienst (work assignment office), ZOW members in, 166
    Arbeitsdiensts (work assignment leaders), 42, 139, 166, 245, 265–266, 275, 281
    Arbeitskommando (camp work detail), 33, 35, 39, 99, 138, 234
    Aufräumungskommando (salvage Kommando), *197, 200–202*
    Auschwitz buildings and roads, construction of, *44*, 56–58, *111–112*, 122–123
    bakery, 276–277, 279–281, 289–298
    barbers, 146–149, 176
    basket-weaving, 255
    Bekleidungskammer (clothing storeroom), as work detail, 248–250, 251
    Bekleidungswerkstätte (clothing workshop), 255
    Brotabladungskommando (bread-unloading Kommando), 276
    carpenter's shops, 60–65, 72, 80–82, 104–105, 114–116, 120–121, 123, 127–129, 132,
        140–141, 167, 215–216
    Camp Commandant's garden, 45, 47–48, 51–53
    crematorium, building of, 34
    escape attempts associated by camp authorities with change in, 266, 280
    Landwirtschaftskommando (farming Kommando), 97
    fish ponds, 167
    gravel in wheelbarrows, moving, 33–35, 63–64
    Harmense, 166–167
    houses in vicinity of Auschwitz, destruction of, 52–55
    indoor work, advantages of, xlii, 48, 60, 104, 110, 112, 116
    inspections of camp, during, 164
    Kiesgrube or gravel pit, 250
    length of time spent in camp and, 48–49, 255
    livestock, work with, 113–114, 146
    orchestra playing in and out of camp, 107–109
    organization of, 31, 33, 39, 104
    parcel Kommando, 255–259, 272, 273, 283, 289
    "physical exercise" (PE) instead of, 39–41, 71
    Poles removed from, prior to transport, 254–255
    rollers, inmates attached to, 40–41
    stove fitter (Ofensetzer), Pilecki's work as, 42–47
    Strassenbaukommando (road-construction Kommando), 58
    surveying, 260
    tannery (Lederfabrik), 114, 140–142, 169–170, 196, 215–216, 228–229
    woodcarving shop, 127–129, 140–141, 167, 215
    ZOW control of, 92–94, 116, 166, 168
Konfederacja Zbrojna Narodu or Nation's Armed Alliance (KZN), 145–146
Konrad (Konrad Lang, inmate no. 18), 94, *96*, 140–142, 158, 167, 215
Koprowiak, Stanisław, 71, 103
Kostecki, Zygmunt, 144
Koszczyński, Antoni (43), 121
Kosztowny, Witold (101), 166, 224, 252–254, 291
Kownacki, Piotr (former member of Parliament; 73), 139, 216, 217
Krankenbau (hospital). *See also* medical issues
    admission to, 138, 179
    barbiturates used to drug SS men for escape purposes, 262
    beds constructed by Pilecki in, 82
    Dering's work at, 98–99, 116, 143, 166
    gassing of patients from, 207–208
    murdered inmates added to mortuary list of, 149–150

Pflegers (nurses), 37, 87, 91, 131, 138, 146, 219–220, 252, 286
phenol, murder of inmates with, 179–182
Pilecki's faking of typhus as part of escape, 283–287
Pilecki's first fever and convalescence (in early 1941), 83–91, 97, 104
Pilecki's second fever and convalescence (in mid-1942), 221–227
Schonungsblock (convalescence block), 120, 138, 220
    in ZOW plan of eventual action, 227
Krankenmann (block chief), 32, 41, 164–165
Kriegsgefangenenlager (prisoner of war camp), 136. See also prisoners of war (POWs).
Krzyś (Krzysztof Hofman), 91
Kuc, Father (160), 240, 320, 321
Kuczbara, Bolesław (161), 244–245, 275, 324
Kukiełka, Leon (129), 218, 226, 239, 241
Kumuniecki, Lieutenant Colonel Karol (24), 105, 165, 184, 232, 249
Kupiec, Antoni, 105n26
Kupiec, Bolesław (Bolek; 18), 105
Kupiec, First Lieutenant Jan (Janek; 20), 105
Kupiec, Józef, 105n26
Kupiec, Karol, 105n26
Kupiec, Władysław (Władek; 17), 105, 115
Küsel, Otto (inmate no. 2), 42, 43, 47, 94, 245, 246
KZN (Pilecki conflates the Konfederacja Zbrojna [KZ—The Armed Confederation] with the
    Konfederacja Narodu [KN—The Confederation of the Nation]), 145–146

L

labor camp (Arbeitslager), 279
Lachmann (SS man), 241–242, 249, 251
Lagerältesters (head inmates), 30, 31, 94, 158, 291
Lagerführers (camp heads), 41, 42, 154, 205, 338, 343
Lagerkapos (discipline Kapos), 63, 138, 158
Lagerkommandant (Camp Commandant), 103
Lamsdorf POW camp, lii
Landwirtschaftskommando (farming Kommando), 97
Lang, Konrad (inmate no. 18), 94, 96, 140–142, 158, 167, 215
latrines, 25–26, 214, 229
Laufschritt (doing things at the double), 25–26, 34, 42, 63, 295
Lech, Tadeusz (42), 121, 128–129
Lechenich, Jonny (inmate no. 19), 94–97, 158
Lederfabrik (tannery), 114, 140–142, 169–170, 196, 215–216, 228–229
Leo (Lagerältester Leo Wietschorek/Leon Wieczorek; inmate no. 30), 30, 31, 65, 80–81, 94,
    353n2
Leon (Leon Wandasiewicz; 178), 319–321
letters to families. See families, of Auschwitz inmates; family, of Pilecki; Jews at
    Auschwitz-Birkenau—letters sent home from
lice infestations, 83–91, 159, 186
livestock, as work detail, 113–114, 146
Lublin pacification, 231–232, 234, 235
Lublin prison, 18

M

Machnowski, Jan (Janek; 97), 140–141, 165
Machowski, Captain Stanisław (159), 240, 274
Majdanek, xii, 156, 264
Makaliński, First Lieutenant Włodzimierz (Włodek; 29), 106, 117, 163, 204, 240
Makowski-Gąsienica, Andrzej (110), 167, 266

mail censorship office (Postzensurstelle), 100–104, 124
main gate guard or guardhouse (Hauptwache), 205, 235, 267
mangelwurzels, 55
Marduła, Andrzej (58), 129, 217
Maringe, Officer Cadet Platoon Sergeant Stanisław (Stasiek; 26), 106, 116, 212, 240
"Mateczka" or "Mom" (Fritz Biessgen; inmate no. 4), 94, *95*, 228
Mauthausen, 186, 273, 359
Mazurkiewicz, Piotr (175), 314–315
medical experimentation at Auschwitz, 36n9, 252–254
medical issues. *See also* Krankenbau
    Aloiz's treatment of sick inmates, 38–39
    dysentery, 55–56
    escape from Auschwitz, during, 308, 309–310, 312, 316–318
    hernia faked by Pilecki to avoid transport to another camp, 271, 273
    lice infestations, 83–91, 159, 186
    liquid foods, excessive reliance on, 26–27
    meningitis, 98, 218
    Pflegers (nurses), 37, 87, 91, 131, 138, 146, 219–220, 252, 286
    Pilecki's first fever and convalescence (in early 1941), 83–91, 97, 104
    Pilecki's second fever and convalescence (in mid-1942), 221–227
    typhus, 159, 169, 182, 186, 216–220, 221–224, 242, 283–284
Meldung (report), 142
meningitis, 98, 218
Michał (Captain Michał Romanowicz; Captain Michał; 7), 47, 53–54, 56, 58
Mickiewicz, Adam, 119n32
Mielcarek, Jan (Wernyhora; 50), 129, 216, 217
Mietek (Arbeitsdienst), 245, 281
Miksa, Cavalry Sergeant Jan (119), 184, 186
military attacks on Auschwitz
    bombing raids, 223
    I. G. Farben works near Auschwitz, bombing of, 223n51
    lack of, xli, xliii–xliv, li, 230–231, 321–323, 325
    Pilecki's post-escape efforts regarding, 321–327
    ZOW plan of eventual action, 183–184, 226–227, 231–232, 243, 268. *See also* ZOW
military career of Pilecki prior to Auschwitz, xliv–xlviii
military promotion of Polish inmates while in Auschwitz, xlvii, 145–146
Młynarski, Janusz (172), 284, 286
"Mom" or "Mateczka" (Fritz Biessgen; inmate no. 4), 94, *95*, 228
money allowed to inmates, 151. *See also* paper money
Montelupich prison, 18, 259
Mosdorf, Jan (former member of Parliament, per Pilecki; 71), 139, 216, 217
motor pool (Fahrbereitschaft), 116
Możdżeń, Andrzej (180), 321–322
Murnau POW camp, lii
Murzyn, Leon, 326
Muselmänner, 120, 138, 179, 208, 220–221
Myszkowski, Tadeusz (Tadek; 52), 128, 167, 168, 215

**N**

Narkun (Auschwitz inmate), 85
Neuengamme, 272
NIE (Niepodległość or Independence), lii
"Nie dbam jaka spadnie kara" lyrics, 54–55
Niebudek, Stefan (former member of Parliament; 75), 139
Niepodległość (NIE; Independence), lii

Niepołomnicka Forest (location VIII), map *300*, 315
Nierychło, Franciszek (Franz), 107
Niewiarowski, Officer Cadet Remigiusz (35), 116, 240
Norwegian inmates at Auschwitz, 209
Nowak, Dr. Edward (12), 87–88
Nowy Wiśnicz (location X), xix, *xlix*, map *300*, 319–320, 323
numbers issued to inmates, 16, 20, *21*
nurses (Pflegers), 37, 87, 91, 131, 138, 146, 219–220, 252, 286

**O**

Oberkapos (senior Kapos), 94, *95*, 104, 115, 121, 140–142, 158
Obersturmführer (the equivalent in the German SS of First Lieutenant), 69
Obojski, Eugeniusz, 37n10
Obora, Mr. and Mrs. (176), 318–319
"Oda do Młodości" ("Ode to Youth," Mickiewicz), 119n32
Ofensetzer (stove fitter), Pilecki's work as, 42–47
office (Schreibstube), 118, 136, 150, 155, 182, 210, 256, 265, 272, 287
"old numbers," 48, 108, 117, 150–151, 255, 281, 287, 288, 290, 292
Olek (Second Lieutenant Aleksander Bugajski; 167), 259–262, 265–266, 280, 289, 326
Olszowski, Second Lieutenant Jan (174), 293
orchestra, 106–107, 121, 146, 164, *172*, 173, 246
organization of inmates. *See* ZOW
organization of inmates, camp authorities' efforts to uncover, 160–163, 184–185, 243–244, 249–250
"organizing," new meaning of word spread by ZOW, 92–93
Ostrowska, Eleonora (sister-in-law of Pilecki; E.O.), 100, 103, 153, 322, 325
Oświęcim (in German, Auschwitz), town of, xxi, xxvii, maps *10* and *300*, 18, 136, 169, 274–275, 303
Otto (Otto Küsel; inmate no. 2), 42, *43*, 47, 94, 245, 246
Our Lady, picture of hanging on bush, 52
Ozimek, Stanisław (Stach; 48), 125, 241

**P**

pacification campaign in Lublin region, 231–232, 234, 235
Paliński, Aleksander (86), 154, 325
Palitzsch, Gerhard
    execution of inmates by, 76–79, 92, 103, 219, 224, 238, 247
    feared by SS and inmates, 69, 71
    "gold lust" of, 282–283
    Grabner, Maximilian, cooperation with, 92
    information box, sabotage of, 160
    Kiesgrube or gravel pit of, 250
    mass shooting of Polish inmates and, 236, 238
    paid "by the head" for shooting inmates, 92
    photo of, *78*
    Pilecki's pictures destroyed and confiscated by, 219
    rank of, 69n19
    Seidler substituting for, 154
    sexual relationship with Jewish inmate Katti, 282
    transport of Polish inmates and, 269
Pańszczyk, Mieczysław, 181
Paolone, Captain Tadeusz (114), 183, 227, 291n66
paper money, 229
parcel Kommando, 255–259, 272, 273, 283, 289
parcels sent by families of Auschwitz inmates, 79, 150, 245, 246, 255–259, 270, 288–290
Parliament, Polish, former members inmates at Auschwitz, 139–140, 167, 187

Pawiak prison, 18, 106, 117, 165, 204, 239, 275, 324
Pawłowicz, Captain Zygmunt (116; in camp as Julian Trzęsimiech), 183–184, 227, 327
Pawłowska, Dr. Helena (83), 152–153, 321
PE ("physical exercise") instead of work assignment, 39–41, 71
"Pearly" ("Perełka," SS man), 65, 75
Pełczyński, Major General Tadeusz, xix, xxxv, 1, 3
Penal Company (SK or Strafkompanie), 19, 32, 65, 155, 158, 211–213, 266, 280, 281, 326
"Perełka" ("Pearly," SS man), 65, 75
perimeter fencing, Auschwitz. *See* Auschwitz—fencing, perimeter and interior
personal details of inmates, camp check on, 150–153, 240
Pflegers (nurses), 37, 87, 91, 131, 138, 146, 219–220, 252, 286
phenol, murder of inmates with, 179–182, 185–186, 226, 232, 242, 254, 277
"physical exercise" (PE) instead of work assignment, 39–41, 71
pictures made by Pilecki of camp life, 219
Piekarski, Second Lieutenant Konstanty (61), 138, 145, 168, 183, 226, 228, 244, 266, 271
Pietrzykowski, Tadeusz (Tadek; 21), 105, 114, 206
Pilecki, Andrzej (son), xx, *xlvi*
Pilecki, Captain Witold, xliv–liv. *See also* beatings experienced by Pilecki; escape of Pilecki
    from Auschwitz; family, of Pilecki; Report on Auschwitz; ZOW
    anti-communist Polish resistance movement, involvement with, xvi, xxiii, lii,
    liii–liv
    arrest of, sent to Auschwitz, xlviii, 11–12
    assumed name, use of, xlviii, 3, 61, 98, 100, 117, 152–153, 320–323
    in Auschwitz, xlviii–liii. *See also* Auschwitz, *and more specific entries*
    birth, family background, and education, xliv, *xlv*
    Christian faith of, xxxix–xxx, xlvii, 157, 230, 254
    dangerous game in Auschwitz, 124–125
    final mission and execution of, xiii, xvi, *l*, liii–liv, 3n1
    illnesses while in Auschwitz, 83–91, 221–227
    in Italy in 1945, xix, xxxv, *xlix*, lii
    marriage and children, xlvii, liii, liv
    military career prior to Auschwitz, xliv–xlviii
    military promotion while in Auschwitz, xlvii, 145–146
    number 4859 issued to, 20
    personal qualities of, xii–xiii, xvi–xvii, xxxvi
    pictures of camp life made by, 219
    political views of, xlvii
    as POW, lii
    pronunciation of name, xin1, xxvii
    psychological adjustments made by, 13, 32–33, 46–47, 60, 86, 118, 124–125, 225,
        229–230, 306, 331–332
    suppression of story of, xvi–xvi
    transport of Poles to other camps, decision to avoid, 270, 271, 273
    on twentieth century "civilization," 109–110
    Warsaw Uprising of 1944, role in, xii, xvi, xxi, lii, 12, 327–328
    weakening of, exertion of willpower to conceal, 58–60
    world outside of Auschwitz after escape, reaction to, xlii, 306–307, 331–332
Pilecki, Captain Witold, photographs of
    after Auschwitz, *xxviii, xlix, l*
    before Auschwitz, *xiv, xviii, xxxvii, xlv, xlvi, 1*
    as Auschwitz inmate no. 4859, *xxxviii, 21*, 97, 323
    with family, *xxviii, xlvi*
Pilecki, Jan (16; no relation to Witold Pilecki), 105
Pilecki (Pilecka), Maria Ostrowska (wife), *xxviii, xlvi*, xlvii, liii, liv
Pilecki (Pilecka), Zofia (daughter), *xlvi*
Piłsudski, Marshal, xlvii
Pohl, Alojz (81), 150

Poland

    anti-communist Polish resistance movement, Pilecki's involvement with, xvi, xxiii, lii, liii–liv

    invasion of (September 1939), map *ix*, xlvii

    location in Europe (1939), map *vi*

    occupied (1939–1941), map *x*

pole, inmates hung by arms from, 75

Polish–Bolshevik War of 1919–1920, xliv, 285n65

Polish conscience, 233

Polish Constitution, execution of Poles on anniversary of ratification of (May 3rd), 127

Polish Home Army (Armia Krajowa or AK)

    Auschwitz inmates and ZOW not considered as active asset by, 242–243

    Auschwitz reports sent to Polish government-in-exile via, xli

    escapes from Auschwitz, response to, 250–251

    formation of, xlviii

    Kedyw, 324, 325

    military attack on Auschwitz, failure to organize, xli, xliii–xliv, li, 230–231, 321–323, 325

    photo of soldiers from, *148*

    Pilecki's letters to family via, 125

    Pilecki's work with, after Auschwitz, xvi, lii, 323–328

    PZP (Polski Związek Powstańczy or Polish Insurrectionary Organization), known as, xlviiin8

Polish language, pronunciation key for, xxvi–xxvii

Polish Parachute Brigade, xliii

Polish inmates in Auschwitz

    active asset, not considered by outside world to be, 242–243

    as best workers, 255, 273

    female inmates, arrival and execution of, 173–174

    frozen by exposure after hot shower, 149

    Kommandos, removal from, 254–255

    Lublin region, pacification campaign in, 231–232, 234, 235

    mass shooting of Polish inmates (28th of October 1942), xl, 233–239

    Pilecki's post-escape efforts regarding, 321–327

    political party members, rapprochement between, xl–xli, lii, 139–140, 150

    political prisoners, Auschwitz used for, xxxix, xlii–xliii, 23

    politicians, as inmates at Auschwitz, xl–xli, lii, 139–140, 150, 167, 187

    sexual experimentation on, 253

    solidarity of. *See* solidarity of Polish inmates in Auschwitz

    survival rates of, 19, 49, 150–151, 186

    transport to other camps, 254–255, 268–274

political department at Auschwitz (Gestapo), 73, 92, 99, 103, 150, 151–153, 160, 166, 182, 184, 212, 233, 240, 249, 268, 269

politicians, as inmates at Auschwitz, xl–xli, lii, 139–140, 150, 167, 187

Polkowski, Corporal Stanisław (91), 165, 216, 217

Polkowski, Stasiek (barber), 65

Polski Związek Powstańczy or Polish Insurrectionary Organization (PZP), Home Army known as, xlviiin8

Poraziński, First Lieutenant Jerzy (Jurek; 27), 106, 116, 212

possessions of inmates

    Bekleidungskammer (clothing storeroom), 196

    burnt in tannery, 196, 228

    "Canada," 196–204, *197–202*, 218, 220, 225, 245, 257, 270, 278

    commandeered or recycled, 196–204, *200–202*, 228–229

diamonds and gold, 203–204, 229–230, 243–244, 246, 257, 275, 282–283
Effektenkammer (storeroom for inmates' possessions), 70–71, 79
    inmates allowed to wear civilian clothes taken from, 278
    Jewish inmates stripped of, 188, 195–204, *197–202*
    parcels sent to dead inmates, 257–259, 270
Postenkette (security perimeter), 51, 137. *See also* Auschwitz—fencing, perimeter and
    interior
Postzensurstelle (mail censorship office), 100–104, 124
Potocki, Antek, 83, 84
POWs. *See* prisoners of war
priests
    assistance to Pilecki during escape, 309–312
    beaten to death, 17–18
    change in attitude toward, 156
    Dauchau, transports to, 156–157
    Kolbe, Father Maksymilian, death of, 127n35
    parish records, changed to protect Pilecki's assumed identity, 152–153, 240, 321
    rollers, inmates attached to, 41
    self-sacrifice to save another inmate, 126–127
    SK (Strafkompanie or Penal Company), sent to, 32
    ZOW chaplain (Father Zygmunt Ruszczak; 87), 157
prisoners of war (POWs)
    Bolshevik POWs at Auschwitz-Birkenau, xvi, xxxix, li, map *10*, 16, 131–136, *134*,
        157, 159, 209. *See also* Soviet Union
    Lamsdorf POW camp, lii
    Murnau POW camp, lii
    Pilecki as POW, lii
    Polish officers spending war as, 72n20
promotions, military, of Polish inmates while at Auschwitz, xlvii, 145–146
Prussic acid, gassing with, 131. *See also* Zyklon B; gas chambers
psychological adjustments made by Pilecki, 13, 32–33, 46–47, 60, 86, 118, 124–125, 225,
    229–230, 306, 331–332
punishments in Auschwitz. *See* beatings and punishments of inmates; torture and
    interrogation
punishment parade. *See* beatings and punishments of imates
Putek, Józef (former member of Parliament; 104), 167
PZP (Polski Związek Powstańczy or Polish Insurrectionary Organization), Home Army
    known as, xlviiin8

**Q**

quarantine
    of inmates to be released, 98, 124, 153
    of sick inmates, 219, 221, 226, 227, 286
*Quo Vadis* (Sienkiewicz), 61n17

**R**

radio room (Funkstelle), 168, 169
radio transmitter built and operated by ZOW, 168–169
Radwański, Kazimierz (nephew of Pilecki; Kazio; 39), 120, 184, 225, 250, 270, 271
Rajsko. *See* Birkenau
Rapportführer (SS officer responsible for discipline and roll calls), 69
Ravensbrück, 326
Rawicz, Lieutenant Colonel Kazimierz (in camp as Jan Hilkner; 64), lii, 139, 140, *162*, 163,
    183–184, 186
records office (Erkennungsdienst), 97, 99, 234

Redzej, Jan (Jasiek, Jasio, Jaś, Janek; in camp as Jan Retko; 170). *xlix*, 276–277, *299*, 319, 323, 325, 328. *See also* escape of Pilecki from Auschwitz
Reichsdeutschen (German citizens), 249, 268
Reklewski, Colonel Tadeusz (Colonel R; 11), 51, 81, 270–271, 291n66
relationships between men (both SS and inmates) and female inmates, sexual or romantic, 281–282
relationships between inmates at Auschwitz, 49–51
releases of inmates from Auschwitz
in 1940, 123–124
in 1942, 173
families arranging for, 11, 91, 114, 123, 125
for good behavior, 206
orchestra members, 173
quarantine of inmates to be released, 98, 124, 153
Surmacki released through influence of friend in German Army, 153–154
religion. *See also* priests; Christmas at Auschwitz; Easter at Auschwitz
church bells, 47, 136–137, 310
picture of Our Lady hanging in bush, 52
Pilecki, Christian faith of, xxxix–xxx, xlvii, 157, 230, 254
praying man, Aloiz's treatment of, 38–39
ZOW chaplain, 157
Report on Auschwitz (Pilecki, 1945)
character of, xxxv–xlii
coding of names and places in, xix–xx, xxv, 37
commercial offers made to Pilecki for, 3
composition of, xii, xix, xxiii, 325
covering letter, xxxv, *1*, 3
editing and translation of, xix–xxi, xxiii–xxvi
facts and feelings, balancing, xvii, 7
family of Pilecki seldom mentioned in, liii
German words in, xxi, xxiv
importance of telling world about Auschwitz, 254
nicknames and diminutives, use of, xxiv
prior reports
June 1943, xii, xix
Autumn 1943 (*Raport W*), xix–xx, 37, 105n28, 106n29, 325
purpose of Pilecki's mission and, xlii–xliv, 36
repetition in, 208
structure, chronology, and highlights, xxv, xxix–xxx, 355–363
time period covered by, xvi
reserve arms store, under Baubüro or construction site office, 235
resistance organization among inmates. *See* ZOW
Retko, Jan (assumed name of Jan Redzej; Jasiek, Jasio, Jaś, Janek; 170), *xlix*, 276–277, *299*, 319, 323, 325, 328. *See also* escape of Pilecki from Auschwitz
road-construction Kommando (Strassenbaukommando), 58
roll call, *16*, 19, 28, 31–32, 35, 48, 57, 68–69, 154, 160, 277–278, 289
rollers, inmates attached to, 40–41
Roman, Józef (181), 323
Romanowicz, Captain Michał (Michał or Captain Michał; 7), 47, 53–54, 56, 58
romantic relationships between men (both SS and inmates) and female inmates, 281–282
Romek (inmate), 230
Romek G. (inmate), 212
room supervisors (Stubendiensts), 24–25, 26, 27, 130, 146, 149
Rosa, Antoni (Antek; 22), 105
Rowecki, Lieutenant General Stefan (Grot), 146, 323
Różak, Zbigniew (56), 129

Różycki, Adam, 24n7
Różycki, Witold, 24
Russia. *See* Soviet Union
Ruszczak, Father Zygmunt (87), 157
Ruszczyński, Zbigniew (77), 140, 168, 243
Rybarski, Professor Roman (former member of Parliament; 69), 139, 150, 166
Rzeczkowski, Warrant Officer Szczepan (Szczepan; 28), 106, 280

**S**

Sachsenhausen, 146n42, 272
salad dressing/vinegar, fed to inmates hung from poles, 75
salvage Kommando (Aufräumungskommando), *197, 200–202*
Salwa, Edek, 86
Scharführer (equivalent in the German SS of Staff Sergeant), 293
Schreibers (clerks), 234, 309
Schreibstube (office), 118, 136, 150, 155, 182, 210, 256, 265, 272, 287
Schonungsblock (convalescence block), 120, 138, 220
Schudrich, Rabbi Michael, xv–xvii
Schutzhäftling, as term for inmate, 20
"Scooter" ("Hulajnoga"; Kapo), 167, 215
Second World War, misconceptions about, xi–xiii
Seidler, Fritz, 19, *22*, 73, 154
"Seidler week," 154
Sęp II (Major Chmielewski, first name unknown; 38), 117, 241
Serafiński, Lieutenant Tomasz (Tomek; 84; with wife referred to as 179)
    Pilecki's assumption of identity of, xlviii, 61, 98, 100, 117, 152–153, 320–323
    Pilecki's plan to attack Auschwitz with, 321–323
    Pilecki's post-escape stay with family of, xix, *xlix*, 319–323
    pronunciation of name, xxvii
Serafiński, Mr. and Mrs. (179), 321–323. *See also* Serafiński, Lieutenant Tomasz
sewers as possible escape route, 259–260, 266–267, 276–277, 280
sexual abuse of inmates
    boys abused by Leo (Leon Wietschorek), 80–81
    female inmates forced to strip and run while being shot by Palitzsch, 76
    Jewish women saved from gas chambers for purposes of, 209–210
    SS men having sex with female inmates, 281–282
sexual experiments on Auschwitz inmates, 252–254
sexual relationships between men (both SS and inmates) and female inmates, 281–282
shoes, 228, 231, 232, 255
shooting, death by. *See* beatings and punishments of inmates
sickness. *See* Krankenbau; medical issues
Siegruth, Johann (Sigrod, Kapo), 53, 164–165
Sienkiewicz, Henryk, 61
Sigrod (Johann Siegruth, Kapo), 53, 164–165
Sikora, Czesław (157), 239, 241, 242
Sikorski, General Władysław, 146
Silesians at Auschwitz, 69–70, 150, 151, 163, 184
siren at Auschwitz, 68, 137, 145. *See also* bell at Auschwitz; gong
SK (Strafkompanie or Penal Company; located in Block 11 [new no.], Block 13 [old no.]), 19, 32, 65, 155, 158, 211–213, 266, 280, 281, 326
Skornowicz, Mikołaj, 105n28
Skrzypek, Alfred, 70
sleeping at Auschwitz. *See also* gong
    arrangements, 11, 25, 91, 143, 213. *See also* blocks/barracks—bunks in
    lice and, 83–86
    SS men, 259, 296, 298, 301
    time on Sundays, 158

Słowiaczek, Tadeusz (Tadek; 19), 105, 131–132, 215, 309, 311
smoking, 27, 145, 302
Smyczek, Wilhelm, 70
Śniegucki, Wiktor (46), 121
Sobibor, 264
"Sokół" ("Falcon") organization of Czechs, 163
Sokołowski (first name unknown; 113), 168
solidarity of Polish inmates in Auschwitz, xxxvi, xxxix–xl, 32, 33, 92, 139–140
Solzhenitsyn, Aleksandr, xxxvi
Soviet Union (U.S.S.R.)
    Bolshevik POWs in Auschwitz-Birkenau, xvi, xxxix, li, map *10*, 16, 131–136,
      *134*, 157, 159, 209
    concentration camps in, xii
    German–Bolshevik war (beginning June 1941), 131
    location in Europe (1939), map *vi*
    Polish–Bolshevik War of 1919–1920, xliv
    in WWII and after, xi–xiii, xxiii, liii–liv, 131, *133*, 147, 159n44, 223n60
    invasion, partition and occupation of Poland (1939–1941), maps *ix* and *x*, xi,
      xlvii
spade used by "the Strangler" to kill Jews in SK, 211
spoons made by woodcarving shop, 167, 215, 302
spring, strongest sense of imprisonment felt in, 175–176
SS (Schutzstaffel—Protective Guard) garrison at Auschwitz
    bakery, escape of Pilecki, Edek, and Janek via, 293–298, 301, 328
    bombings of Auschwitz, reaction to, 223
    burial of inmates alive by, 71–72
    escapes using uniforms of, 204–205, 245–246
    female camp authorities in SS uniforms, 282
    Gawron's painting of portraits of, 166
    human feelings, Pilecki's consideration of, 46–47
    inmates, SS men killed by, xl
    liquidation of inmates by, fears of, xliii, xliv
    parcels of dead inmates consumed by, 257–258
    possessions of gassed Jews commandeered by, 196–204, *200–202*
    private arrangements with Auschwitz workshops, 42–47, 108–109
    relationship to inmates and internal camp authorities, 31
    stove fitting at SS apartment, 42–47
    strength of, xliii
    Totenkopf (Death's Head) cap badge, *22*
    typhus-infected lice released by inmates on, 159, 186, 216
    ZOW, SS men working with, 268
Stach (Stanisław Ozimek; 48), 125, 241
Stalin, Joseph, xi
Stammlager (main camp at Auschwitz), 122, 163, 180, 279. *See also* Auschwitz
standing bunker (Stehbunker), 74, 158
Stasiek (Officer Cadet Platoon Sergeant Stanisław Maringe; 26), 106, 116, 212, 240
Stasiek (Second Lieutenant Stanisław Wierzbicki; 156), 232, 239–242, 250–251, 274
Stawarz, Colonel Aleksander (23), 105, 165, 184, 187
Stawiszyński, Stanisław (41), 106n29, 121, 207, 233, 239, 241
Stehbunker (standing bunker), 74, 158
Stępień, Senior Uhlan Stefan (123), 204
sterilization experiments on Auschwitz inmates, 252–254
storerooms
    Bekleidungskammer (clothing storeroom), 196, 248–250, 251
    "Canada," 196–204, *197–202*, 218, 220, 225, 245, 257, 270, 278
    Effektenkammer (storeroom for inmates' possessions), 70–71, 79
    smell of food from, 58

Stössel, Second Lieutenant Alfred (Fredek; 4), 37, 91, 116, 168, 226, 241–242
stove fitter (Ofensetzer), Pilecki's work as, 42–47
Strafkompanie (SK; Penal Company), 19, 32, 65, 155, 158, 211–213, 266, 280, 281, 326
"the Strangler" (Izak Gąska), 211
Stransky, Karel (89), 163
Strassenbaukommando (road-construction Kommando), 58
straw, making shoes out of, 255
Stubendiensts (room supervisors), 24–25, 26, 27, 130, 146, 149
Stulgiński, Tadeusz (96), 165
"subhumans" (Untermenschen), 108, 282
submarine, rumors of, 268
Suchnicki, Captain Dr. Henryk (146), 224, 226, 239
suicides by inmates, 28
Sundays at Auschwitz
    concert, 121, *172*
    free time/Blocksperre (confinement to blocks), 121, 157–158
    letter writing, 102, 210
    roll call, 278
    work on, 143–145, 157–158
"supermen" (Übermenschen), 108, 113, 257
Surmacki, Colonel Władysław (Władek; 1), xx, xxvii, 36–37, 59, 106, 149, 153–154, 165, 240
surveyors' Kommando, 260
survival expectations/death rates at Auschwitz, 19, 49, 150–151, 186, 328–329
Świerczyna, First Lieutenant Bernard (76), 140, 184, 225–226, 240, 243, 249, 275, 291, 292
Świętorzecki, Karol (31), 24, 113
Szczepan (Warrant Officer Szczepan Rzeczkowski; 28), 106, 280
Szczerbowska, Zofia (13), 97
Szelągowska, Maria, *xlix*
Szklarz, Second Lieutenant Henryk (165), 259
Szpakowski, Sławek, xxvii, 12, 49, 54–55, 58–60, 63, 97–98, 102, 324
Szydlik, Platoon Sergeant Tadeusz (40), 120–121, 291
Szymkowiak, Officer Cadet Witold (Witold; 15), 105, 186
Szyszko-Bohusz, Second Lieutenant Marian, *xlix*

**T**

Tadek (Second Lieutenant Tadeusz Burski; 6), 37, 87, 91
Tadek (Tadeusz Myszkowski; 52), 128, 167, 168, 215
Tadek (Tadeusz Pietrzykowski; 21), 105, 114, 206
Tadek (Tadeusz Słowiaczek; 19), 105, 131–132, 215, 309, 311
Tajna Armia Polska or Polish Secret Army (TAP), xlviii, 36, 145, 239–240, 280
tannery (Lederfabrik), 114, 140–142, 169–170, 196, 215–216, 228–229
TAP (Tajna Armia Polska or Polish Secret Army), xlviii, 36, 145, 239–240, 280
"Tata" or "Daddy" (Hans Bock; inmate no. 5), 94
tattooing of inmates, 16
*10 z Pawiaka* (*10 from the Pawiak Prison*) (film), 204
testicles, crushing of, 65
Third Reich, xi, 17, 23, 35, 80, 87, 158, 187–188, 308
Tierpflegers (animal or veterinary nurses), 146
time, sense of passage of, 49
titles and honorifics, inmate abandonment of, 51
tobacco, 27, 145, 302
toilets, 25–26, 214, 229
Tomek (Lieutenant Tomasz Serafiński; 84). *See* Serafiński, Lieutenant Tomasz.
torture and interrogation
    of Auschwitz inmates, 23, 46, 48, 75, 76, 174, 242, 248, 250, 251
    of Karcz, 160–163

of Pilecki on return to Poland, xvi, liv
ZOW's efforts to avoid discovery via, li, 106
toys, woodcarving inmates making, 142, 167
transports to Auschwitz, xii, xlviii, 12–13, 17–19, 48n12, 70, 93, 106, 149, 151, 165, 175–176, 184, 187–195, *189–193*, 232, 239, 257, 259
transports from Auschwitz, 125, 156-157, 186, 269–273, 291n66
Treblinka, xii, 156, 264
Triebling, Captain Eugeniusz (Geniek; 30), 106, 217–218
Trojnicki, Captain Ferdynand (Fred; 8), 60, 61, 64, 168
truss worn by Pilecki to fake hernia, 271, 273
Trzęsimiech, Julian (assumed name of Captain Zygmunt Pawłowicz; 116), 183–184, 227, 327
tunnel from Block 28 as possible escape route, 226, 241
turnips carried into camp, 143–144
"twenties," 47, 53, 56, 99, 121, 132, 142
Tyniec (location IV), map *300*, 313
typhus, 159, 169, 182, 186, 216–220, 221–224, 242, 283–284

**U**

Übermenschen ("supermen"), 108, 113, 257
Uhlan regiment colors, hiding place of, 204
Uhlan, Senior (rank in a Polish uhlan cavalry regiment equivalent to Private First Class), 204
underground fuel tank converted to submarine, rumors of, 268
Unterkapos (deputy Kapos), 47, 144, 278, 281, 292
Untermenschen ("subhumans"), 108, 282
Uris, Leon, 36n9

**V**

Verkehrsabkürzungen (German cipher keys), 169
Vernichtungslager (extermination camp), 279. *See also* Auschwitz
vinegar/salad dressing, fed to inmates hung from poles, 75
Virion, Cavalry Captain Jerzy de (3), 37, 59, 102, 240
Virtuti Militari (Poland's highest award for gallantry), 250
vodka, 205, 262, 281, 287
Volksdeutschen (ethnic Germans), 53, 60, 150, 184, 249, 268, 342
Volksliste (German People's Register), 233
Vorarbeiteren (foremen), 34, 45, 47, 53, 60, 61, 69

**W**

Wagner, Mieczysław (55), 129
"Wall of Tears," 75–79, *77*, 242
Walter (Walterscheid; Kapo), 121, 141, 145, 229, 283
Wandasiewicz, Leon (178), 319–321
Warsaw, Pilecki's post-escape work in, 323–327
Warsaw Rising. *See* Warsaw Uprising of 1944
Warsaw Uprising of 1944 (Warsaw Rising), xii, xvi, xxi, lii, 12, 327–328
Waschraum (washroom), 26, 84, 180. *See also* washing facilities; latrines; toilets
washing facilities, 20, 26, 84, 141–142, 149, 214
Wąsowski, Corporal Czesław (Czesiek; 9), 62–64, 104, 153
Ważyński, Zygmunt (158), 239–242, 320
weather, 48
Weinhold, Reinhard, 283
"went for the wires," 28, *29*
Wernyhora (Jan Mielcarek; 50), 129, 216, 217

*Wesele* (play by Stanisław Wyspiański), 129n39
Westrych, Wilhelm, 60–62, 64, 80–82, 98, 104, 328
Weszke, Wacław (92), 165, 216, 281, 292
wheelbarrows
       corpses on, 70, 195
       carrying coal in, 297
       carrying turnips in, 144
       moving gravel in, 33–35
       "on the barrows," 35, 63–64
       putting bread in, 19, 55
White August, 53, 58
Wicek (Wincenty Gawron; 44), *21*, 106n29, 121, 128, 141, 150, 165–167, 322, 328
Wiejowski, Tadeusz, 66
Wieliczka (location VII), map *300*, 315
Wielopolski, Aleksander, 37n11
Wierusz, First Lieutenant Witold (168), 260–262, 265
Wierzbicki, Second Lieutenant Stanisław (Stasiek; 156), 232, 239–242, 250–251, 274
Wietschorek, Leo (Leon Wieczorek; inmate no. 30), *30*, 31, 65, 80–81, 94, 353n2
Wilk (Major Karol Jabłoński; Zygmunt), 325
Winkels, *16*, 17, 20–23
Wiśnicz prison, 18
Witold, Cavalry Captain (Witold Pilecki), 3
Witold (Officer Cadet Witold Szymkowiak; 15), 105, 186
Władek (Captain Dr. Władysław Dering or Dziunko; 2). *See* Dering, Captain Dr. Władysław
Władek (Colonel Władysław Surmacki; 1), xx, xxvii, 36–37, 59, 106, 149, 153–154, 165, 240
Władek (Władysław Kupiec; 17), 105, 115
Włodarczyk, Alfred (80), 70, 150, 218, 221, 291
Włodarkiewicz, Major Jan (Janek W.; 82), *xlvi*, 17, 125, 146
Włodek (First Lieutenant Włodzimierz Makaliński; 29), 106, 117, 163, 204, 240
women inmates. *See* female inmates at Auschwitz
woodcarving shop, Pilecki in, 127–129, 140–141, 167, 215
work assignment office or leaders. *See* Arbeitsdienst; Arbeitsdiensts
work assignments or details. *See* Kommandos; Arbeitskommando
World War II, misconceptions about, xi–xiii
Woźniak, Sergeant Antoni (Antek; 14), 104–105, 153, 240
Wyspiański, Stanisław, 129n39

**Y**

"youngsters' block" (located in Block 5, old no.), 80–81
Yugoslav inmates at Auschwitz, 209

**Z**

Z (Babice/Bochnia), 153, 240, 283, map *300*, 308n67, 317, 319, 320, 352n1
Zabawska, Helena (177; wife of Edmund), 318
Zabawski, Second Lieutenant Edmund (164), 259, 276, 283, 317–318
Zagner, Roman (5), 37, 241
Zakrzewski, Dr. Zygmunt (120), 184, 241
Zalewski, Lieutenant Colonel Jerzy (63), 138
Zaturski, First Lieutenant Eugeniusz (117), 184, 240, 241, 243, 250
Zettel (camp assignment card), 287–288
Zofia (Zofia Szczerbowska; 13), 97

ZOW (Związek Organizacji Wojskowych or Union of Military Organizations). *See also* "fives," ZOW organized in
    able to take over the camp, 230–231
    active asset, not considered by outside world to be, 242–243
    arms store, reserve under baubüro or construction site office, 235
    Bolshevik POW camp jobs scorned by, 135
    camp authorities' efforts to uncover, 160–163, 184–185, 243–244, 249–250
    camp court set up by, xl
    chaplain for (Father Zygmunt Ruszczak; 87), 157
    death at Auschwitz and, 92
    escapes, opposition to, 126, 262
    escapes, organization of, 166–167, 226, 241
    establishment of, xlviii, 36–38
    goals of, xlii–xliv, 36
    information box, sabotage of, 159–160
    Kapos used by, 94–97
    Kommandos, control of, 92–94, 116, 166, 168
    Kuczbara's betrayal of, 324
    leadership of, lii, 129–130, 139, 183–184, 227, 275–276
    mass shooting of Polish inmates, decision to not resist, 235–239
    "organizing," spreading new meaning of word, 92–93
    plan of eventual action, 183–184, 226–227, 231–232, 243, 268
    political cell, 139–140, 150
    post-escape work of Pilecki regarding, 323–327
    reliance on Krankenbau (hospital) and Arbeitsdienst (work assignment office), 166
    reports and communications, xli, li, 37, 125, 129, 167, 168–169, 204, 231, 260
    senior officers in camp under own names, problem of, 105–106, 138–139, 160
    SS members working with, 268
    transport of Poles to other camps, Pilecki's decision to avoid, 270, 271, 273
Zugangs (new arrivals), 18, 24, 51, 64, 108, 116, 117, 143, 164, 166, 169, 182, 214, 244, 269, 270
Związek Organizacji Wojskowych or Union of Military Organizations. *See* ZOW
ZWZ (Związek Walki Zbrojnej or Union for Armed Combat), xlviii, 146
Zygmunt (Major Karol Jabłoński; Wilk), 325
Zyklon B, gassing with, 134, *194*, 195. *See also* Prussic acid; gas chambers

*THE AUSCHWITZ VOLUNTEER*

DISCUSSION QUESTIONS

*Preceding page:*
Witold Pilecki with his young nephew Marek
Ostrowski—son of Eleonora Ostrowska, 1940.

# DISCUSSION QUESTIONS

1. On the first page of his report, Captain Witold Pilecki writes that he has been advised to "stick to the bare facts without any kind of commentary." Was he able to do that or are there moments in the book when his feelings are revealed?

2. During his incarceration at Auschwitz, the author survived the relentless brutality that felled so many of the other prisoners. What techniques did he use to stay alive?

3. What did Pilecki hope to accomplish during his undercover mission at Auschwitz? Was he successful?

4. Pilecki's intelligence reports smuggled out of Auschwitz were among the first reports to reach the Allies about the Germans' treatment of Jews and the establishment of an extermination camp. What impact did these reports have?

5. When the author volunteered to undertake his dangerous mission in Auschwitz, he put himself and his family at grave risk. "How much easier it would have been simply to lower the brim of one's trilby and take the quiet route to anonymous obscurity," notes translator Jarek Garliński. What do you think motivates heroes like Pilecki to act as they do?

6. Under what circumstances is it legitimate to endanger the lives of others to further your own laudable goals? Give examples from history.

7. What role—if any—did the author's Catholic religion play during his imprisonment?

8. Eventually the author concludes it is time to escape from what he calls "hell." What finally prompts his decision?

**9.** A strain of patriotic pride runs through Pilecki's report. For example, he writes of "the Poles' fine physiques," and that "Poles were always the best workers in every kommando." What role does pride play in the face of dehumanizing treatment? Is it ballast for the soul and spirit?

**10.** In what ways did *The Auschwitz Volunteer* enlarge your knowledge of World War II, the efforts of the Polish Underground, and the part played by Auschwitz during the war?

**11.** Pilecki was the married father of two young children when he volunteered to organize a resistance and smuggle intelligence out of Auschwitz. Discuss the personal sacrifices made by heroes like Pilecki—men and women who believe it is their duty to risk their lives for the greater good of society.

**12.** Pilecki wonders how he could inspire anyone else if he admitted that he was overwhelmed by the situation. Discuss the qualities that distinguish a leader.

**13.** At one point, Pilecki says: "The mask of apparent passivity was a burden, when we were ready and eager for action." In order to carry out his mission, Pilecki had to submit to brutal, punishing domination for nearly three years, instead of acting forcefully against the enemy. This is one type of heroism. Discuss all the different types of heroism. Can they be measured against each other?

**14.** Pilecki dutifully followed the Polish military motto of "God, Honor, Country" above all else. How do you think this applies, if at all, to military combatants in recent conflicts?

**15.** Why did the Germans establish Auschwitz? How could it have been seen to further German war aims? How did Auschwitz evolve during the period Captain Pilecki was there?

**16.** What categories of people were sent to Auschwitz by the Germans? How did their treatment vary?

**17.** Was there any historical precedent for this sort of treatment of such prisoners, and if so, what was it?

**18.** Why did the Germans not respect the Geneva Conventions on the Eastern Front, but instead sent Soviet prisoners of war to a concentration camp rather than a POW camp? How did the Germans treat other Allied prisoners of war?

**19.** What was the German motivation for the "Final Solution" and their decision to begin murdering Jews in cold blood at Auschwitz? What could they hope to gain?

**20.** Discuss the German legal concept of *Schutzhaft* (protective custody).

**21.** Discuss the implications of the phrase "Arbeit macht frei."

**Captain Witold Pilecki** (1901–1948), a cavalry officer in the Polish Army, was one of the founders of a resistance organization in Nazi German-occupied Poland during World War II that quickly evolved into the Polish Underground Army.

Pilecki is the only man known to have volunteered to get himself arrested and sent to Auschwitz as a prisoner. His secret mission for the Polish Underground: smuggle out intelligence about this new German concentration camp, and build a resistance organization among the inmates with the ultimate goal of liberating the camp.

Barely surviving nearly three years of hunger, disease and brutality, Pilecki accomplished his mission before escaping in April 1943. He subsequently fought in the Warsaw Uprising (August–October 1944).

After the war Pilecki, who was married and the father of two children, volunteered to return to Poland to liaise with the anti-communist resistance organizations and report back on conditions within the country. He was captured by the postwar Polish communist regime, tortured and executed in 1948 as a traitor and a "Western spy." Pilecki's name was erased from Polish history until the collapse of communism in 1989.

Pilecki was fully exonerated posthumously in the 1990s. Today he is regarded as one of Poland's heroes.

Translator **Jarek Garliński** was born in London, England, and grew up bilingual in English and Polish. His father was noted historian and author Józef Garliński, a former prisoner at Auschwitz-Birkenau. His mother Eileen Short-Garlińska was one of only a few Britons who spent World War II in Warsaw. Both parents served in the Polish Underground Army during the war.

Educated at the University of Nottingham, the University of Grenoble, and the School of Slavonic and East European Studies at the University of London, Garliński is fluent in English, French, Polish and Russian, with a distinguished career in education.

Garliński is a member of the Polish Institute of Arts and Sciences of America and has been decorated by the Polish Ministry of Defense and the Knights of Malta for services to Polish culture.

He has translated numerous books of Polish literature and history, specializing in the World War II era.

## Also From Aquila Polonica Publishing...

### Maps and Shadows: A Novel
by **Krysia Jopek**
- Hardcover: 978-1-60772-007-2 ($19.95)
  Trade Paperback: 978-1-60772-008-9 ($14.95)
- 160 pages. Eleven black and white illustrations and map;
  Bibliography; Reading Group Guide.
- Fiction. **Winner of the 2011 Benjamin Franklin SILVER Award for Historical Fiction.**

Stunning debut novel from poet Jopek illuminates little known chapter of WWII—the Soviet deportations of 1.5 million Polish civilians to forced labor camps in Siberia. Told from the points of view of four members of one family, *Maps and Shadows* traces their journeys from Poland to Siberia, on divergent paths to Persia, Palestine and Italy, to Uzbekistan and Africa, converging in England and finally settling in the U.S. Fresh stylistic approach fuses minimalist narrative with lush lyricism. **"Jopek... shows how very talented she is."** —*Nightreader.*

### 303 Squadron: The Legendary Battle of Britain Fighter Squadron
by **Arkady Fiedler; Translation by Jarek Garliński**
- Hardcover: 978-1-60772-004-1 ($27.95)
  Trade Paperback: 978-1-60772-005-8 ($21.95)
- 368 pages. Nearly 200 black and white photos, maps and illustrations; contextualizing historical material; nine appendices.
- Nonfiction. A Selection of the History Book Club® and the Military Book Club®. **Winner of the 2011 Benjamin Franklin GOLD Award for History and SILVER Award for Interior Design.**

The fighter pilot, "his sworn duty to protect... hurls himself at the enemy with the momentum of the thousand horses harnessed in his engine." Thrilling action story of the famous squadron of Polish fighter pilots whose superb aerial skills helped save Britain during its most desperate hours. Underdog heroes who rose to defend against the deadliest German Luftwaffe attacks, the pilots of 303 Squadron were lionized by the British press, congratulated by the King, and adored by the British public. **"About as exciting as it gets... a must-read."** — *The Washington Times.*

### The Mermaid and the Messerschmitt: War Through a Woman's Eyes, 1939-1940
by **Rulka Langer**
- Hardcover: 978-1-60772-000-3 ($29.95)
  Trade Paperback: 978-1-60772-001-0 ($19.95)
- 468 pages. More than 100 black and white photos, maps and illustrations; contextualizing historical material; Reading Group Guide (included in paperback; online for hardcover).
- Nonfiction. A Selection of the Book-of-the-Month Club®, the History Book Club® and the Military Book Club®. **Winner of the 2010 Benjamin Franklin SILVER Award for Best First Book (Nonfiction).** *Continued*

Continued from preceding page

Thoroughly modern, Vassar-educated career woman risked her life and relied on her wits to keep her two small children and elderly mother out of harm's way during first months of WWII: the Nazi German invasion of Poland, Siege of Warsaw and Occupation. Engaging, clear-eyed chronicle sparkles. **"Absolutely one of the best."—Alan Furst, bestselling author of** *The Foreign Correspondent* **and** *The Spies of Warsaw.*

### The Ice Road: An Epic Journey from the Stalinist Labor Camps to Freedom
**by Stefan Waydenfeld; Foreword by Norman Davies**
• Hardcover: 978-1-60772-002-7 ($28.95)
  Trade Paperback: 978-1-60772-003-4 ($18.95)
• 400 pages. More than 70 black and white photos, maps and illustrations; contextualizing historical material; interview with the author; Reading Group Guide.
• Nonfiction. A Selection of the History Book Club® and the Military Book Club®. **Winner of the 2011 Benjamin Franklin SILVER Award for Autobiography/Memoir.**

Fourteen years old when WWII began, Stefan Waydenfeld and his family were deported by cattle car in 1940 from Poland to a forced labor camp in the frozen wastes of the Russian arctic north. Coming of age was never so dangerous—but Waydenfeld recounts the experience with a teenager's irrepressible curiosity and subversive humor. **"Extraordinary."—Anne Applebaum, Pulitzer Prize-winning author of** *Gulag.*

### Siege: World War II Begins
**Filmed and narrated by Julien Bryan**
• DVD Video, all regions; 978-1-60772-006-5 ($14.95)
• Black and white newsreel, newly restored (10-minute run time); plus Special Features: 26 color screens of text, still photos and maps; historic 4-minute audio essay by Bryan for Edward R. Murrow's famous 1950s radio show "This I Believe."

A "must have" for every WWII collection! First time available on DVD. This rare historic newsreel was among the first WWII film footage to come out of Europe. Renowned American photojournalist Julien Bryan's gut-wrenching images of the Siege of Warsaw in September 1939 shocked the American public into awareness of the devastation of modern warfare and the looming danger posed by Nazi Germany. **Nominated for an Oscar** in 1940. **Inducted into the U.S. National Film Registry** in 2006 as one of the nation's most "culturally, historically or aesthetically significant films." **"First-rate."—***The New York Times.*

**... Where Heroic Stories Make Epic Reads™**

www.AquilaPolonica.com

 **green press**
INITIATIVE

Aquila Polonica is committed to preserving ancient forests and natural resources. We elected to print this title on 30% postconsumer recycled paper, processed chlorine-free. As a result, we have saved:

48 Trees (40' tall and 6-8" diameter)
20 Million BTUs of Total Energy
4,883 Pounds of Greenhouse Gases
22,018 Gallons of Wastewater
1,396 Pounds of Solid Waste

Aquila Polonica made this paper choice because our printer, Thomson-Shore, Inc., is a member of Green Press Initiative, a nonprofit program dedicated to supporting authors, publishers, and suppliers in their efforts to reduce their use of fiber obtained from endangered forests.

For more information, visit www.greenpressinitiative.org

Environmental impact estimates were made using the Environmental Defense Paper Calculator.
For more information visit: www.edf.org/papercalculator